ALSO BY RICH BENJAMIN

Searching for Whitopia

TALK
TO ME

TALK
TO ME

LESSONS FROM A FAMILY

FORGED BY HISTORY

RICH BENJAMIN

Pantheon Books, New York

All rights reserved. Published in the United States by Pantheon Books, a
division of Penguin Random House LLC, New York, and distributed in
Canada by Penguin Random House Canada Limited, Toronto.

Pantheon Books and colophon are registered trademarks of
Penguin Random House LLC.

Library of Congress Cataloging-in-Publication Data
Names: Benjamin, Rich (Richard M.), author.
Title: Talk to me : lessons from a family forged by history /
Rich Benjamin.
Description: First edition. | New York : Pantheon Books, 2025. |
Includes bibliographical references.
Identifiers: LCCN 2024021561 (print) | LCCN 2024021562 (ebook) |
ISBN 9780593317396 (hardcover) | ISBN 9780593317402 (ebook)
Subjects: Benjamin, Rich (Richard M.)—Family. | Benjamin, Danielle,
1944—Family. | Fignolé, Daniel, approximately 1913–1986—Family. |
Fignolé family. | Haitian Americans—New York (State)—New York—
Biography. | Exiles—New York (State)—New York—Biography. |
Haiti—Politics and government—1934–1971. | Port-au-Prince (Haiti)—
Biography. | New York (N.Y.)—Biography.
Classification: LCC F128.25 .B45 2025 (print) | LCC F128.25 (ebook) |
DDC 929.3747/1—dc23
LC record available at https://lccn.loc.gov/2024021561
LC ebook record available at https://lccn.loc.gov/2024021562

pantheonbooks.com

Jacket inset photograph: National Palace, Port-au-Prince,
Haiti (detail) by Paul Popper/Getty Images
Jacket design by Madeline Partner

Printed in the United States of America

First Edition

2   4   6   8   9   7   5   3   1

For my mother

TALK
TO ME

Prologue

———

WE PLUNGED OUR FORKS INTO THE BLACK PELLETS OF short-grain rice, my mother and I, then scooped up the sofrito shrimp, mussels, and calamari, the bits to savor for last, polishing off the pan of paella. After we left the restaurant, we made the short walk to catch a late screening of Chaplin at a nearby arthouse cinema. I snuck glances at my mother as she cackled at Monsieur Verdoux's ridiculous disguises, his attempts to seduce a rich old widow. Leaving the theater, I relished the satisfaction of having chosen just the right movie to please her.

Later, back in my apartment in Brooklyn, I offered her my bed to sleep in and settled myself into a sleeping bag on the living room floor.

In the middle of the night, I heard wails from my room.

"No. Please don't kill me. Please don't kill me."

Never had I heard her shout out in sleep, and with such terror. Her sobs woke me with a ferocity that my own nightmares never have.

I walked toward the bedroom, planning to sit on the bed beside her and take her hands in mine. Suddenly my feet couldn't move. What would this gesture lead to? So late in the night. What would I say? What conversations would I commit myself to by offering that touch?

I returned to the sleeping bag. That's all I could think to do.

Since that night I've had my own nightmares of my mother bawling. When you've been to hell and back, she used to say to me when I was small, nothing can ever destroy you.

Only now do I have some sense of the pain fenced in by those cries.

ANOTHER NIGHT, FAR FROM my mother's terror—Columbus Avenue, Manhattan.

The cold hit my face as I stepped outside the lobby of the Lincoln Center Theater, holding the door for my date, who followed a pace behind me. Outside, the temperature hovered around freezing, so the splashes on the already-slick pavement could have been rain or sleet. Ian foisted an enormous black golf umbrella into the air above our heads, his gloved hand clutching the leather handle. I noticed the name PRINCETON stretching across the fabric and winced.

Ian leaned into me. I wrapped my right arm around his shoulder. My cashmere overcoat felt snug and dry on my small frame, though my feet felt cold and damp. Ian placed his free left hand around my shoulder and landed his lips on mine. Half my mind reveled in the moment; the other defaulted to my habit of critiquing something even as I'm enjoying it. I pulled away, not wanting to surrender yet to his posh self-assurance, and play-slapped him on the cheek. Hand in hand, we walked toward the stone fountain in the middle of the plaza. Water shot up from the reflecting pool, glistening in floodlights, casting a glow on the buildings nearby: the Philharmonic, the opera house, the ballet.

"What's the plan?" I asked, knowing he'd invite me to his loft.

"Do you want to get a nightcap at my place?"

"We'll need a cab." I exhaled for emphasis.

Ian waved his free hand in the air and, in no time, a cab braked in front of us, almost drenching our coats.

We piled in and Ian took my hand in his.

"I can't," I said. "I just can't."

"Can't what?"

"How could the lead single-handedly ruin that production?"

"It wasn't single-handed. He had a lot of help from that awful direction."

"Truly," I said. "The director didn't conjure a hint of magic, let alone add any subtlety to the social commentary. She just moved traffic."

"I told you, we should have left at intermission."

"I'm sorry, baby." I pecked Ian's lips. "I was thrown by the free fall."

"Free fall?"

"Free fall. That play kept getting worse faster than I could lower my expectations."

I snickered and Ian slipped his hand between two buttons of my soft combed-cotton dress shirt, finding my chest. His was a muscled hand, chafed and frayed at the cuticles, handsome, blunt, unmanicured. I leaned into his face.

We were kissing when suddenly I heard it. The driver started to cough. I looked up at him through the rearview mirror. And as I leaned back into Ian, the driver screeched to a stop at a red light. Ian and I crashed into each other, his front tooth scratching my lip. Ian laughed, but I caught the driver's eyes and shot him a scowl. He ignored Ian and turned to look at me. His wrinkled eyes squinted. Age spots pocked his dark, wide face. His shoulders drooped toward the wheel as if seeking support. His gaze became purposeful.

"You talk different," he said to me. "You have an accent."

"Do I?"

"Where are you from?"

"New York."

"No, really. Where are you from?"

"New York. I was born in New York."

"I mean originally. Where are you from originally?"

"I originated in New York."

Ian laughed.

"That makes me American."

"You sound Caribbean," the old man said. "And you have a Haitian face." He paused, as though offering me a new opening, room to recant my stories. Finally he said, "I am from Haiti."

"Really?" Ian said, removing his hands from my torso and sitting up straight. "One of my favorite nannies was Haitian. I adored her. What was her name? Rosaline? Marie-Louise? Shit. Anyway, her parents died in 1989. AIDS. One after the other."

I heard Ian's voice go soft. Eyes swimming in pity, he looked at the cabdriver. I turned to the window, pretending not to listen.

"I'll never forget her," Ian said. "What an unlucky people. But so lively. Resilient. Isn't Haiti the poorest country in the world? When will it ever catch a break?" He turned to me. "Have you read Graham Greene's Haiti stuff?"

"Can't say that I have. I've never been very interested in Haitian culture. But did I tell you I'm reading early Julian Barnes?"

"Which?"

"Flaubert's Parrot."

"Really? I've been meaning to read that!"

"The thing about Barnes is that you have to read his latest novels first—before the early ones. I read *England, England* and *Arthur & George* before *Flaubert's Parrot*. That way, I can savor all three of them more."

Ian looked into me. "So. What's the story? When do I get to see you again?"

"You see me now. I'm here."

"No, I mean later."

"Well. I'm gonna be at the writers' colony for at least four months."

"Four months!" Ian said. "Why didn't you tell me?"

I said nothing, not having decided what I intended next in life.

"That's a big stretch. Like asking me to eat steak with chopsticks."

I kissed Ian again, shushing him.

Months later, I vanished on him.

But that night, holding Ian's hand, I caught the taximan shake his head, eyes cursing, muttering under his breath.

What he didn't know is that I could understand his French patois.

I swear that nigger is Haitian!

This has been the bane of my life. Perceptive people—they see right through me.

•   •   •

HAITIAN. FOR MOST OF MY LIFE, just hearing the word—in a cab, on television, anywhere—could overwhelm me with dread.

Haiti lies six hundred miles from the U.S. coast, though it hovered inches from my mind at times, threatening like a skin-close machete. At others, it felt light-years away, a distant comet, vaguely menacing. Voodoo. AIDS. Boat People. Poorest Country in the Western Hemisphere. I had no interest in the island, I told myself, and even less interest in the shameful stereotypes that caricature it, the shorthand that defines Haiti for so many Americans.

During the second Bush presidency, I remember a friend telling me a joke, not realizing I had Haitian blood coursing through my veins.

Then president George W. Bush had been presiding at a press conference, packed to the hilt. An eager cub reporter got his attention.

"Mr. President! Mr. President!" the reporter shouted. "What do you think about *Roe v. Wade*?"

The president paused. "Well, I don't really care how them Hayshuns get to Florida!"

My friend doubled over in laughter in the retelling.

My family doesn't look like boat people. And what of it? What if we did? It shouldn't have mattered. Yet still, I avoided the topic, the place. I was chronically embarrassed by my mother's weird Haitian tics, by the vagueness of our background. We hadn't been boat people, but our passage to America hadn't been neat. Ours had been an unromantic arrival, a messy birth, and to conjure Haiti meant to think of that bloody past.

"Please don't kill me," my mother had shouted in her nightmare.

I only now realize, foolish me, that I cannot understand my mother without understanding her motherland, and my long-standing avoidance pains me. The opposite of love, after all, is not hate. It is indifference.

Chapter 1

MY MOTHER CARRIES MANY NAMES. MY WHOLE LIFE I HAVE called her Mommy. She insisted on it, appalled by my friends who called their mothers by first name. But *Mommy* suggests a maternal warmth my mother never had, and it imparts an infantilizing smallness on those who utter it. It would embarrass me in high school, college, and even now when my friends overhear me on the phone: "Okay, Mommy. I'm doing my best." My sisters, middle-aged women, use the word *Mommy* sometimes with a cutting sarcasm they don't quite intend. "Would someone call that woman an Uber? Mommy got lost again."

Her sisters called her Danny, especially when they needed something from her. It showed affection, but it also brought her down a peg or two. "Did you hear what Danny did?" an auntie would snicker, making my mother sound like some dumb teenager. But also: "Oh, Auntie Danny [flattery, flattery, flattery]!" a broke cousin would crow, angling for yet another in a lifetime of handouts. Danny is a name of approach, familiar, endearing, a versatile catchall for the many roles my mother plays to extended family.

Her friends and staff at the United Nations used to introduce her as Danielle Benjamin, which is also how she signed all her correspondence. It's a posh sort of name, worn by the kind of person with more luxuries than problems. In my twenties, I would pick her up at the UN complex in Manhattan so we could go out to lunch. Danielle, beaming, would grab my hand and shove me toward her colleagues.

"This is my son Richard. He's a professor. He's come all the way from California—especially to see *me*." And her colleagues, UN officials, would say with excitement, "You're the son of Danielle Benjamin?" I would smile, proud. That name made her formidable, a powerful, independent woman, even though she'd inherited it from two men, her father, Daniel, and her husband.

To Pops, our father, she was always "your mother." "Your mother said so," he'd explain as he denied we siblings something we wanted, putting on his helpless, remote face. He got to be light and easy by making his wife—"your mother"—a shrew. One Saturday afternoon sometime in the nineties Pops turned up with a brand-new SUV. My siblings and I circled the golden Lexus in the driveway, jumping up and down. Pops had bought it on a whim for thirty thousand dollars. Mommy screamed at him for hours, then wouldn't speak to him for days. She was the one who had to bring things back down to planet Earth. It was her refugee mentality that kept us bathed, educated, fed. He got to gallivant the world and be the popular one. She had to make the tough choices. Those choices got us where we are today.

JUST AS HER NAMES STIR a nest of contradiction, so too does her demeanor. Closed off and harsh in some instances, she is also a devoted humanitarian. Wherever I travel around the globe, strangers corner me, recite all the things that Danielle has done for them: bought braces for their daughter to straighten her teeth; shipped books to their broke, crowded school; slipped them money so they could flee their war-ravaged country. Never have I met anyone with the capacity to be so noxious one moment, so generous the next.

I never know which version of her will turn up, the damning judge or the empathic Samaritan. Years ago, I visited her at her independent senior–living community in suburban Maryland. We came upon her neighbor in the third-floor hallway, sprawled on the floor in front of her own door.

"I fell," she cried.

"One second!" I said. "Let me help you up." Her face brightened, but then we heard my mother bark:

"Don't help her! Just leave her on the floor."

"Excuse me?" said the old lady. Her face froze and her voice hardened on the question.

Mommy ignored her and turned to me. "When some granny falls, you're not supposed to move them. Just call nine one one."

"Please don't call nine one one," the woman croaked. "My son had to pick me up in the emergency room last week—then his wife threatened to put me in a nursing home."

My mother looked down at her neighbor, her filmy blue eyes hopeful and pleading.

"C'mon. Just give me a little boost. Once I grab that doorknob, I can do the rest myself. Please?"

The lady did a small wave of her hand, jewels blinking from her wrinkled knuckles, as if to remind me how close she was to reaching her door from the floor.

"Don't touch her!"

"Sorry." I shrugged. I reached for my phone and called 911. I spoke slowly and cheerfully to the dispatcher, so as not to panic the woman.

For an awkward fifteen minutes, I made small talk with the woman between her pained whimpers, while my mother checked her email on her cell phone. As soon as the paramedics arrived, Mommy announced, "Great. Let's go."

EVEN AS DANIELLE ABANDONS you to your own devices, she won't miss an opportunity to control you. So ingrained are her refugee tics, she will impose her anxiety on you and shatter your calm in an instant.

Years ago, on yet another visit, my mother and I got ready for bed in my Brooklyn apartment. She appeared to be in a jolly mood when she emerged from my bathroom, traces of her night cream pocking her cheeks.

"What time do we need to be up?" she asked as she settled into my bed.

"No specific time. Sleep in and we'll have a leisurely morning before I head to work."

The next day I woke to an amber flush of light shining on my face from the large living room windows. I took a deep breath, savoring the sensation of a beautiful mind, that rare, primordial morning clarity when my writer's head is spacious. I rolled out of the sleeping bag and onto a yoga mat. Each long, slow breath lent a small bliss to the syncopated release of my muscles. After Ustrasana, a generous, heart-opening stretch, I sat on my off-white tufted couch, meditating, then rose, put on a kettle, and arranged my Japanese tea leaves into the infuser. I slowly poured the boiled water to steep the aromatic loose-leaf sencha and watched with well-versed patience, waiting for the leaves to release just the right sweet grassiness.

My mother vaulted out of my bedroom, eyes bulging, brow scrunched, mouth crimped.

"Wake up! You're late! Hurry up!" she hollered. Her cheeks drilled down, compressing her mouth into a tight, ugly pucker. "What time is it?" she yelled, her eyes darting across the kitchen, searching for a clock. There was none. "You're late!"

Seeing no reaction from me, she thrust her index finger in my face. "You're going to lose your job!"

My chest tightened. "Am I late for work?" I wondered. My shoulders clenched. I checked my phone: It was barely eight. I wanted to slap her that instant. I could practically see my beautiful mind on the kitchen floor in a small pile of ashes.

And then a smile crept on my lips. My mother's expression transported me directly to my childhood; she'd been screaming at me since I was a baby. I was certain my nervous system had been shot thanks to shouting sprees like this, growing up with her dramatics. She had a penchant for beginning every school day, every shopping outing, every vacation, in a frenzy, certain that the worst was about to ambush us. Staring at her now, I wanted to remind her of what I'd said the night before, that there would be no rushing this morning.

Instead I said nothing. I turned to my cup and wriggled the brew basket. The leaves had steeped too long; I knew that my tea would taste bitter.

TO HER CHAGRIN, Mommy's antics often boomerang back at her. I am more like her than either of us cares to admit. Her sensibilities—her outbursts, her aggressions—grate on me because they hold an unflattering mirror to my own, and I suspect my mother is often caught off guard, in turn, by how my impatience, my aloofness, lasers on her.

Once, walking down Sixth Avenue from Penn Station, I looked, midsentence, to my right: I'd been talking to no one. I swiveled and saw my mother many feet behind me. She was in her midseventies then, standing next to her small pull-along suitcase, panting.

"This thing," she moaned. "Can you take it? My asthma is killing me." She started exhaling some loud, dramatic breaths.

"C'mon," I snapped. "Stop faking!"

Mommy did a double take. "It's heavy." I could see her eyes tear up.

"Next time don't pack so many shoes. One pair. That's all the sneakers one needs for a weekend."

I looked her in the eyes for punctuation, turned around, and kept walking.

Another evening, she told me she had news. Doctors had found a precancerous lesion in her breast. She asked me to go to the hospital with her for the surgery. I eagerly volunteered to call her a car to get her to the operation on time. Nothing else. It took years for me to realize my misunderstanding, the cold idiocy of my reply. Mommy was seeking company and comfort through an unnerving ordeal, not transportation to an appointment. But it was a time in my life in which I genuinely believed that organizing her car service to the hospital covered my bases for being a good son.

As much as I hope to demonize this woman, I find that I can't. I am but a photonegative of her. So, notably, it is not just the way we fight that bonds us, it's the way we laugh.

We used to go on occasion for ice cream on the Upper East Side. To kill time waiting for the bus back downtown, we'd play one of our favorite games, Facelift Punchbug. Whoever saw a facelift first swatted the other on the shoulder. Once, I saw a woman with skin snapped back so tight her smile looked shrink-wrapped on her jaw, like Heath Ledger as the Joker.

"Facelift, Mommy!" Thwack! "Punchbug."

There was no shortage of facelifts floating on Fifth Avenue, so by the time the M3 arrived, Mommy had beat me four to two.

Unlike all those Upper East Side matrons, my mother and I have always looked much younger than our ages. Big almond-shaped eyes bracket her pert nose, both complementing her bright, manicured smile, her smooth, medium-dark skin. Busty and pear-shaped, she looks the way you might imagine an upscale librarian—bookish, sensibly dressed, a woman who isn't missing a good meal. Meanwhile, I am gangly. Still we share a haunting resemblance. Strangers often point out how much we look alike—the inquiring eyes, the wide nose, the mouth that can whipsaw from raucous smile to damning scowl. Both of us like to make our faces go blank, organic Botox. We freeze our faces so our adversaries have no idea what we're really thinking. The enemy is thrown off guard, made to feel uncertain, insecure, even less than. It is our resting-empress face.

No matter our similarities, for years I sensed an intense grief in my mother that kept us from connecting in a deep and real way. I didn't know the circumstances of her upbringing. I hadn't heard about the violence she'd suffered. Her aversion to addressing that agony, and my inability to ask about it, corroded our relationship.

When my mother was thirteen, her father, Daniel Fignolé, became the president of Haiti. A fiery orator, he addressed the dreams of an entire generation of voiceless Haitians, impoverished and working class, who worshipped him. He was one of the most charismatic, popular figures in that country's history—Haiti's own

Juan Perón or Huey Long. But his presidency collapsed just nineteen days after his inauguration, and he was ejected from his country into America. That coup brought his once-close friend Papa Doc Duvalier to power and launched one of the most brutal dictatorships of the twentieth century. Roughly fifty thousand people were imprisoned, tortured, or executed.

Even though my mother came from an important political family, she never spoke of her childhood. And when questions about her father came up, she went deaf rather than hear the query. I came to know at an early age that if I persisted, the family temper would be unleashed in an ice-hot slap, a palm of flame stinging my cheek.

"Your grandfather was obsessed with politics—to the point of mental derangement," my *tante* Gigine, my mother's aunt, once told me when I was a boy, shaking her head. "It was his malady."

This small rant was a notable exception to my family's studied silence. As I was growing up, my family revealed virtually nothing about this history or their feelings. Only generic snippets of my grandfather surfaced—a vague nod to his legend here, a salute to his good looks there. Otherwise, he was purged from our dinner-table conversations, banned from Christmas Eve reminiscences, hushed from summer family reunions, when my aunties would sit on the porch, clutching their caftans between their legs, fanning themselves, gossiping about anything but him and their childhoods.

I used to pester my mother for details all the time. Now, mostly, I let her be. She is eighty-one years old. She absolutely does not want to tell this story. It is not her choice to salvage damage from history. It is mine.

As my mother ages, I worry I am squandering a vanishing chance to really know her—our history.

My family's existence in Haiti, those disremembered years, dwell like a caesura in our minds, lost stanzas in an epic poem. If ever I am to understand my mother, I must speak to that void.

Chapter 2

———

JUNE 13, 1957. A HOT, CLEAR THURSDAY NIGHT. DANIEL
Fignolé's cabinet was waiting for him as he slipped into a sedan,
his lips pursed in the purposeful way that his family knew so well.
He'd eaten a light supper with his wife, Carmen, and their seven children and was headed back to work. His three oldest daughters—
thirteen, twelve, and ten—had just completed their homework; the
four younger children had long since been put down to sleep. Daniel
said good night to the older girls—terse, unremarkable—and met
his chauffeur in front of the house. Not far away, the city was crackling as the jet set sipped rum punch at the smartest rooftop bars
or petered into the nightclubs. But in Carrefour Feuilles, the hilly
Port-au-Prince neighborhood where the Fignolé family lived, all
was encased in quiet, a thick, total dark.

No one knows why exactly Daniel assembled his cabinet so late
that night. Fine-tuning his plan to stave off recession, finalizing
ambassadors for top posts—he had so much to do. Just before entering the meeting, he talked to Lyonel Paquin, a former student of his.
Daniel had offered the businessman and scholar the post of under-
secretary of finance—or if not that, almost any diplomatic post he
wanted, except Washington. That ambassadorship would go to someone more experienced, more trusted, to be determined once Daniel
could suss out the international landscape. The two were in the hallway considering Lyonel's options when the secretary of health interrupted them. He nudged the president—the cabinet was waiting.

Daniel began the meeting at roughly eleven o'clock. But just a few moments later, he heard footsteps, slow and heavy, thumping up the stairs. Everyone he'd invited was assembled already. The sound of the heels striking the marble grew louder and louder, the sharp footsteps closer and closer.

The door burst open, kicked in by General Antonio Kébreau, the nation's chief military officer. A squad of troops waving Thompson submachine guns stormed into the chamber after the general.

"*Ti-cock, ou caca,*" the general announced to the president. "Little cock, you're shit."

Captain Jean Beauvoir, a top officer, approached Daniel. "This meeting is adjourned," Beauvoir said, staring at him. "Put your hands in the air."

Daniel turned to his startled cabinet members. "Gentlemen, this session is over," he said calmly, then raised his hands above his head. Four soldiers—Beauvoir, Leon, Nelson, and Rey—surrounded the president. He was galled when he recognized one of them—a former student. Determined to remain dignified, he said nothing to the man. The show of force infuriated him. Unlike his predecessors, he had yet to arrest a single person during his presidency.

Officers handcuffed the cabinet members and carted them into waiting trucks. A soldier gathered all the papers scattered across the table and put them into a military satchel. Their machine guns trained at his back, the officers loaded Daniel into one of the presidential vehicles, then sped off into the night.

AT THE SAME TIME, soldiers descended on the Fignolé home. My mother, thirteen at the time, had fallen asleep in her room. Natacha, the maid, heard loud knocking and hurried to the door. She cracked it slightly and a soldier demanded to see the First Lady. Shaking, Natacha insisted the stranger tell her what he wanted. But having already heard the racket, my grandmother Carmen came down the stairs and opened the door fully.

"Madame, the president needs you urgently at the National Palace."

"What is the matter?" Carmen's breath started to quicken.

"Don't ask any questions, madame!" the man shouted.

She was startled at all the soldiers crowding her front porch and property; she couldn't tell how many there were. She was still wearing the linen dress she'd had on during the day. She grabbed her purse and took the maid by her shoulders.

"Watch after the children. Please. I'll be right back."

When she stepped out of the house, a soldier waved his rifle at a waiting car. "Get in. Your husband needs to speak to you."

Awakened by the ruckus, Danielle looked out her window as the car disappeared. Soldiers had come to her home before, looking for her father, but not once had they ever taken her *maman*.

THE VEHICLE CARRYING the president bolted north on the major road leading out of Port-au-Prince. Lieutenant Nelson looked ahead, his foot on the gas, and Lieutenant Rey sat in the front passenger seat. Daniel sat in the back, wedged between Captain Beauvoir and Lieutenant Leon. Daniel decided he would not beg for his life when the two men executed him. He had no intention of granting them the satisfaction of hearing him plead.

They drove for roughly an hour. Then, rather suddenly, the car pulled onto the shoulder. The officers in front whispered among themselves.

"N' ap ba li la?" Daniel heard Lieutenant Rey say to the driver. "Let's give it to him?"

Lieutenant Nelson didn't respond.

Daniel wondered what the soldier's silence meant.

Then Lieutenant Nelson restarted the engine and continued driving.

After a while, the sedan slowed, stopped once more. The soldiers parked the car in the entrance to a deserted wood.

Daniel thought that this was his end.

• • •

ANOTHER SEDAN SHUTTLED Carmen through Port-au-Prince. She wondered why Daniel had summoned her, then grew nervous, slightly, that she might not be able to address, to provide, whatever it was that he needed. She steadied her mind, calmed her annoyance that such an aggressive escort had been sent to deliver her to his office.

But the maneuver was sharp, her realization sudden. When the car made a bad turn, she shouted, "What is going on? The palace is the other way. We are not going anywhere near the direction of the palace."

"Shut up, madame!" a soldier barked. "And don't ask questions."

The car headed north on the highway. What if soldiers have assassinated Daniel at the palace? Carmen wondered. And where are they taking me? She trembled, knowing that they knew she was a wife and a mother and still they were sneering as they held her, defenseless, at gunpoint, headed to an undisclosed nowhere. She shut her eyes for an instant and made a small prayer that no soldiers would return to her home that night, banging down the door once more, this time coming for her children.

CAPTAIN BEAUVOIR took out a piece of paper from his military attaché case and a flashlight from his pocket. From the front seat, Lieutenant Rey pointed his machine gun at the president.

"Sign," said the captain, showing the president where to put his signature.

Daniel took the paper and read it over. He decided that forged words on a letter should have no value. And if the words had no meaning, he thought, there was no good reason to risk his life by refusing the order.

He signed his resignation to the presidency. It was only nineteen days after his inauguration.

The car made a U-turn out of the woods and continued north.

•   •   •

THE SEDAN CARRYING Carmen rolled to a stop. She looked over her captors and out the window. There was a deserted road—leading where, she could not tell.

"Behave yourself!" one of the officers said with a smirk. He noticed her eyes darting. "And don't try to escape."

They'd stopped at the small town of Cazeau, where the four officers got out of the car and whispered among themselves. She could not make out what they'd said. The fear rattled her head more loudly, more urgently. *What about my children? Where is Daniel? Where are they taking me?* Whatever else might happen to her, she thought, she must keep herself alive for her children.

And almost as abruptly as it had stopped, the car got back on the road for what seemed like infinite time. When it finally stopped again, she noticed three cars nearby, parked side by side. The soldiers ordered her out of the sedan and led her over to them. They opened the door of one and Carmen saw Daniel. Daniel took his suit coat off and put it around his wife's shoulders to shield her from the chill. He shrugged—baffled, silenced.

They'd been taken to a seaside town in northwest Haiti. The soldiers escorted them to a small wharf, where they were forced onto a tiny Coast Guard vessel, the *Crête-á-Pierrot,* which crossed the Gulf of Gonâve. The soldiers kept their machine guns trained on their backs. Soon after, they were led from the Coast Guard cutter to a rowboat, then rowed to dry land ahead, where a Haitian military plane sat waiting.

Môle-Saint-Nicolas. On the northwestern coast of Haiti, this tiny fishing village was precisely where Christopher Columbus first landed on December 6, 1492. He established a colony, which he named La Isla Española, taken into English as Hispaniola, the first long-lasting European settlement in the Americas. I don't know whether the kidnappers told Daniel and Carmen where they were taking them, but if they did, I doubt the irony of being forcibly ejected from his homeland in the exact place where Christopher Columbus had first settled was lost on my grandfather. They were not an accidental couple captured in a senseless stickup. Their bodies bore the weight of empire.

Chapter 3

DANIEL'S LIFE HAD BEGUN JUST ACROSS THE BAY FROM Môle-Saint-Nicolas, in a town called Pestel, a cozy seaport where fishing dinghies drifted in the humble harbor, but momentous vistas stretched above the colorful, generous farmland.

Pangs struck Leonie Fignolé as she tended her garden near the small village one day in November 1913. She lugged herself back to her neat thatch-roofed hut. She swallowed the pain squeezing her belly and did a kind of squat, placing the *choukèt*, her small wooden birthing stool, under her hips.

The baby wrenched himself away.

Leonie sat up, cut her cord, washed the baby off, and laid him down on an immaculate patch of cloth next to her in bed. She sank into a deep unconsciousness and awoke, hours later, to find her husband, Camille, and their neighbors staring down at her as the baby, Daniel, bawled.

Camille held Daniel in his arms for a moment, a stern look on his face. Then he went back to work. He wasn't one for idleness, joy, or tears. And besides, his wife had delivered other babies. He rationed his hours working both as a struggling shopkeeper, selling the villagers basic staples, and as a low-level part-time civil servant, verifying and notarizing the townspeople's official papers. Like his confrères in the civil service, he considered himself lucky if he received his pay late, rather than not at all.

Ultimately, Daniel and his younger brother, Necker, would be the only ones of Camille and Leonie's children to survive. Their four other siblings all died from sickness or malnutrition before reaching their sixth birthdays, a grief not uncommon in their village. The nearest cemetery felt like a cenotaph to hard luck, with its makeshift shrines to the lot of crying children who had died before growing to potential.

PESTEL SITS BETWEEN rust-colored hills on three sides and a bay on the fourth. Since the dirt was red, like rusting metal, the villagers, huts, and animals glowed with the same colored dust. As dawn cracked into morning light, the pale gray air feeling cool, the roosters would shout in the yards, beating their wings and scratching at the dirt. Getting feisty, they seemed to think, would provoke the farmers into throwing them some corn.

Every day was a reckoning with the earth. The villagers churned it, opened it, pounded it, over and once again, sowed it, and pounded it some more. They filed into the fields in a race against time with the scorching sun. Up went the hoes, sun-glint light like sparks of fire, then down they crashed with terrible force and certainty. The farmhands stepped forward, one next to the other, lifting their hoes, moving, moving, moving, in uniform rows, work songs ringing in one solid voice.

Some villagers seemed to spend years trekking the hills on errands, wading through the low surf to get to their fishing boats, trudging through the rice or sugarcane fields, carting water back home in cisterns balanced on their heads, nothing on their feet. Others searched constantly for a jug of water fresh enough to drink. As a child Daniel spent his days ferrying charcoal from the vendor back home, cutting wood to help repair a fence, fixing a hole in a roof's straw thatch, making and setting traps to catch the birds. Besides his own chores, his parents were always loaning him to neighbors. Favors were the currency of the village: Today I help you, tomorrow you help me.

Sitting one day outside the two-room, one-story, dirt-floored thatch-roofed house, staring past the silhouette of the hills, Daniel sighed.

"Papa!" he said, not realizing he was shouting. "Why can't I choose where I was born?"

His father swatted him smartly across the nose. The slow-shuffling boy's dreamy spells, his constant wheezing, aggravated the man. Daniel, underweight and anemic, was forever coming down with respiratory infections, but he knew not to whimper to his father and risk a real beating.

Daniel croaked out a cough. Maybe he wanted to say something, but *gran-gou*, "big hunger," soured him with bile, gurgled up his tongue, so he didn't. The words might've come out too bitter.

Camille stood and left Daniel to wonder what lay beyond the green crests, what life entailed for boys like him, scattered elsewhere about the country. Electricity and stores and plumbing had yet to arrive to Pestel, and he knew nothing of phonographs or tommy guns or chewing gum. The small village felt less like a valley, more like a prison.

AS INSULATED AS PESTEL SEEMED, it still was caught in the larger power struggle that seized the country. When Daniel was still a baby, in 1915, the president, Vilbrun Guillaume Sam, had granted himself total authority, as though he were a uniformed monarch, and the country's rich mulattoes—*les milats*—revolted. The president responded by curtailing most civil liberties. He ordered the execution of 167 political prisoners, including a popular former president. The country rose up against him; he went into hiding. An infuriated public, including rebels backed by the mulattoes, broke into France's embassy, where the president had taken refuge, and beat him to death.

Following the assassination, President Woodrow Wilson dispatched U.S. marines to protect "foreign lives and property" and "to preserve order." The First World War was heating up and Wilson claimed that he wanted to deny the kaiser's Germany a staging ground so close to America. German merchants had established

U.S. forces in Haiti, 1915

outposts in Haiti in the early 1900s, and their families enjoyed great social and economic power on the island, controlling 80 percent of the country's international commerce. In truth, a tight tapestry of bankers, railroad magnates, industrial barons, and Wall Street lobbyists had pressured Wilson to invade, not only for the tactical advantages of controlling Haiti but the strong financial ones. American companies, from sugar producers to banks, had their claws sunk into the island.

From all over America the marines came, from all kinds of backgrounds, but because the military was segregated, they had one thing in common: they were white. And they all reported to Colonel Littleton W. T. Waller, the grandson of rich Virginia slaveholders. "I know the nigger and how to handle him," he once boasted to fellow marine commander John A. Lejeune in a letter. "They are real niggers. Make no mistake, there are some fine-looking, well-educated, polished men here, but they are real nigs beneath the surface."

Not long after setting foot ashore, the marines installed a puppet mulatto president, dissolved the legislature at gunpoint, imposed a new constitution—one more favorable to U.S. business interests—

and took control of Haiti's finances, including its national deposits. The country and its finances were turned over to American "conservators," who ruled its purse strings carte blanche. American companies had long had their hands on Haiti's money. A year after Daniel was born, U.S. marines had seized five hundred thousand dollars' worth of gold from the vault of the Haitian National Bank. They shipped it in wooden crates for "safekeeping" to a Wall Street bank, which had already taken control of the Haitian National Bank and charged the Haitian government for every deposit and withdrawal that it made. Some of the fattest profits the American bank reaped in the 1920s came from the transaction fees it imposed on Haiti; that bank later became Citigroup.

The marines also seized the country's ports and customs offices. The United States helped itself to the profit collected from the duties on all that coffee, bananas, sugar, and so on. And from the rubber plants to the factories to the massive plantations, U.S. businesses exploited cheap labor, stole fertile land, and seized abundant natural resources without any rules or consequence. American "investors" muscled in to acquire some of the nation's best assets—including railroads, sugar mills, and tens of thousands of acres of Haiti's most arable farmland.

When the marines attempted to coerce Haitian office workers and tradesmen to help them reorganize the ports and the customhouses, the Haitians stared back with arms akimbo. They performed *marronage,* the national art of protesting by refusing to work. And when the occupiers drafted peasants for backbreaking labor, such as road laying and construction, the Haitians gathered together, drank rum, delivered bits of political theater, sang, danced—this was *rara,* a folk tradition of protest through carnivalesque celebration.

The marines, determined to build roads to allow quick mobility across the island, revived a punitive custom, *corvée.* Dating from the plantation days of the 1800s, corvée had allowed mulatto landowners to conscript so-called peasants to till their land for free. The marines took advantage of old corvée laws and forced "peasants" either to pay a road tax or to work as road builders without pay. The rural Haitians had no money for arbitrary taxes, so the soldiers rounded them up, bound them, and ordered them to work. Thousands of people were kidnapped from their homes and forced into labor, on the roads, or in camps, poorly fed and guarded by surly Americans, rifles at the ready. Anyone who tried to flee was shot on the spot. A white Baptist missionary was horrified to discover one Sunday morning a crew of Haitians, including his fellow pastors and members of his congregation, "roped tightly and cruelly together, and driven like slaves."

News ricocheted village to village, including to Pestel, about family and friends and neighbors shackled by whites and ordered to work. The stories, the sights, the experiences, were too redolent of slavery, supposedly banished just a few generations before.

While the marines had taken the capital and the army rather handily, guerrilla resistance to their occupation stiffened in the north. Daniel, by then a teenager, watched village rebels—called Cacos, or "bandits"—join the native uprising. The Cacos took up ancient armaments to fight the invaders—Spanish cutlasses, Napoleonic sabers, machetes, and their ancestors' horse pistols. They mounted such a terrific challenge to Wilson's military that he increased its presence in the country, even dispatching airplanes to squelch guerrilla gains.

Villagers were tortured by marines to turn over information on rebels' whereabouts. The marines committed arson and murder, as they pleased, against the Haitians, then confiscated whatever property or supplies they needed. An estimated 11,500 Haitians, civilians and Cacos, were killed by U.S. forces over the course of the occupation.

The marines tracked down the north's most ferocious, celebrated rebel leader, Charlemagne Péralte, and shot him point-blank in the heart. They pinned his corpse to a door and photographed it days later, rotting in the sun, and blanketed the country with the photo, a pointed warning against resistance. But handsome, Christlike Péralte became an instant martyr. His image only rallied the troops.

The Cacos were fighting not just for their lives, they were rising up for national pride. A fierce patriotism extended the depth, rippled the breadth, of their resistance. As such, the battle against the occupation didn't take place only on combat fields but also in the living rooms of everyday people.

Village uncles would regularly crowd the small salon of Camille's candlelit home to conjure the past. They made verbal jabs at one another over cups of *kleren,* sharing the lore their elders had passed along. Daniel would sit in the corner on a wooden stool, listening in rapture. Their forefathers were the first in the New World to slaughter their masters and successfully revolt. *Really now, how did Louverture lead that uprising?* Again and again, the men narrated Haiti's independence from its colonizers, again they debated the story-details of their heroes' finest exploits, parsed again the ripple-effects of Haiti becoming the world's first black republic. Thus spoke the uncles. On those nights, Daniel imbibed in big thirsty gulps a sense of his own potential to think and act for the country, his mind cognizant of its blood-soaked past. The sickly boy, who could never serve in a platoon, gleaned that his only life arsenal would be the defiance of storytelling, the stuff of words. He absorbed from the uncles a pride in the country's history of triumphant slave revolts, a hunger of memory, a yearning for would-be legend to crowd out all the current, evident defeats, which no uncle could talk away.

THEN, IN 1927, Camille dropped dead from a stroke. Daniel knew that if he didn't leave Pestel immediately, he would die there too. After the funeral, he asked to be sent away to school. Leonie agreed to ship him off to live with her brother André, a former government bureaucrat, who had the good fortune to live in his own apartment in Port-au-Prince.

Slave-built roads linked the small nation, but the distance from

The road out of Pestel, 1934

Pestel to Port-au-Prince, or anywhere else, seemed infinite to Daniel. It took days by donkey or horse buggy to get to the closest place, Jérémie, itself one of Haiti's second-fiddle cities. All of fourteen years old, Daniel sat on a mule with a guide and set out for the capital.

He arrived days later, wearing his flour-sack breeches and the stink of the provinces.

Chapter 4

*H*ONÉ?" CAME DANIEL'S HESITANT VOICE OUTSIDE HIS uncle's front door. Honor?

"Respé!" his uncle answered. Respect!

Daniel was anxious to heed the old ritual greeting that governed homes.

Tonton André and Pamela, his only daughter, were wary when they heard Daniel rapping on their door, unsure how long he planned to stay. Tonton André hugged Daniel, then took his hands in his own, giving him a once-over. Tonton was taken aback—such thickness and roughness on Daniel's touch, his calluses like a sales receipt, a certificate of authenticity for someone who'd grown up in the bushes.

Daniel unpacked his belongings: a couple of books and two outfits. He hesitated over where to put them; there was hardly a meter to spare in the apartment, though the place contained little itself: an old kerosene lamp, its glass dark, dingy from age and use, and some unmatched bric-a-brac, the ornamental touches Tonton André had sprinkled throughout: an old plant in a cracked clay vase, a fading painting of the countryside, the lace that covered the headrest of the frayed love seat. A tin ashtray sat on the lone coffee table, near the plastic drinking glasses they kept around, in perpetual reuse, all of which André had haggled for at the nearby hardware stall.

Daniel was allotted a corner in the small apartment. He unfurled a slim mattress behind a curtain, an improvised wall, stripped to his underpants, and went to sleep. Since André had no bathroom, Daniel made sure to relieve himself before bed, saving himself a walk in the middle of the night to the communal latrine in the alley alongside the cinder-block building.

That week, when he had enough energy left for walking after finishing the household chores that André had assigned him, Daniel spent as much time outside the apartment as he could. He wandered the narrow, dusty streets of the surrounding neighborhood, came to memorize their contents: the baguette shack, the barbershop, the old man's dry goods store, the coal peddler squatting on the corner, whistling to get his attention.

Some days, Daniel went to Market Square, winding his way through the labyrinth of tin stands crammed together. Cassava and cabbage, clove and chili pepper, the merchants sang out their wares. He held his nose at the refuse lying in the bazaar's tight walkways, trying not to slip on the rotting mango pits. He could see the women coming and going in their slow, easy gait, baskets of dried fish balanced on their heads.

The marketplace, Port-au-Prince, 1926

And when Daniel ventured even farther from the market, he saw the city pulse with work, bodies heaving crates on the docks, muscles hacking cow carcasses at the butcher. He stared at the boot-black, little just like Necker, tramping down the avenue beating a wooden spoon against a tin box to lure customers, his thin fingers and indented cheeks blotted with black wax.

Beyond that were the big promenades in the city's center. Daniel strolled into the Champ de Mars, gazing at the park's volatile reds and blues, the lush green surrounding the flowers. Though Daniel's neighbors called it Chanmas in Kreyòl, the public park was an homage to the Champ de Mars in Paris, the illustrious park between the Eiffel Tower and the École Militaire.

Years earlier, the wide boulevards near the Champ de Mars had been used for official Haitian parades, but now they showcased American military spectacles. Sitting on one of the park's marble benches, Daniel noticed the radio speaker dangling from a metal pole. The occupation government had installed the public speaker system to blast American entertainment programs, radio serials in English and French, as well as "educational programs" in Kreyòl, which André called propaganda.

Daniel wandered the empty racetrack abutting the park, certain that he'd never be able to afford to lounge in its wrought-iron viewing stands during a race. Across the way was the National Palace. An elegant dome rested atop the main entrance, something like a crown, so the building looked as though a church had been hatched from an emperor's manor. Daniel had heard from tonton's neighbors bitter-sweet accounts of the palace: the country's most beautiful building, designed by a Haitian architect in French Renaissance splendor, but engineered and constructed by occupying forces.

And without word to André, Daniel crept out one Saturday night and walked the city's dingier blocks. He saw white soldiers staggering out of a dance hall and pale Dominicanas standing around waiting. He couldn't tell if he wanted to watch or run away. A marine saw and cursed him with a look. The marine's face was bronzed, his hair yellow, his eyes blue, just above his Henley shirt and blazer. A cigarillo dangled from his mouth and a Dominicana had cemented her lips to his veiny neck. Another woman stood watching, not far away, a plot of a breast swelling past her meager, sheer chemise. The courtyard was a checkerboard of her friends—charcoaled brows, rouged cheeks, fat eyelashes that clapped—all looking and acting nothing like Daniel's neighbors. They stood in tight dresses, spoke to one another in zealous, chopping gestures, caressed and whispered at the men. Why? He wasn't sure.

He found his way too, one afternoon, to the city's major bookshop, a flagship pride for the rich. There was no such place in his village, and he studied the men in fine suits who came, made purchases, and left, books cradled in the pits of their arms. He couldn't drum up the gourdes to buy goodies—a new bicycle, cinema passes to the Parisiana—and certainly not novels or treatises at the store. He decided then to locate the library so he could borrow them instead.

Onward he walked, carried along most afternoons by his longing for independence. And each street seemed to make the city livelier, sharper than the last. He thrust himself into their commotion, even as he retreated into his head. It was a singular shot of joy that he felt, his solitude and belonging to the crowd.

The city mesmerized Daniel, not just the palaces and the estates, with their handsome profiles, or the flamboyant, leisurely parks, which felt decidedly different from Pestel's cornfields—it was the whole of the place. All those bodies, walking the boulevards, shopping the markets, spilling from the universities, churning, bustling him about, their voices a welcoming cacophony not unlike the crunching trolley wheels. More and more, Port-au-Prince drew him out, and he was awaking to its provocations and treasures.

BACK IN PESTEL, Leonie missed Daniel fiercely. Mothers, whether they hailed from the hinterland or the capital, spoiled their oldest boys as a tradition, and Leonie was no exception. One year after Daniel moved to Port-au-Prince, in 1928, Leonie left Pestel to reunite with him, bringing Necker with her. When she arrived, André could see her bones more prominently than he ever remembered, in her face, her hips. Her body had been pelted by the years, by life's bad surprises. To make it to Port-au-Prince, Leonie had deprived herself of a thousand comforts. She had no dresses for calypso dancing, no nice red lipstick, no cowhide purse, which even her most modest neighbors carried. And when she hugged Daniel, she said nothing about his hole-specked, outgrown overalls.

Leonie set herself up in the apartment, much to Pamela's annoyance. Pamela did not especially like her tante or that her household had doubled. Leonie could be so formal and Pamela could never seem to rinse the stewpan and the utensils soaking in the basin to her satisfaction. And when Leonie cooked, boiled yam on a good night, smoke from the small coal stove poured onto Pamela's things. Quarrels befell the apartment. Neither woman was used to following orders from another or sharing three rooms among five people.

The bloated household lived as it could, ate as it could. Even when Camille had died, Leonie had always insisted that Daniel share her trials with stoicism. She did not shower Daniel in weeping sentiment or hugs. The measure of her love was how he dispatched life's persistent discomforts, or any day's burdens. Leonie, like Camille, did not like whining children who made their woes, themselves, conspicuous: routine beatings were administered to ingrain in a child a constant fear of expressing himself. She beat Daniel so he stayed polite, focused, brave. Things might get harder, but he better not debase himself by that hardship. Pride was foremost: stooping to frailty or charity was no way to get their daily bread.

Daniel focused on his schoolwork. He read with abandon, lingering in the libraries, retreating to his corner turf in the apartment with all the books he'd borrowed. Come nightfall, he would read by candlelight or walk to the nearest thoroughfare and stand under the streetlamp, placing the book under the hanging bulb. The children passing by snickered.

But soon enough, he'd earned a spot at Lycée Pétion, the country's most prestigious high school, which drew boys from the wealthiest families. Generations of famous Haitian men had attended Lycée Pétion since its founding in 1816, including nearly every civilian president of the republic.

Daniel rose at dawn to walk to his new school. Slow, long swills of the morning dew moistened his nostrils, soothed his brittle lungs. Arriving to school, he was self-conscious of his feet, his skin. "Big-toed nigger, splay-footed nigger," the petite bourgeoisie in Pestel had said about the farmhands. "Peasants have their big, flat bare feet planted in dirt." Daniel looked at his skin, which had shone lighter, a medium hue, next to Pestel's croppers, who tilled the fields all day, but was darker—much, much browner—than that of the mulatto boys he sat next to. Thankfully, the school required pupils to wear uniforms. But his classmates could still sniff the difference. Daniel's country accent sounded thick and rude. The sheen on his one pair of uniform khakis was already fading on his backside. His ramshackle appearance—Afro, pockmarks, shoes—made them laugh.

He's got roosters on his feet. The bastard's sandals squawk!

Daniel had bought his shoes for a pittance from a roadside hawker selling footwear, oranges, and herbs off a straw mat. But the shoes had fallen apart to the point that they looked like sandals. His class-mates, meanwhile, wore leather loafers and Oxfords hand-stitched by a cobbler. Most of them, he learned, lived in Pétion-Ville or Ken-scoff, posh neighborhoods on the hill.

Status was inscribed into the city's altitude. The lower parts of the capital burst with people and stench, rows of small wooden homes ringing the wharves. Those streets overflowed with makeshift mar-kets and yakety vendors shouting and skirting the sewage.

Up the hills, meanwhile, the temperature dropped about ten degrees, the leaves grew more verdant, the air fresher. In Pétion-Ville and Kenscoff, high above the center, the well-to-do occupied fine villas, ensconced in green gardens with dashes of red, red poin-settia. Well paved and clean, the hilly streets emanated an old-world European charm, hosting top-of-the-mark restaurants and hotels and cafés, where *le beau monde* met to discuss politics and books and world news in German, French, and English. Skin color mapped itself onto this geography of privilege: the higher Daniel went, the lighter the skin.

Since the country's founding in 1804, French, Syrian, British, German, Dutch, and white Americans had emigrated there, commingling only with one another and the country's existing mulatto population. Thus the light-skinned elite consisted of the descendants of European slave owners, the landed gentry, and an ongoing influx of light-skinned newcomers. They socialized at exclusive clubs, patronized the best restaurants, dispatched their kids to the most respected private schools, and vacationed abroad together. The milat class kept the most coveted positions in law, industry, medicine, letters, the academy, and Foreign Service for themselves—jobs Daniel dreamed of breaking into.

In class, Daniel began devouring the European classics, Racine and Voltaire, Shakespeare and Montaigne. He consumed there, also, *So Spoke the Uncle* and *Le Vieux Piquet,* literary anthems to patriotism, which became his favorite books. He read the articles of the black journalist, who'd died around the time of Daniel's birth, Louis-Joseph Janvier, "Haiti for the Haitians" and "The Equality of the Races." Then he trailed his teachers in the afternoons as they went to cafés or the park near the school. Once he'd gotten their attention, he ambushed them, desperate to dissect the questions raised in his books. His classmates often mocked him for following one of his favorite teachers, uninvited, to his home—the legendary professor J. C. Dorsainvil, who had written three acclaimed histories of black Haiti. Dorsainvil, like Daniel's other revered instructors, had declined firearms in favor of pens; for them, the country's liberation would not happen in guerrilla trenches but in the refuge of the best schools.

But Daniel couldn't afford to vanish entirely into his reading. "No one can feed a family on books," Tonton André liked to say with a sneer. Daniel's uncle and mother demanded he supplement their meager incomes. Frail, he was in no position to tax himself with physical labor. Since he was near the top of his class, he decided to become a tutor to his high-society classmates.

Inside his pupils' houses, he smelled and saw what their families ate—hors d'oeuvres of chicken liver, seafood casserole, pork roasted into succulent submission, salted cod, rice and beans, fried plantains, *gâteau au chocolat,* sorbet grenadine, Rhum Barbancourt spiced with fresh cinnamon bark, and French red wine. When the lessons were over, he would return to the threshold of his door. Would there be food on the charcoal stove or the table? A boiled yam or cornmeal? Often the cupboard was bare.

And still Daniel's body was maturing, in pace with his mind. Soon he fell for one of his students. Her name was Chantal, a mulatto girl with long, silky hair. Her vacuous eyes suggested a boredom with her perfumed, cocooned life. The first time they met, she shot Daniel a quick, flirtatious smile, and over the coming weeks, that attraction grew. She began receiving Daniel for lessons in her bedchamber. After they'd studied, she'd sneak him foie gras, or they'd disappear on long walks to the patisserie, where she bought him warm shortbread. This went on for months until finally her father noticed the romance. Intermarriage between mulattoes and dark-skinned people was unacceptable; the union would diminish the milat family's standing—unless a highly successful dark-skinned man married a dim, homely mulatto woman, which Chantal was not. Chantal's parents fired Daniel, literally ejecting him out the villa's back door. He left with a wounded heart, deflated pride, and a practical tutorial on his place.

NOT LONG AFTER, Leonie was able to move with Daniel and Necker into their own one-bedroom apartment downtown. They settled in, glad for the space, wary at the steeper price.

Leonie had found new work, helping a milat who ran a small export business; she also did odd jobs in his home. She was just about breaking her neck working for that skinny swine. He and his cronies thought of themselves as white, but with faint traces of Negro blood. But not all whites were created equal. Making her way up the city, Leonie understood, there were *les petits blancs* (shopkeepers, reverends, professionals) near sea level and *les grands blancs* (plantation owners, industrial tycoons, the president's circle) in the upper altitudes.

Two stern lines had hardened near each crease of her mouth. She was exhausted from winding her way down the hill from work to home. Her calves stung after the long walk from the trolley depot. As soon as her braids hit the pillow, she fell to sleep. Working for that little white was mincing her nerves like a garlic clove in her mortar. When she awoke, she thought about the rent to pay, the new skirt she needed, the medicine that another little white had prescribed for Daniel's breathing. Daniel made do instead with gingerroot and tea brewed from a crushed herb, something the Vodou healer had told her about.

The stack of gourdes that Leonie kept in a tin toolbox hidden in the bureau in the bedroom—her life reserves—was dwindling. A world depression was decimating global prices for exports. Businesses were teetering. Tonton André, Pamela, Leonie: they watched their incomes shrink. Their neighbors who were lucky enough to have jobs also saw their paychecks dissipate. Soon, Daniel, at twenty-four, came to a realization: his prospects were bleak, even though he'd finished his studies with distinction at the most prestigious high school.

As the global depression shrank their incomes, however, it surprised them with a silver lining. The country's colonizer decided that it no longer had the resources, nor the political appetite, to occupy her. President Franklin D. Roosevelt called the marines home in 1934. The cynicism of the decades-long charade hadn't fooled a soul. When the ships sailed off, the true purpose of the occupation was just as clear as when they'd first docked: "I helped make Haiti and Cuba a decent place for the National City Bank boys to collect revenues," Marine Corps general Smedley Butler reported later in a memoir. General Butler, who'd won a Medal of Honor for his exploits fighting

Haitians, later revealed in a newspaper that he'd spent thirty-three years as a "high-class muscle man for Big Business" and "a gangster for capitalism."

When the marines packed their weaponry and left, their absence was palpable to Daniel, the household, most everybody. For as long as he could remember, the marines had been a blight on the land-scape; they spattered from the taxis, from the roadside restaurants, from the dance halls, toting their loaded pistols, faces often crimson, heads plastered. "You are likely to run into groups of marines in the little cafés, talking in 'cracker' accents, and drinking in the usual boisterous American manner," said Langston Hughes in Port-au-Prince, speaking for more than a few Haitians. And when the gunboats sailed off, tax collection and policing were returned to Haitian control. There would no longer be a colonial governor but an elected Haitian president.

The atmosphere was heady; people felt new possibility. The just-departed occupying force created government-job vacancies, opening space for young, brilliant minds to imagine themselves with a direct hand in steering the country. Daniel enrolled in the University Law School, the nation's best, in 1936, with the dream of becoming a barrister. He loved it. Conversing with his classmates in the law school's courtyard during recess, Daniel was certain he was arguing with future cabinet members, supreme court judges, and presidents. But after two years of study, he had to abandon his dreams. The economic depression had worsened, and his mother needed him to bring in cash. He dropped out of law school to teach full-time at his alma mater, Lycée Pétion.

Daniel was more a doer, less a dreamer. He did not sulk in what-ifs. Even though he was a law school dropout—or maybe because—he continued to nurse his thirst for fame and prominence. A still greater determination to shine possessed him, even if the exact avenue were not yet clear.

He stole moments when his mother and Necker were out running errands or still on their work shifts. Alone, he took a mirror to the kitchen and practiced his delivery as a speaker, polishing his voice, rehearsing his gestures. He tried to imitate the thunderous speaking styles of the world's most celebrated speakers, in all their musicality and allure. He'd heard their voices drifting out of Leonie's radio or humming from the phonographs that his professors switched on in class. "I am Professor Fignolé," he said in the apartment. "Today, let us comb the legacy of Lucius Quinctius Cincinnatus!"

On weekdays, Daniel would strut into his classroom at Lycée Pétion and dust off the blackboard. Sunrays from the lacquered-blue sky would flood through the windows, illuminating the chalk dust in the air and the students' faces. As if on cue to a maestro's baton, the young men would rise to their feet the second after he entered. "Good morning, Professor," their voices called out in unison. He'd hold his students' gazes for a beat with his deep-set eyes, then the young men would sit back down on their wooden benches, aligned in rows, their elbows settled on the plank-wood tables in front of them, alongside their marked-up books.

Daniel would launch into his lesson, reporting episodes from the country's history as though he'd been there himself. He professed on the foreign capture of the people's natural resources and delivered tart assessments of the ruling class. His long arms waved, words sprang from the pink of his tongue, distracting students from the heat, even as sweat beaded their pressed shirts. The chalkboard he'd clean upon entering the classroom would brim with his scrawlings by the end of the lesson. Once he'd finished his lecture, the air would ring with applause. He'd stand for a beat to take in the adulation, the stage he craved to elevate his voice. Students swarmed him after class, followed him out the door to drag out the lesson; they wanted to draw more from the breadth of his knowledge, the cold lucidity of his analyses. His lessons opened for them a new way of understanding the burning social realities of the day. Buzz spread through Port-au-Prince: enroll in that young man's courses.

"He was the joy of his students," Lyonel Paquin recalled years later. "He was a born actor, terribly sure of himself, amusingly overbearing, and a show-off. His students loved his antics. He had a tremendous ego and enjoyed his students' teasing and flattery."

"I knew Fignolé to be very extravagant at times," recalled René Depestre, a milat student, who became one of the most celebrated writers in the history of Haitian literature. "At one point he wore unusual clothes, dressed eccentrically to attract attention. He had a particular way of asserting himself, with a kind of awkward aggressiveness, almost burlesque. But students always listened to him with great attention. He would say, 'You, Depestre, are not a mulatto'— and intend that as a compliment to my intelligence. Fignolé was always looking for a way to express his sarcasm and racial insults."

Daniel knew that his students exercised different means to get to his classroom, which was tucked among the school's elegant archways and handsome columns. The school had been designed in French Renaissance elegance by Georges Baussan, the same architect who had designed the City Hall, the Supreme Court building, and the National Palace. Some of Daniel's students were driven to the school by servants, some pedaled their bicycles to class, and some walked a long path to the door, miles on foot, just as he had.

His keen attention to political suffering, students noticed, did not make him a gentler teacher. When a mousy student provoked him with a halting, disjointed remark, Daniel stared into him with a slow, sarcastic silence, then returned to the chalkboard. Or if a student blurted out a dumb, brash answer to one of his questions, Daniel would kick him out of class.

"I ultimately loved the man," Henock Trouillot, his student, once recalled. "Although his judgments always disturbed me—even if they seemed just." Trouillot went on to become a renowned historian and dean of one of Haiti's most prominent literary families.

OUTSIDE OF WORK, Daniel was eager to make friends beyond his slender social circle and far from Leonie's constricted flat. Across the city, other young idea-hungry black men were too. Incensed by the occupation and uninterested in the vapid obsessions of a feckless elite, the men began fomenting their own social scene. After teaching class, Daniel visited local cafés and started rubbing shoulders with other black learners, accumulating smart connections as his cousin Pamela had once collected dolls.

Milling through those emerging circles were three men, confident beyond their twenty-odd years. They had formed a clique and dubbed it the Three Ds. François Duvalier, Lorimer Denis, and Louis Diaquoi first met as high school students at the Lycée Pétion in the mid-1920s and inaugurated themselves the Three Ds as early as 1929. They met regularly in Lorimer's rented house in downtown Port-au-Prince, not far from Daniel's, and lost themselves discussing global politics. But in 1932, Louis died suddenly at the age of twenty-three; François wrote an anguished tribute to him in the city's oldest daily.

In Louis's absence, François and Lorimer continued on, fashioning themselves as griots, enchanted storytellers. They believed that Africa was the origin and soul of their civilization, and that to be an authentic Haitian, you had to embrace the country's most African elements. They read up on Vodou and insisted there was a special sensitivity to the black creative temperament. They denounced Catholic priests as racist apostles of imperialism; the French-colonial values that Haiti had internalized, they believed, were a cancer stunting her healthy growth.

Lorimer had known Daniel separately for years, but in the late 1930s, he introduced him to François. All three had attended the same high school, though at different times.

Lorimer and Daniel were the kind of men who women gawked at and asked to dance. François was not. He had a fat, oblong head. It was so dark, it was even midnight purple. Coke-bottle glasses obscured his beady eyes. His thick lips seemed to never smile: he looked like a disgruntled eggplant. As if to distract from his homely face, he dressed in tailored suits. Buffing his confidence in this striving uniform, François trotted out decorous, old-fashioned manners, rolling out his French r's, bowing his head when he spoke.

François's family had always hovered near poverty, so he'd overcome obscene odds when he'd graduated from the University of Haiti School of Medicine in 1934. At the mostly milat medical school, François, a middling student, had studied just enough to pass his courses. Outside class, he was a brilliant thinker, more interested in black history and folklore than in medicine.

François and Daniel got to know each other over coffee one afternoon in Lorimer's living room or sitting in the grand park nearby; they found they had so much in common. Daniel hadn't been able to purchase his own books as a young student; François had also relied on the goodwill of a few classmates who'd loaned him their books. They both had been infuriated to see the Stars and Stripes fly over their country's greatest landmarks and could name their elders who had been humiliated in public by white boy-soldiers. Their friendship was baptized by a gritty shared history and a cutting determination to land a toehold in the black bourgeoisie, or at least to scrape out of poverty.

Chapter 5

———

D ANIEL'S CATCHPENNY DIET, HIS NEVER-ENDING WORKLOAD, exacted a tax on his health. After working his handful of teaching jobs, he ignored the increased troubles he was having breathing, hoping the problem would clear free of cost. But he was rushed to the general hospital in 1940 on two separate occasions with a chronic sinus infection. The doctors feared also that tuberculosis would strike him. He nearly died during the last-minute visits, his immune system and lungs failing.

He was undergoing treatment for his second sinus infection when Leonie collapsed from a heart attack. She lay for hours, thirsty, fever-hot, nauseated, on a straw floor mat in the hospital reception bay. No matter the squeezing twinge in her arm, or her pants for breath, she was left beside all the other emergency patients who had no cash to pay for decent care, relegated among other poor women to wait for hours without a doctor or even a bed.

At her plain funeral, Daniel lauded his last parent, his best living connection to the past. He was still wheezing the day he buried her, the woman who'd delivered him from a life of countryside starvation, who'd skipped meals and luxuries so that he could have a chance at a different life, the person on the planet who loved him most, and whom he loved most in turn.

HIS GRIEF HAD HARDLY EASED in his chest when he first set eyes on her. Carmen Jean-François was barely twenty-one, practicing piano inside a chic hair salon in downtown Port-au-Prince. It was the summer of 1941, and Daniel's cousin Arnold had dragged him to the salon, where he was going to meet a friend. Carmen glanced up and saw Daniel looking at her. She averted her eyes. He moved closer. She glanced up again, noticing him still watching, and stumbled over her notes. Carmen blushed and turned the page. When he caught her stealing another glance at him, Daniel arched an eyebrow and cocked a grin. He shifted his weight to lean his frame on the instrument. Flustered, she launched into Debussy's *Préludes*, fingers pirouetting to the melody. He left without a word.

Later that week he returned to the salon, and then again the next. He could afford only so many haircuts, so he invented excuses to turn up. He dragged his cousin along for cover, then promptly ignored him. Daniel went to linger near the piano. Not long after their first meeting, Daniel began sitting on the piano bench next to Carmen, demanding to meet her mother.

"Why?" the astonished girl replied, a little unsteadied by his nerve.

Daniel grinned and told her he was toying with her.

Carmen spent every afternoon that summer at the salon, to keep the owner, Madame Renee Chevalier, company and to enjoy the camaraderie of wealthy women who gathered there to have their hair done. With her broad, shiny face, Madame Chevalier looked like the round toe of a polished boot. She offered Carmen a wellspring of impromptu lessons on running a business. Carmen didn't tell her dour old mentor that she thought her crush dashing, his face stony and soothing at once.

When she wasn't playing piano, Carmen taught preparatory one classes at Notre Dame Sisters of Perpetual Help, a grade school. She'd once dreamed of becoming a nun, had even gone to a convent to make inquiries as a teenager. Instead, at her mother's urging, she'd settled on the more practical, comfortable vocation of teaching children.

Daniel sometimes bought them lunch at the roadside canteen to impress Carmen at the salon. Between forkfuls of rice and goat, the two teachers traded stories of their childhoods and of their work. Teaching consumed Daniel whole, but for Carmen, it was more a choice than a necessity. She had taken her teaching job mainly as a placeholder until she landed a husband, and she adored the work more than she coveted the money.

Playing piano in the elegant salon was a natural pastime for Carmen. She'd grown up among the landowning coffee-harvesting black upper class of Jacmel, a town in the south. Her parents had planted and traded coffee and owned general stores. But her father had died suddenly, and her widowed mother, Madame Claire Mina Alexandre Jean-François, was left to fend for her five young children: two boys and three girls. A shrewd, cheap businesswoman—she hounded down every gourde—the widow would buy two-bit properties, fix them up nice, and rent them out at a tidy markup.

Around the time that Carmen turned eight, her mother sent her off to a *pensionnat,* a communal boarding school for girls in Port-au-Prince. The widow paid room, board, and tuition in exchange for her daughter's classical education. Founded in 1913 by an order of European nuns, the school was run by Madame Debordes, a white Frenchwoman. The nuns condemned the girls' supposed African folkways, garnered in the outback—wiggling their butts, sucking their teeth, invoking their mothers' superstitions. The nuns were determined to make the boarding school a dutiful replica of Europe and wanted to exorcise the Vodou, the nigger, out of their charges. It was there that Carmen had learned to play Debussy and Brahms.

Among the sisters, one took an especial shine to Carmen. Sister Marie Nathalie had been the first to guide her toward teaching. Some girls had focused on learning embroidery, on hospitality service, on fine arts; under Sister Marie Nathalie's doting tutelage, Carmen focused on training to be a teacher, all the way until her graduation from the high school.

Inside the academy, Carmen and her classmates had been forbidden from reading or speaking in Kreyòl. Because every last lesson in every last classroom across the country was conducted in French. So was official business. Contracts, laws, news reports, public IDs: all done in French. But it was in Kreyòl that people did their everyday business—they borrowed sugar from the neighbor, cracked a joke, cursed, fucked, in Kreyòl.

Daniel, though, told Carmen sweet things in French—how he admired her face, so clear and bright. Her skin looked smooth, delicate, like that of a woman whose sleep had never been littered with nightmares. She had a fawn's eyes, relaxed and generous. She was virtuous, but no schoolmarm. She never left her house without a good lipstick, a garnish to her high fashion. His peers also did their *parler français* when chasing girls. The language, Daniel felt, lent him the prestige he wanted courting Carmen, and winning over her mother. Speaking a good French, people in those circles thought, would pay a lifetime of dividends: not only did it show an appreciation for the great treasures of Western civilization, it let a person participate in the progress of the modernizing city.

And so, Daniel talked to Carmen about history, rebellion, politics, in a language and manner they cherished. She was taken in by his stories, his matinee-idol looks, his attention to his students, and his evident concern for the injustices that had been visited on his mother—and on total strangers. In spite of her quiet, finespun education at Madame Debordes's, or perhaps because of it, she wondered whether this feisty backcountry man was the one for her. Carmen had no father and four siblings. A choice marriage was her ambition, her only assurance of a stable, comfortable future—more so than even her learning.

Daniel understood quite plainly that he was foraging out of his league. Carmen, he likely felt, had just the right traits to make him an ideal wife: medium complexion, and an education and social grace to match his former tutees' and the milat elite. Although he was falling in love, courting Carmen was also a meticulous step in career planning: He wanted to marry an upper-middle-class black mademoiselle—refined, poised, sociable—who would facilitate his ambitions: raise good children, govern his household, decorate his public profile. And at twenty-eight years, he was rather old not to be married.

So, not even half a year after first setting eyes on Carmen, Daniel wrote her mother *une lettre de demande* in his Frenchest French, requesting Carmen's hand in marriage. Then he made the journey to Thomazeau to ask Madame Claire Mina Alexandre Jean-François for her blessing in person. But the widow wanted her daughter to marry Monsieur Gérard Jolibois, a milat from a big, robust family. The more family a man had, the widow felt, the more prosperous and assured her daughter's future—larger families meant softer safety cushions. After all, only one of Daniel's five siblings had survived past infancy, and her daughter's suitor looked himself to be about one mishap away from the food line. Carmen, though, determined in her own way, chose to marry the smarter, poorer, good-looking guy from the south. Some people, starting with her mother, saw Daniel as a commonplace hustler on the make, but Carmen swore that she saw in his bearing and heard in his voice a singularly gifted man, the kind of talent who comes along once in a generation. She wasn't alone in that.

In September 1942, Daniel and Carmen wed in Thomazeau. It was a speck of a village, deep in the country's interior, near the border with the Dominican Republic, the plains so flat, no wedding guest had reprieve from the unrelenting sun. As they gorged on the feast that Carmen's aunties had prepared for after the ceremony, including sumptuous cake, it would not occur to Daniel and Carmen that they were among the legions making a historic migration from the countryside to the capital, a black mass swelling its ranks, many of whom had no political caretakers, nary a leader. They could not have fathomed the distance that their marriage would wrest them from their born worlds, roosters thrashing their wings near plots of sweet-potato growth, banana trees fluttering in the wind's kiss, neighbors thatching one another's roofs after a storm, no; rather, they danced to the tempos of the rumba and *djaz Ameriken,* limbs whisking in unbridled joy.

Chapter 6

Daniel and Carmen, Port-au-Prince, 1952

THE NEWLYWEDS MOVED IN WITH CARMEN'S BROTHER AND his family in Port-au-Prince immediately after the wedding. Daniel begrudgingly agreed to the arrangement—it was temporary, he told Carmen, just until he got his income sorted out. What an embarrassment: he'd barely finished his wedding vows, and already his mother-in-law's skepticism about his bank account had proven well founded.

He disappeared from the normally bustling house just after dawn most mornings and boarded the bus to punch in to one of his jobs. He still taught mathematics and history at his alma mater. Once his courses were done there, he'd haul himself to Petit Séminaire Collège Saint Martial, a quality all-boys Catholic high school, to teach again, or to Collège Odéide. It was a reckoning with his stamina: Daniel was impatient to earn his own keep and have a home free from relatives, his or hers.

Despite all that, he still found time in the evenings to feed his growing interest in politics, informed by the brutality he'd witnessed during the occupation, the slights he'd suffered in the homes of his tutees, and the shabby medical treatment that had hastened his mother's death. The same fall that he married Carmen, he and some friends founded *Chantiers,* a pro-black newspaper. Its title meant "work yards," and there Daniel published emerging black voices, including that of his friend François, who frequently contributed to *Chantiers'* pages.

"It is time that all conscious Haitians raise their voices," Daniel advised in *Chantiers.* "We are black and we will stay black, proud of our origins and proud of our glorious past."

What he had endured day in and day out, Daniel understood, had its roots in how the country ordered itself. Each gilded-skinned grandee had but one aim: advantage for himself, servitude for blacks, and a system to control it all. Take the newly elected president, Élie Lescot, a milat: he made one concession after another to other wealthy milats, which amounted to a state-organized looting of the national treasury. At the United States' urging, the president had ejected poor black people from roughly one hundred thousand acres of land, bulldozing their homes, as well as over one million fruit trees, so that wealthy industrialists could cultivate rubber, an industrial project that ultimately failed. And still another law dictated that a police officer be present any time workers met, preventing blacks from peaceably assembling to discuss the harsh conditions on the ravenous plantations and factories, American- and milat-owned.

Haiti remained "the property of sixty privileged families," Daniel wrote, asserting that the milats' "lazy, selfish, egotistical, and sectarian bourgeois way of life is an insult to the poverty of the peasant who works for the pleasure of a class swollen with prejudice. And the descendants of Toussaint and Dessalines are abandoned in filth and ignorance."

Most of Daniel's fellow teachers and writers danced around the autocracy, fearful of directly criticizing the president. Daniel, though, plainly denounced Lescot, publicly calling the president a tin-pot dictator who ran the country for the benefit of the wealthy milats. Lescot retaliated by shutting down *Chantiers* and banning all of Daniel's writings. Daniel, unfazed, simply started a new journal, *Le Réveil*—a call to awakenings—and wrote under a pseudonym, Jean Sadors.

Daniel was coming into his calling. He had lived the poor masses' circumstances and was becoming a role model for their aspirations. *Le professeur.* That's what he insisted people call him. On an island where nine in ten people could not read or write, where colonialism depended on keeping people illiterate, and where parents made punishing sacrifices to educate their children, the sobriquet rang like a clarion of inspiration.

Daniel's darts grew so regular, so pointed, that the president didn't just shutter his journals, he fired him from his teaching posts—the schools were all government owned. He took occasion personally to dismiss Daniel from Lycée Pétion, both men's alma mater, in a blustery speech to the parliament. "We have our eyes on him and on all those who surround him," Lescot declared. True to his word, he put Daniel under strict police surveillance.

And so Daniel—in the middle of a term—was booted out his classroom door. No dignified conclusion to his lesson plans, no befitting goodbye to his beloved students. The abrupt loss of his teaching posts infuriated him. The president had unwittingly unleashed a pent-up mind, a coiled fuse. Daniel took the firing as license to turn full-time from the classroom to politics.

If Carmen had expected her honeymoon glow to stretch out indefinitely, she was mistaken. Daniel's budding interest in politics drew more and more of his concentration from the marital oath he'd just taken. His new vow was to confront injustice, and it was growing ever more sacred. To fill her own time, Carmen started teaching again. And soon she was expecting, pregnant with their first child.

Chapter 7

———

THE MIDWIFE WHO'D BEEN HIRED MANY MONTHS PRIOR BY Madame Claire Mina arrived to a modest house. Carmen was a twenty-one-year-old in robust health, and the *fanmsaj* had proficient talent, so the baby slipped into the world without incident. In February 1944, Daniel and Carmen welcomed their first child, a daughter, to a world smoldering under global war, a premonition, perhaps, to the tenor of her future. Daniel had wanted a son, so he split the difference and named his daughter after himself.

He admired Danielle's medium-brown complexion, her large, inquiring eyes. She was born with her father's asthma, but still, not long after her birth, was crawling across the floors of their home, very sure of herself. Curious about her surroundings, she learned quickly, picked up on words, moods, sounds. Daniel grew besotted with her clear confidence and smarts. Cooing at her papa, Danielle would smile, make entertaining faces, then turn coquettishly away. She seemed to have a knack for theater, a taste for self-image. Daniel had been cultivating his bold strain of individuality, bordering on eccentricity, and could sense his passion in her face. She was the star of the small house, and she enjoyed his fatherly attention all to herself—until her baby sister Raymonde arrived two years later.

The Fignolé family, in those years, had struck out from Carmen's brother's into Poste Marchand, a working-class neighborhood in downtown Port-au-Prince. Carmen had set up house in their *lakou*, a cluster of one-family homes surrounding a shared rear courtyard. Neighbors, comprising several generations of families, living close together, helped one another with money, food, favors. Their tradition of collective living had begun on mulattoes' plantations in the countryside, not long after slavery was abolished. Exploited sharecroppers pooled their means, built shacks surrounding small farming plots of their own. The Fignolés now lived in the modern, urban version of this, just across the courtyard from their old friends the Duvaliers.

Since Daniel had gone from employed teacher to independent writer, a modest house in the bargain neighborhood suited him just fine. Money was tight. World War II was raging, and Haiti had its own problems. By the time Danielle had started crawling, its economy was flagging and suffering was mounting, in no small part because of the president's corrupt botched attempt to produce rubber for America's wartime efforts. Not only was precious land destroyed, ninety thousand Haitians lost their jobs. Unrest percolated. Low-ranking black soldiers conspired to overthrow the pro-American light-skinned puppet from power, but were caught; many were then executed without trial. Soon after, Lescot unilaterally extended his term from five years to seven.

BY THE TIME DANIELLE had started walking, her father's focus was concentrated on the political unrest, not her.

"Tonton François! Tonton François!" little Danielle would holler, tugging her mutt, Tou-Tousse, across the courtyard to her uncle's, in search of attention and mischief. Daniel hated the ragged, yelping Tou-Tousse. Danielle pretended not to care, and their neighbors laughed at the scene; they couldn't tell whether the mutt's name, "cough-cough," referred to the panting dog or her wheezing owner.

Tonton François was in his late thirties then and, like Daniel and Danielle, seemed always to be sick, but more severely so. He was diabetic and nearly blind. His knees, elbows, joints, all jutted out everywhere; he looked like a short, flimsy skeleton trying to jiggle out of its suit. His wife, Simone, towered over him, as did tall, lean Daniel.

François too had little money to speak of. "I just want to focus on what I love best: my social and anthropological research," he liked to remind Carmen, as if making a pointed dig at the grime of money-making or politics. He cared deeply about ideas and so planted his family in the run-down working neighborhood to save himself from financial pressures. He had few to no patients and scraped by on a small salary he drew as a medical consultant to an old-folks home south of the city. He was so thrifty he refused to buy even a refrigerator; instead, he pestered neighbors to borrow ice.

Daniel had chosen Lorimer Denis as Danielle's godfather, but enlisted Tonton François to serve as Raymonde's. Living cheek by jowl, Daniel and François honed their friendship through an exhaustive, roaming conversation about the country's *noiriste* movement, which they'd helped establish, a pro-black philosophy championing the interests of the dark-skinned majority.

The noiriste movement blossomed in tandem with a worldwide pro-black consciousness, spanning from Dakar to Paris to Chicago, often called the negritude movement, that had flourished most famously years earlier, during the Harlem Renaissance. Many of the central writers of the Harlem Renaissance, including Langston Hughes and Zora Neale Hurston, drew inspiration from Haiti, as did Aimé Césaire, a celebrated poet and one of the founders of the global negritude movement, who'd spent seven months there the year Danielle was born, a time when Haiti was still the only independent black republic in the Americas. The poet had gushed that the noiriste movement had spiritually been born in Haiti.

François and Lorimer had been working since the 1930s to recruit someone—a kind of extrovert and political oracle—who could bring their ideas of black pride and economic uplift to the masses. François was politically inexperienced, so the two men had been searching for a live wire who could turn their worldview into concrete political and economic wins. They believed Daniel was that someone.

While François liked and respected Daniel, he adored Carmen. She was the more vivacious, open, and generous half of the couple. And Carmen loved him and his wife, Simone, in turn. François had a whiff of the humanitarian intellectual, having traveled the country to vaccinate the poor before throwing himself into his writing. And even though he had medical training from the University of Michigan, François fancied himself a *houngan*—a Vodou priest. A medical expert moonlighting as a Vodou philosopher: François could be grand, original company. The foulest things slipped out of his mouth—salty jokes, greasy gossip. Carmen visited the couple frequently, and the Duvaliers enjoyed her soirees and card parties—always irresistible, if sporadic, events.

They shared their families, their noiriste philosophies, their courtyard, even their ice, but Daniel and François had different ways about them. Daniel could be sour—an insufferable pedant who scolded Carmen every chance he got. He retreated into his work, his discipline. The courtyard of their lakou was a place for neighbors to sit, to show delighted surprise when another neighbor appeared unannounced, but even on Saturdays, Daniel rarely took part in the gossip-slinging, rum-slugging, merengue-pulsing impromptu get-togethers. It was there, though, that François charmed.

The public merriment aside, Danielle had been told throughout her childhood to keep her mouth shut about the neighbors' private business—including the fact that Tante Simone was born a "bastard." A well-known mulatto merchant, a man called Jules, had bedded one of his maids in 1913. After the maid got pregnant, Jules fired her, dismissed her existence, and rejected the newborn. Simone's mother then left her to an orphanage. In a rare stroke of luck for Simone, since few people could attain higher education, she was offered vocational training through the orphanage; she chose to train as a nurse's aide. She met François on duty. François's ambitious, upwardly mobile fellow doctors never married beneath their social class, but lucky for Simone, her height, her high cheekbones, and her light skin made up for her "illegitimate" birth into poverty. She was too striking for François to turn from.

François had confided to Danielle that he was a *loa*, a spiritual protector, an intermediary between mere mortals such as she and Bondye, the Vodou god. While foreigners and the city's light-skinned elite thought that Dr. Duvalier was an enigma shrouded in a riddle,

Danielle adored him. She found Tonton François intriguing, funny, and his Vodou flotsam never bothered her. He snuck her chocolates, regaled her with folktales from the country. Once he even gave her a book: Machiavelli's *The Prince*.

MADAME CLAIRE MINA VISITED often at the lakou, though not as often as she or Danielle would have liked. Grand-mère Mina and Daniel annoyed each other; they kept an unspoken, peaceable amnesty that dictated how often she came through. Madame Claire Mina, deep in her temperament, was a *commerçante,* one of those practical people who could take a gourde and transform it into two. She was baffled that her daughter's husband wouldn't get a job, like any normal man, or at least start a business. On top of all that, she was bothered by his highfalutin ideas, never mind the soaring way he explained them to her. She shot him direct questions about his intentions. Why, for instance, had it been she who thought to secure for Carmen a top midwife? She gave him unsolicited opinions in her business voice. Daniel, for his part, found her charmless, a petty old woman with a shallow mind. A nosy shrew. But elders were elders, so he treated Grand-mère Mina with his utmost formal manners: he held the door for her, asked repeated questions about her physical comfort, made sure she had enough servings at supper.

No matter how she irritated him, Madame Claire Mina had a point: Daniel and Carmen had difficulty getting by on his patchwork earnings, so she felt no choice but to slip them money. She loaned them cash for rent on their tumbledown house, or to pay the family's mounting bills. Her loans were supplemented by Carmen's salary from teaching. It was thanks to that income that Carmen was eventually able to hire two maids, Selavi and Natacha, determined to re-create for her daughters, however vaguely, the gentility she'd known as a girl.

Daniel studiously divorced himself from the vulgar details of money; the banality of running a household, he felt, was beneath a man and an intellectual. Though he played aloof, he bristled inside—he was a grown man having to subsist on his wife's and mother-in-law's purse strings.

DANIELLE, ONE LATE AFTERNOON, yanked Tou-Tousse across the courtyard to visit Tonton François. She skipped along, suddenly noticing Tou-Tousse's paws etching faint prints in the dust, then smacked into Marie-Rose, a little girl, dark, big-eyed, with a striking resemblance to her—so much so, she might as well have been staring in her bedroom mirror. Her mother had sold Marie-Rose to a nearby family to work in their house in exchange for meals and a roof over the girl's head. She endured as a *restavek,* a child castaway, a serf. Danielle hugged Marie-Rose without a word and scampered away, feeling uncharacteristically shy. To look into Marie-Rose's eyes was a pointed reminder of her own good fortune. Just weeks before, Marie-Rose had been coughing hoarsely, blood projecting from her tongue. Her boss lady, rumor had it, had thought hard about whether Marie-Rose was worth saving. Her tuberculosis could, after all, infect the family. Still, the woman heated up blankets on a charcoal stove, then made Marie-Rose sleep in the courtyard under the hot cover, in the fresh air, a makeshift sanitarium. Watching this, Carmen thought, there go I but for the grace of God. Her family, she felt, could find itself someday one tuberculosis diagnosis, one house fire, one jolt, away from destitution themselves. They wasted nothing because they had so little, and because Daniel and Carmen knew that no matter how tight things were in their own home, they had it much better than so many others. If they felt their girls took for granted their privilege, the exacting punishment was swift.

On one such occasion, three years later, Daniel was away. Danielle, six, and Raymonde, four, waged battle. It began when Raymonde showed her ceramic bowl of corn porridge to Selavi, the maid, who was washing dishes at the kitchen sink.

"See?" Raymonde said, tears streaming. "She spit in it." The girl nodded toward Danielle, which sent Raymonde's braids jangling. Selavi laughed, more entertained by the zany fashion that Raymonde's hairstyle had turned out than concerned by the girl's bitter complaint.

Later, Carmen emerged from the bedroom and noticed Raymonde seated at the kitchen table, her bowl of *mayi moulin* fresh and unmoved. She paid no mind to the girl's groans.

"Raymonde, eat your dinner. So many are starving, and you of all people will not waste that food."

Raymonde stared back at her mother. She did not understand why she in particular should not have the gall to waste her dinner. She took her corpulent little fist and shoved the bowl away. Bits of porridge went flying like golden confetti blessing a parade, and the unexpected spectacle that she had created delighted Raymonde. She laughed.

Selavi, who was prone to dramatics, let out a shriek of anger when she saw the table she just had scrubbed decorated with Raymonde's food. The maid steadied herself and turned back to the dishes, not wanting her own theatrics to undercut whatever move her mistress was about to make. And indeed Carmen delivered the worst threat of all: "Then you will not leave the table until every spoonful of your dinner is gone. And your father might have some ideas about that."

Through all this, Danielle lounged nearby, reading. Often her mouth ran nonstop in the evening—except when she thought talking might make matters worse for her. She was learning when to tattle and when to stay quiet in the ongoing clash that had developed between her and her sister.

Raymonde looked to Selavi, who calmly dried a dish. "Attention, yo!" said Selavi in Kreyòl with a cutting grin. "If Papa sees you, he will slap you, *vlap! vlap!*"

Danielle and Raymonde had never formally been taught Kreyòl; their parents had forbidden them from speaking it in the house, so they picked up its saltiest put-downs from Selavi and from the street. Raymonde glared at the maid and muttered something in Kreyòl about her sister, sucking her teeth, which was quite a bootleg pleasure.

When Daniel walked in the door hours later, shoulders slumping,

Carmen studied his face. She, Danielle, and the maids had grown used to inspecting his walk, his expression, for clues to his temper. If his lower lip pouted subtly downward, they knew to retreat from him, as they did if he was grinding his jaw or tilting his head at a small angle. But that night he had an air she could not grasp; his eyes escaped all definition.

When Daniel noticed Raymonde at the dining table, falling asleep and startling awake before her bowl of hardened porridge, his eyes blazed. Bits of grain, looking like cruddy chicken feed, lay scattered across the nice wood. He set down a briefcase heavy with work papers and undid his belt buckle, then heaved Raymonde from her seat and pelted her with his leather belt. Once he was satisfied by her wails, he ensconced himself with a coffee in his favorite armchair, his eyes lost in nowhere.

Danielle went to join her father in his chair, a small snicker overtaking her lips. Sobbing from the floor, Raymonde studied her, now on their father's lap.

Carmen paused writing her lesson plan. She called out toward the bedrooms over her left shoulder for Natacha to fetch the crying child and carry her upstairs. There Natacha put the girl in a tin washbasin full of warm, sudsy water and massaged her bleeding wounds with a homemade pomade that reeked of wax, charcoal-burning smoke, and wild plants. She kept the greasy balm on hand for the girls' insect bites, play scrapes, and beating welts.

"Ça ira," Natacha murmured to Raymonde. "Ça ira"—it'll be okay.

Natacha returned Raymonde to the living room, kissed her, and put her back where she'd sat before. Raymonde tugged at her pajamas, which were sticking to her oiled, clammy skin. She drilled her eyes into Danielle and said nothing. Danielle was once again mocking her, from the safe nest in their father's arms. She could smell Raymonde from across the room and glared back at her with a slight devil's smile.

Carmen had long known her husband was just that type of professor to sit in front of his students barraging them with challenges, stoking their rivalries to spark electricity in his classroom. Le professeur could not be troubled to hide his preferences, rewarding the victors, scorning the losers. That night she saw how he enjoyed pitting his daughters against each other just as he did his students and his political underlings. He seeded their fighting to raise the stakes of their devotion to him.

Chapter 8

O N SUNDAY MORNINGS, DANIEL AWOKE IN CONCERT WITH the rooster's crow, as if it were a weekday. He was a light eater who nourished himself on his nervous energy, so only nibbled at the scant breakfast that Selavi delivered to him: the heel of a baguette, warm and buttered, with a tranche of papaya. Daniel and Selavi were the only ones to work on the Sabbath. He muttered no more than a few words to her as he hurried to his den.

Papers drowned his desk in the study, his favorite room in the house, the place where he went to hide from his wife and daughters. Books sat stacked in neat piles on the bureau, in towers on the floor, spilled from the bookshelves. They expounded on a gamut of topics, but mostly mathematics, history, and economics. Between the desk and bookshelves stood a blackboard, crowded with geometric figures and mathematical equations. Daniel contemplated, calculated, scribbled for hours on the blackboard for relaxation.

Carmen could not hear Daniel in his den. She got up and put on her finest cotton, as she did most Sundays, to take Danielle and Raymonde to church. Carmen stopped inviting Daniel to worship since he ignored her appeals. For Carmen, religion was a balm to life's inevitable tribulations. Agnostic, Daniel refused to accompany his wife to those churchy functions—and certainly not to Sunday service. He told his wife how he loathed the clucking congregants with their insatiable thirst for gossip—Who had died? Who was dying? Who was gonna die next? He cringed in the homes of her friends, all those tacky holy paintings. He mocked the religious frippery of the bourgeois Catholics striving to climb Port-au-Prince's social ladder.

Daniel had plans of his own for the day. He got dressed to leave—he never stepped out without a jacket and tie, especially the dark gabardine and light linen suits he loved so much, always tailored, polished, with a silk cravat. He complemented his suit with a fedora. Then he walked twelve minutes to a speakeasy in Bel-Air, a working-class neighborhood like theirs.

As soon as Lescot had begun to feel his grip on power waver, he had banned his political opponents, especially Marxists and socialists, from meeting in public. In response, back-alley discussion clubs sprang up throughout the city. Daniel knew, as he arrived to his destination, that his peers, his former students—and much of the intelligentsia—would soon descend for this week's secret meeting. The gatherings moved throughout the city—from art galleries to private homes to threadbare joints such as this speakeasy. They were always in one of the city's more popular working-class neighborhoods, such as Bel-Air and Bas Peu de Chose.

Entering the bar, Daniel would take a seat at an empty table. Sunlight hit the bare wooden walls. The floorboards creaked. The no-frills place looked like a small, modest warehouse. The heavy-bodied, rich aroma of Haitian coffee beans roasting floated from the kitchen, less acidic, bitter, and aggressive smelling—more forgiving—than most darker roasts, beans harvested, surely, not far from his wife's childhood village.

Then a former student of his, Fritz-Claude, walked in. He didn't appear so different from most of the other young men streaming through the door, the speakeasy filling up. He had a wide, inviting dark face framed by a trimmed Afro, and wore a neat, simple outfit: pants and a pristine, well-pressed guayabera. The young man smiled and reached into his satchel. Daniel smiled too—he knew what was coming. The man pulled out a plastic bag of checkers pieces and a folded board. Daniel beckoned the waiter to bring him and his unemployed protégé a coffee and a juice. They arranged the checkers in place.

The perfume of hibiscus and orange and grenadine permeated the air; celebrants clutched their drinks. Men sat at the half dozen tables dotting the center of the room. At one, two men played bridge, straddling the backs of their chairs. A cluster of men were standing in the back corner, wisps of cigarette clouds floating from the Chesterfields they favored. The din of animated voices rose.

Daniel slid a checker piece, slowly, demurely, across the varnished plastic. Glancing to the side, he could see other young men whom he had taught. There stood René Depestre, who had just dazzled the capital with his debut collection of poems, *Sparks*. The twenty-year-old poet, who moonlit as a communist activist, stood near the bar, beautifully turned out in a suit and an ascot. Most of the young, debonair mulatto idealists in the speakeasy were ready to discard their upscale social origins in the interest of combating fascism and worker exploitation, not racial differences, as the noiristes in the room were. Max Menard, a mulatto communist student and friend of René's, had said, "For us Marxists, the color question does not lie at the heart of the Haitian problem." René, who would soon sail for Paris to stretch out his education, shuddered at the thought of Mussolini and Franco, not the persistence of racism. But swilling drinks in the snug speakeasy, they made common cause with the noiristes: all were post-occupation reformers, not wanting to see their republic become a piggy bank for faraway powers and nearby kleptocrats.

Then Jean-Henri, in a lavish smoking jacket and overpriced panama hat, strode to Daniel's table, extended his hand. Daniel gave him a short nod and returned to his game. He favored his old students, such as Fritz-Claude, with rapacious appetites for politics—diligent, bookish, erudite—pupils who could clinically dissect his arguments, yet devoutly evangelize them, at once obedient and defiant. He felt a nasty scorn for the wannabes such as Jean-Henri, who feigned serious intentions but mostly chased women and spectacularly smoked their pipes.

Daniel pretended not to notice his growing queue of opponents tableside, alongside his spectators. He glanced around for François, but his friend was nowhere to be seen; Daniel didn't know if François preferred his bed, or if, pushing forty, he felt too old and shy to spend his day in a bar. Sensing a rapt audience, a choice moment, Daniel opened his mouth and delivered a lecture on recent political history, keeping his eyes on his game. He marveled at the country's unmet need for a good labor union. He gloated that the Sunday Clubs were practically the only space in his city where young men across the political divide, from communists to democrats, across classes, across all shades of color, could go to debate their lives.

Many of his Sunday Club students, Daniel knew, had more reason to be embittered than he. For le professeur, racism was a pressing political question. For his pupils, it was life. Fritz-Claude had been born into an illiterate family but had excelled in his studies. His dazzling mind could dart around in French, English, Spanish, German, and Kreyòl. Still, his future felt like a trap. He'd have to dump some white man's shit bowl with his educated hands. His hard-earned learning next to his master's inherited riches would make his exploitation feel all the more scorching. Flagrant. Learned but dismissed, Fritz-Claude and other members of the Sunday Clubs had to waive their dreams and work as garbage collectors, street sweepers, sanitation workers, ditchdiggers.

And they risked so much to attend those clubs. If the president's henchmen stumbled upon a public congregation of animated young men on a Sunday morning, they'd immediately understand that they weren't gathered to discuss westerns or girls—they'd shut down the meetings and jail the congregants. An arrest record could snuff any hope from a black student's already-precarious future.

Chapter 9

B Y THE EVE OF DANIELLE'S SECOND BIRTHDAY, JANUARY 1946, President Lescot had put the country in a ditch. The government was bankrupt. Businesses struggled. People resented how little they had. The president redoubled his efforts to hold on to his power by attacking still more of the people's liberties. He puffed up his security forces, in authority and in numbers, his personal guard, an elite corps of light-skinned military officers, and authorized a system of rural police chiefs to crack down on dissent by force.

On January 1, 1946, a citywide group of students issued a special New Year's edition of their journal, *La Ruche,* denouncing the country's "fascist oppression." Lescot confiscated the journal and arrested its top editors. Inspired by the Spanish Revolution, the released editors and their compatriots decried the dictatorship and demanded an end to the intrusion of the U.S. government and the exploitation wrought by American corporations. Empty pockets, squelched freedoms, fleeced futures. So many students felt they had the most to gain, the least to lose.

And so, one bright morning, ten o'clock on Monday, January 7, a group of law, medical, and agricultural students marched out of their classrooms. They clenched their fists high above their heads and headed toward the streets in their uniforms. They stopped at Lycée de Jeune Filles nearby, where they collected their female high school compatriots, then made their way to other preeminent high schools, Lycée Pétion and Saint Martial, to corral even more students. Their throng multiplied, not quite aware of its strength, and the air shook with their cries: *"Vive la révolution!"*

Police fanned across the city. The officers slammed their *kokomakaks*—Vodou nightsticks—against the students' backs and shoulders and took them into custody. The flatbeds of the police trucks and the cabooses of their jeeps swelled with a sea of khaki, of starched beige skirts, of white blouses, of dress shirts. Students crammed into the jail cells of the central police station and flooded its lobby, as though in a school gymnasium. Less than twenty-four hours later, they were set free, on the president's orders. They were shocked.

That night on the radio, government officials scolded parents city-wide, calling on them to better supervise their children and warning the students, above all, to abandon any plans for future demonstrations. Earlier that day, Lescot had instructed the head of his secret police to refrain from harassing the students: "The youth are not dangerous," he said dismissively. "They are only dialecticians."

The next day, even more students, from both high schools and colleges, swarmed into the streets. Walking down the avenues, they linked arms and sang the national anthem. They chanted for the president's ouster. Hearing the music, the shouts, still more students thrust their heads through their classroom windows, dashed out of their schools to join the procession. The melody of their songs seemed to harmonize with the faint grind of the axles on the trolleys. Some students swatted at the fruit flies; others took shade under the Haitian flags they brandished, which billowed ahead, beckoning their march forward.

Workers all along their route heard the yips, the laughter, the feet thumping the asphalt. Secretaries and pharmacists and blacksmiths all stopped what they were doing and poured into the streets. And so Fritz-Claude, the philosophy student, clutching his guitar case, marched right next to the avocado woman, her rough blouse tattered and loose, bunches of ripe avocados arranged like a baby in a sling across her back. Her mind was swaying, her hips spinning, infected by the buoyant mood.

The crowd wormed its way toward the president. A stream of bodies broke off into a city square. Mulatto socialist students, including René Depestre, read poems under the foliage. "1946 will be the Year of Freedom, when the voice of real democracy will / Triumph over all forms of fascist oppression. / Down with all the Francos!" Other students flooded the capital's commercial district, downtown near the palace, overwhelming the area. Workers made their way to the Champ de Mars and, arm in arm, chanted outside the palace, angry and dizzy with glee. Lescot had badly miscalculated: the initial crowd had been only several dozen strong. This crowd numbered four thousand.

Daniel surfaced in the Champ de Mars standing on a marble bench. He was close to the statue of Dessalines, the black general who had beaten the French and declared Haiti's independence, sculpted on a pedestal, hoisting his stone sword. Daniel could see from his perch his former students, his Sunday Club followers, workers who lived near his lakou. He always had a knack for knowing where to be and when, helped by select students who scurried to him in person with hot news and tips. Pacing the bench, he berated the government. He pointedly spoke in Kreyòl and in his best bass painted for them unforgettable images of an ideal society. He gave the protesters unflinching encouragement, a steely backing to their aims: "Mr. Lescot, the hour of the people is at hand."

"The charismatic leader of Port-au-Prince's urban masses was a born orator in the native creole language," Lyonel Paquin has written about that moment. "His speeches were biting, witty, and sardonic. He was an artist in the coinage of new words and expressions which were not part of the Haitian vernacular. His sword was his words."

Anyone listening to Daniel would have been able to connect his speech to his published writing. *Chantiers* had become a primary platform for the opposition's demands, even though no more than ten issues of the journal had ever been published. "*Chantiers* had a decisive influence on the revolution of 1946," a leading foreign newspaper correspondent noted. It had made an indelible mark on the student protesters, as the most public, fearless, direct critic of those in power.

For two days, the city stood at a standstill. The students refused to continue their studies until their list of demands was met, namely, enforcement of the four liberties, as ratified by the UN charter: freedom of speech, freedom of worship, freedom from want, and freedom from fear. They also demanded the reinstatement of all banned publications and the full allowance of political parties. And they were joined in their demands, for the first time in the history of Port-au-Prince, by a widespread movement of workers: bakers and butchers and civil servants and bus drivers went on strike with them. The U.S. corporate heavies—Standard Fruit and the Atlantic Refining Company, a division of Standard Oil, which had an exploration and drilling program in Haiti—had to shut down for lack of workers.

Lescot and his police, much as they wanted, could no longer snuff out the uprising. Finally, at three in the morning on January 11, 1946, President Lescot and his family scrunched into the back seat of a police car and were driven to Bowen Airfield. Five days after the protests began, the president resigned and he and his entourage fled the country.

The January Revolutions, as they came to be called, were a pivotal moment in the country's history—the people called them the "five glorious days." Not since the slave revolt of 1804 had ordinary Haitians stood up to ruling powers and shown them the door.

Chapter 10

———

HAVING OVERTHROWN THE MULATTO DICTATORSHIP, HAITI stood poised, if anxious, for change. Those five glorious days of January 1946 had heightened the urgent call for a democracy free from occupiers or elite milat rule. A temporary military junta presided over the government, until legislative, then presidential, elections could be held months later.

The political field was wide-open. The success of the January Revolutions emboldened more than two hundred candidates, most of them black, to compete for just fifty-eight legislative seats. Daniel decided to joust for the congressional seat representing Port-au-Prince. He campaigned feverishly over the radio and in the streets, his appeal burnished by *Chantiers,* his prominence in the Sunday Clubs, and his conspicuous tenacity during those five glorious days.

The young leader was "slight, bashful, with embers for eyes, and a rare magnetic timbre to his voice," described a *Time* magazine journalist that year. The popular sentiment in Port-au-Prince held that he would run to a decisive victory.

He lost.

Daniel's defeat to some obscure politician sent shock waves through the nation. His supporters took to the streets. Candidates and public servants on the left accused the body overseeing the election, the Ministry of the Interior, of forging the result. The U.S. embassy agreed: it confided to Washington in a classified cable that the military junta, organized by the head of the ministry, Colonel

Paul Magloire, had fixed the election. Election observers discovered hundreds of ballots had been sold the week before the vote.

"Police clashed tonight with disorderly groups roaming the streets of Port-au-Prince as unofficial returns from yesterday's parliamentary elections indicated defeat for Daniel Fignolé," *The New York Times* reported on May 14. "A group of his supporters yesterday stormed the headquarters of an opposition candidate shouting, 'Down with the middle class, down with mulattoes, and hail the proletariat.' Police used tear gas in attempts to restore order as Leftist groups in trucks jammed the downtown area and defied the Government."

THE NEXT DAY, the air clapped with crackles. A pop rang out. Smoke followed the bang, then billowed into disordered balloons. Danielle, two at the time, scratched at her nose and eyes, started crying, then coughed and gasped.

Soldiers were firing on the Fignolé home, detonating tear gas. The military junta had opened fire on his followers throughout the capital, and now on his house, in broad daylight.

By instinct, Selavi went frantically searching for le professeur, but neither he nor Carmen were home. Caught in her panic, Selavi forgot about the children, who had never been her priority. Raymonde, as it turned out, wasn't home either, but Danielle was crouched in her bedroom closet, bawling. When Selavi found her there, the girl pleaded, "I want to go to Tonton François's house. Take me to Tonton François's house."

Danielle had been left to fend for herself, her abandonment a baptism, an early initiation to close, immediate danger.

THIRTY HAITIANS WERE WOUNDED protesting Daniel's defeat. Two of his supporters were killed by military police.

This was the first time people had died supporting Daniel's political endeavors. Many students and workers collectively grieved those deaths and agonized that the promise of the January Revolutions was now doused in blood. I wish I knew whether my grandfather felt the pain of these lost lives, or whether he considered them the going price for majority "liberation." I cannot find any evidence in the historical record that he attended their funerals.

LATER THAT SUMMER, the parliament elected the handpicked candidate of the mulatto elite, Dumarsais Estimé, to be president. He became the country's first dark-skinned president since the end of the U.S. occupation, though it was a hollow victory for the black majority. The mulatto military and political elite didn't care about the new president's skin color, so long as he played *la politique de doublure*—"the politics of doubleness." Estimé could appear to rule the country impartially but was serving his true masters. Rattled by the January Revolutions, les grands blancs had given a nod to black power without conceding any real authority. They supported a black figurehead, who wore a pleasing mask, so long as he wouldn't ingrain his actions with the needs of actual blacks.

"Estimé's election was received with surprise and disbelief throughout the city. As he made his victory tour through the streets of Port-au-Prince, people shouted threats and slurs at him, while many women were, according to one observer, 'on their knees wailing miserably,'" writes the historian Matthew J. Smith. "Small groups of Daniel's supporters marched through Port-au-Prince, calling out 'Vive Fignolé.'"

THE DAY AFTER THE ELECTION, the new president invited Professor Fignolé and Dr. Duvalier to a secret meeting. As a top Fignolé deputy in the noiriste movement, Duvalier was nursing a profile in opposition politics. His stature as a griot championing Afro-Haitians was ascending, even after Fignolé's and the left's supposed parliamentary defeat.

The president said he wished to honor the January Revolutions by beginning a constructive chapter in the country's history, inclusive of black and poor people. So he invited the two noiriste leaders to join his "coalition government." The president offered Daniel the position of minister of education and public health and invited Duvalier to manage the country's public health service as its director general. Estimé was attempting a masterful maneuver: He wanted to placate the urban leader with a high-profile position and co-opt his irascible followers. He also wanted to keep his fiercest rivals close at hand.

Daniel accepted the president's appointment with pride and skepticism. On the one hand, he believed he had a profound first-hand understanding of what education could do to transform a Haitian's life. And the cabinet post would, he felt, give him the practical means to improve poor people's access to schools, doctors, and better jobs. But he wondered whether the new president would be radical enough to advance the country to the degree Daniel felt necessary. He understood that politicians wore masks. How open was this man to change?

Either way, Daniel had gone from fired itinerant teacher in 1942 to his country's chief educator and health authority by 1946.

And that was just the beginning.

Chapter 11

CARMEN, IN THE BACK SEAT OF THE FAMILY'S CAR BESIDE Daniel, cosseted Danielle, two years old, in her arms. Daniel's closest friend, Rodrigue Casimir, sat up front. Having met Daniel in high school, Rodrigue had been one of the few editors of *Chantiers* at its founding and then became a leading adviser in Daniel's inner circle. The family's driver, Sonny, was taking them all to Morne-A-Tuff, a neighborhood in the heart of Port-au-Prince.

As the car rolled to a stop, Carmen could hear the thud of bodies pounding against the door, hear their hands beat the fenders like a drum. She stared into the faces lurching toward the car, their bullet eyes not far from her window. She held Danielle tighter. Carmen watched waves and waves of people dancing and chanting. Stern faces, carnival-happy faces. One massive, mixed choir.

"Daniel!"

Daniel got out of the car and the crowd ripped open like cloth, crisply giving him passage. Rodrigue set a crate on the ground and Daniel stepped onto it. He paused. The crowd grew still around him, some men in their mechanic's coveralls and work boots, some men shirtless, some women in headscarves, arms dangling from their sleeveless nightgowns.

Roughly ten feet behind him, Carmen watched as Daniel's erudite eyes narrowed, as his lips curled into a faint smile.

Then he thundered against colonialists. He told bottling-plant workers to strike. He demanded more primary schools be built across the country to serve the ballooning number of school-age children, especially in poor neighborhoods such as this one. He insisted that the government could not address their poverty without improving access to public education. For dramatic effect, he lowered his voice to a sonorous, professorial timbre, then popped up into a squeal. He teased the crowd that he had plans up his sleeve for the weeks ahead—they should wait for his cue, then hit the streets.

The crowd hooted its approval at Daniel's colorful speech, flecked with salty Kreyòl. *"Santi bon koute che"*—"Smelling good is expensive." They cheered at his Africanisms, the way his Kreyòl cut through with gut wisdom, poetry, how he repeated his points to drive them home. All the oral farts in everyday life, in everyday sound, crept into his talk. The *élitaire* will fall on its buttocks—*ban! ban!* Spanish words floated into his Kreyòl too, as though they'd migrated from the Dominican Republic, as did English, as he twisted the occupiers' vocabulary against itself. *I will mop this system of the elites' dirty antics.*

For decades, politicians had spoken to this crowd in high French, then sent the police to crack its skulls. Politics was a monologue of the deaf: the powerful talked forever but did not hear. Government leaders spoke to the generals. They spoke to *les grands blancs.* They spoke to Paris and to Washington. But ordinary dark-skinned people had other needs. *Non, non, non,* they yearned. *I don't understand. Forget your political patronizing. Come and talk to me.*

"Daniel's Creole was as good as his French. It menaces. It charms," Carlo Desinor, a Haitian journalist and historian, would later recall. "On his lips our vernacular is a creative laboratory. The people absorb his tumult of eloquence, which makes them see another vision of the world, of themselves, of the future."

"Koute yon lodyans!" the people said in the streets. "Wait'll you hear this! Listen up." It was the rallying cry for the daily gossip-fest, every Haitian a born storyteller. On a street, on a sidewalk, in a market, on a porch, the self-appointed raconteur, with urgent descriptive gestures, would launch into a colorful story as people gathered around. Daniel's supporters loved the *teledjol,* the grapevine. Just listen to what Daniel said, they'd whisper down the line.

Watching Daniel, Carmen knew he felt as delirious as his crowd.
A roar of voices, singing, drowned out his own:

Roulez, lez, lez, Daniel
Roulez, lez, lez, Daniel
Pez buton and let us roll!

Roll, roll, roll, Daniel
Roll, roll, roll, Daniel
Push the button and let us roll!

Applause rang out, in sync with the shouting. Daniel bowed,
stepped off the crate, grinning broadly, a labyrinth of hands, a mass
tangle of fingers, grabbing at him, reaching for his suit, his skin, anything of him. *"Roulez, lay, lay, Daniel!"*

Carmen snatched Danielle's hand, eased her away from the crowd,
and they returned to the back seat of the car. Danielle felt content
tagging along with her papa, since he had told her she was allowed
on this excursion not only as his oldest and his namesake but as his
darling. Watching her husband through her window, Carmen could
not tell whether she enjoyed his swollen public family—still more
competition for his attention. Their bodies pressed closer to him, to
the car, with tender reaching hands. He yearned to embrace them
back in a way he so rarely did the girls.

Eventually, Rodrigue and Sonny hustled Daniel back into the car.
He smiled and waved through his window. Bodies clawed at the vehicle, hopped onto its front fender, hugged the back bonnet, until Sonny
shooed them off. Once he and Rodrigue managed to squeeze themselves through the crush and into the car, Sonny ignited the engine.

With that, the sedan belched and evaporated on the horizon in a
plume of exhaust.

BACK HOME, alone in his den, Daniel read the major newspapers.
Sitting at his desk, he picked up an article in *The New York Times*.

"The greatest political weapon here is known as Fignolé's Steam-roller," the paper reported. "It consists of an aroused population sweeping out of the slum districts and rolling everything before it. On most occasions M. Fignolé has been reluctant to set loose this force, but when it starts moving it spreads terror and destruction."

Daniel had the power to flood the streets with his followers in spontaneous protest, his *woulo*—steamroller. He ignited his steam-roller to intimidate his opponents and to punctuate his political demands. He liked to remind the plantation owners, the business executives, the politicians, that he had his finger on "the button." With one speech, one phone call, one radio broadcast, he could push it and thousands of his supporters would choke the capital in protest.

"Fignolé, in one half hour, could mold a listening crowd of thou-sands into a quivering mass of obedience," writes the historian Eliza-beth Abbott.

Once Daniel made his wishes known, the message spread like fire and the steamroller started to rumble.

Attention! Woulo compresseur deyò!

Beware! The steamroller is outside!

The big whites could hear it too. The noise came as a murmur at first, then a husky thundering. Words rattled and crescendoed from the lower wards, a human rumble ricocheting up the hills to the supine villas, the exclusive social clubs, to Le Port-au-Princien, with its quarters commanding forever city views, to Le Cercle de Bellevue, with its billiard tables and Viennese-style grand ballroom, to the Turgeau Tennis Club. A wave of dark bodies chanting, sing-ing, dancing, protesting, clogging the streets below.

Daniel!

Urgent shouting—some of it menacing, some of it rapturous.

À bas la misère!

Down with misery!

DANIEL HAD MADE QUICK work as head of the country's education and health. Not long after he was sworn in, he began dropping in on public schools unannounced to get an unvarnished view of the institutions he was reforming. Daniel bristled to the president that some elite high schools excluded poorer students. They required subject matter and preparatory study beyond poor people's reach. The prestigious girls' high school in Port-au-Prince, for instance, effectively closed its doors to the lower classes by virtue of its admission design. Daniel required it to add a surrogate junior high school, a pipeline to elite learning for lower-income girls.

He seethed that the education system punished the lower classes by maintaining the better schools in wealthier neighborhoods and created a plan to build more schools in working-class neighborhoods. And he forced those new schools to create more academic levels, to expand their enrollments, and to update their standardized, classical curricula, which had long favored the rich. He set about raising rural teachers' shabby salaries and cracked down on booksellers who had long charged exorbitant prices for new editions of classic books. Days later, a journalist and firsthand witness, Baron von Holbach, dubbed this "the most promising action ever taken by the National Ministry of Education."

"Never before or after in the history of Haiti has any Minister done so much for national education in such a short time," von Holbach would later write.

And Daniel had just as much passion to reform the public health system. To stave off discomfort and disease, he mandated that the streets of the capital be kept clean and that household trash be collected both day and night. The sidewalk garbage generated by homes and businesses was a breeding ground for typhoid; he helped thwart an emerging epidemic before it ravaged the capital and the towns of Jacmel, Jérémie, and Gonaïves by instituting new sanitation measures and medical-preparedness practices in public hospitals. Appalled at the superior treatment enjoyed by elites in the country's General Hospital, he eliminated the private ward. Perhaps he was motivated by the memory of Leonie dying for lack of medical attention, and his own two hospitalizations for sinus infections that had nearly killed him.

He bolstered his cabinet actions through his public speeches, goading his followers into amplifying his message. A sugar mill worker would park his truck roadside, blast its radio, and one hundred more listeners, crowding the sidewalk, would hear Daniel. A seamstress did the same in the doorway of her atelier, and dozens swarmed around her front stoop to listen. A barber blared the speech through the open window of his shop, and there were one hundred more again.

Popular voice, government position. Daniel's personal and public power were growing hand in glove. "If anyone thinks they can stop what I am doing for my people," he declared on the radio, "I will be forced to use my *woulo* to destroy them!"

DUVALIER, MEANWHILE, took a different tack in his work. As Daniel revved his steamroller, Tonton François plodded along as a bureaucrat, running the government's medical apparatus as director general of the National Public Health Service. Though François was almost a decade older than Daniel, Daniel's efficiency and reputation far outshone his friend's.

"In 1946, le Professeur Daniel Fignolé made his political debut with all the fanfare of a comet blazing toward the earth," Lyonel Paquin has noted. By contrast, after riding in a car with François in the 1940s Paquin wrote, "I glanced furtively at him and noticed his likeness to a sad frog with a heavy lower lip and almost painful wryness in his countenance." Another historian, Robert Rotberg, has characterized Duvalier at the time as "singularly non-aggressive. Lack-luster. A little man who listened so intently. Inscrutable. Comparatively competent. Seemingly honest, shy and not particularly impressive."

Daniel, meanwhile, was growing into his legend. *Demain,* a newspaper, issued an editorial that dubbed Daniel "The Moses of Port-au-Prince." One of his supporters wrote a poem of adoration, published in the journal *Rasoir*:

Young teacher of the proletariat,
black friend of the blacks,
sincere comrade loved by the crowd on whose orders they
   swell into an immense sea,
we love, adore, and adulate Daniel Fignolé.

While he may have been Moses to his people, at home he was a Houdini. Carmen needed help around the lakou and Daniel seemed always to be absent. He'd delegated the rearing of his girls to his wife and maids—he felt he had so much else to do. Carmen had come to rely more on Selavi, Natacha, and Sonny. Selavi served le professeur breakfast, took his dirty suits to the launderer à la Parisienne, and mended Carmen's ripped skirts. And both maids tidied up and looked after the girls. Carmen's milat friends marveled that she could manage with such a meager crew—and hold down a job. They kept a staff of at least six or seven: a few maids, a houseboy, a cook, a gardener, a driver, and *le guardian,* armed, to mind their gated villas.

More and more of Daniel's hours were devoured by his cabinet responsibilities, and he had less time for Carmen, Danielle, and Raymonde. He was becoming ever more remote. Opaque, even. The family all had to dance around the inscrutability of his moods. The air of intimidation he cultivated for his political enemies drifted right through the front door. Staring through them, walking past them, standing over them, leaning into them: Over six feet tall, Daniel knew just how to organize his body to intimidate his wife and children.

They measured their nerves by his sounds. When he shuffled papers or the telephone rang in his den, Selavi reminded Danielle to tiptoe. If he cracked his knuckles and exhaled loudly after a long day inspecting hospitals, everyone knew better than to ask him anything. Daniel didn't seem to notice his wife, his daughters, and their maids shadowboxing with his moods. His growing cachet shielded him from their demands, his increasing importance licensed his surly bent. Le professeur is a complicated man, moody and morose, Carmen said to her friends.

Many could tell what she meant: his temper and sarcasm were prolific even in public. Soon after he took his cabinet job, Daniel stumbled upon a mulatto, in a fussy uniform, guarding the black, black president.

Daniel stared the bodyguard down and chortled, "I thought the marines left in 'thirty-four."

His admirers laughed at his rapier wit. Carmen and his deputies often found it mean and condescending.

DANIEL RAILED AGAINST the Establishment, even as he was firmly planted in it. He stoked unrest in the streets even as he worked as a cabinet minister. That had big consequences. His unique standing, as an outsider-insider, inspired jealousy among his peers, drew attention to him from corporations, and put a bull's-eye on his back.

Carmen and the girls always set the radio on the credenza near the dining table so they could listen to Daniel's weekly fifteen-minute broadcast during dinner. He used those speeches to lob attacks at his cabinet colleagues and his boss, but what Carmen heard on October 21, 1946, shocked her, as it did the country. Daniel denounced the minister of commerce and agriculture, an elite mulatto lawyer, for trying to pack key government positions with his wealthy cronies. Even more pointedly, Daniel accused his light-skinned cabinet colleague of trying to overthrow the president.

The address caused quite a scandal. Soon after, the commerce secretary's allies scolded the president for failing to reprimand Fignolé for his incendiary attacks. Critics of President Estimé ridiculed him for tolerating Daniel's cantankerous "fireside chats." Laughing, they dubbed the president Esti-Mop.

For Estimé this was the final straw, though he had no desire to take sides between his dark-skinned education and health secretary and his mulatto commerce secretary—each well connected and each leading important political constituencies.

So, three days after Daniel's broadcast, Estimé fired his entire cabinet.

Chapter 12

————

THE NIGHT AFTER DANIEL LOST HIS CONGRESSIONAL RACE in 1946, he gathered his closest circle—Rodrigue, François, Lorimer—and made plans for the future. His ultimate goal was as clear as it was ambitious: the presidency. He knew, though, that the force of his growing reputation and the work he'd done in the cabinet could not on their own assure his political aims. He needed to get more organized. He needed a group to propel his efforts. He told his deputies that he wanted to start a labor party.

Months earlier, Daniel's former pupils had come to him determined to transform their underground Sunday Clubs into a fearsome organization. They called their nascent movement "mop," with an eye to mopping up Haiti's top-down politics. The students' lives seemed destined for cleaning up after the rich, but they also aimed to cleanse the country's foul political system. What delicious Haitian humor: the word mocked their plight and announced their intentions. They yearned for le professeur to help them guide the organization.

He accepted happily. His internal goals, and these external circumstances, he felt, were marvelously aligned.

So, in May 1946, he formally founded his labor party. He kept the name MOP, which tickled him, and turned it into an acronym: Mouvement des Ouvriers et Paysans, or Movement for Laborers and Peasants. In a momentous radio speech, he lionized the January Revolutions, commended the students for their courage, and declared that together they would mop the country clean of corruption and inequality.

"We have formed MOP which will assure the majority class effective direction of the country," Daniel announced in his journal, *Chantiers,* newly relaunched. "Our party is strong and put to the service of our class."

The party got busy fast. Daniel created a literacy program for workers, with a night school at MOP headquarters, and launched a day school for members' children, eventually extending those offerings to rural areas, schools for a few outpost unions. In a small building next to the headquarters, Daniel created Institut Mopique, a type of think tank offering free lectures to the public on history, geography, and politics. He called on his circle of populist thinkers, including Tonton Rodrigue, to teach grassroots courses in Kreyòl, and they also hosted biweekly documentary film screenings on world affairs. Alongside the institute, the party formed Club Mopiste, a social lodge that hosted sporting events and wedding receptions. It had a youth league and a youth-driven journal, *Notre Jeunesse.* This remarkable, unparalleled hive of activity, Daniel believed, would lure new members and keep existing ones engaged and in the fold.

"Under his leadership, MOP became the most organized labor party in Haitian history," writes Matthew J. Smith. "MOP incorporated unions from the largest companies in Port-au-Prince and its environs, including workers at the Bata shoe factory, dockworkers, hydraulic workers, gas station workers, confectionaries, and barbers. Fignolé's charisma and popular appeal guaranteed MOP a following wider than the unions."

Determined to grow the party, Daniel delegated administrative tasks to François and put him in charge of the party's health initiatives. The party work afforded François a hands-on object lesson in political organizing. Indeed, in those years, Daniel and Lorimer "were to provide the early momentum in Duvalier's climb," as one Duvalier biographer later wrote.

Inspired by the bustle, Carmen set to work. She founded and ran the feminist arm of MOP, the Bureau for Women's Action, and launched a journal to amplify its efforts, *La Famille.* The January

Revolutions had opened space for her: the new revolutionary mood, with its surge in leftist thinking, infused her and her allies with clarity, daring. As Selavi put Danielle and Raymonde to bed, and Daniel was toiling in his den, Carmen lit the kerosene lamp and placed it on the dining room table. At the Underwood, she composed a letter addressed to the president seeking the right for women to vote. She typed up letters to members of parliament, which her group had drafted, demanding more public schools for girls and reformed family laws that better served women on the job, in divorce, and through inheritance. She and a bureau member would physically deliver the letters to the National Assembly. She made a plan to pressure the cabinet to include a women's advocate in the Ministry of Labor. And her group conceived of ways to pressure top businesses to grant women maternity leave and to raise women's wages so that they were at parity to men's. Indigenous, black, mulatta, poor, middle-class, wealthy, Marxist, black nationalist: women around the country were working together in a sisterly collective that transcended their differences. And no matter the women's ideological and human divisions, leading feminist organizations settled on one supreme objective that was clear and paramount: the right to vote.

The most active feminist leaders were well-heeled professionals, such as Carmen, and wealthy mulatta housewives. They were the women who could carve out the time to attend daytime gatherings, or craft political statements in French, or deliver flyers to parliament, or raise money to host get-togethers with allies from around the world. The country's leading women's political group, the Feminine League for Social Action, was presided over by Madame Alice Garoute, a light-skinned, highly educated wife of a milat attorney. The second-most-influential feminist organization in the country was the women's arm of MOP, founded by Carmen.

Carmen drew a sharp boundary between her friendships with noted feminists, including the educated mulatta elites, and her bureau's work. She did not let Daniel's statements and strikes rile those friendships, nor did she let her bonds with them bleach the

distinctly pro-black, pro-worker tint to her group. Historians cite
her as one of the five most consequential feminists in the country
during the twentieth century.

Daniel lauded Carmen's work, though he never called himself a
"feminist" in public, nor, likely, behind closed doors. It was considered such a bourgeois, emasculating, and Europeanized label by men
such as him, a noiriste patriarch leading a brass-knuckles union. But
he passionately and publicly supported girls having equal access
to education as boys, better wages for women, job protections that
helped mothers better care for children, and women's right to vote.

DANIEL ADVOCATED for improved political rights and better wages
for women, but it was Carmen who did the labor of raising the girls.
And now there were two more. The first came at the tail end of 1946,
Marie-Jose. Mathematical odds, Daniel was certain, would grant
him his wish for a son the next time. Imagine his distress: another
daughter! She came in March 1949, and he named her after his
mother, Leonie.

Not long after Leonie was born, Georgina Jean-François, Carmen's favorite and baby sister, turned up at Daniel's house carrying a
suitcase. Gigine, as she was known—even more feminine and exqui-
site than Carmen—had gotten pregnant at twenty. Carmen told her
that abortion was not a question: she had to marry the guy. So it was:
Gigine, the father, Jean Desse, and their newborn were all installed
in the lakou. In turn, Gigine, seven years younger than Carmen,
bathed Danielle and sang to her. Some days, she ironed Danielle's
tangles stiff-straight, favoring the girl with a head of "good" hair.
Hand in hand, she took Danielle to the confectionary and to the
library. Danielle felt that her young aunt was the big sister she'd
never had, and Carmen appreciated the small miracles that Gigine
left around the house. Thanks to her doting sister, she could focus on
her work, with some fugitive moments for herself.

But Gigine's own baby died—suddenly and inexplicably—at nine
months old. Carmen took charge of disposing of the body. Days on

Carmen poses baby Marie underneath Daniel's portrait,
circa 1947–1948

end, she sat and prayed with her sister. She drew Gigine her bath and put her to bed at night.

Carmen saw how furious Daniel grew when her care for Gigine interrupted the small rhythms of their days—Carmen making her deadlines running the women's bureau, her hosting guests in the courtyard, her arrival to bed. One night, he heard voices in the living room and stalked out of his den to see what was going on. When Daniel saw Gigine crying next to his wife, he dispatched her to fetch him *Le Nouvelliste,* as if to limit the attention Gigine received from Carmen. He'd already read the day's news: the paper was vengeance. He would wait on the couch for her return.

Carmen stood up from the table. She looked into Daniel's sagging eyes and shook her head with a soft remorse. She sat next to him on the sofa and put her arm around his shoulder. He pushed it off, got up, and returned to his den.

His house on the lakou was bursting at the seams. His focus was solely on MOP.

• • •

SOON, HE'D CAUGHT WIND from his deputies that the business class and his political rivals were whispering lies about him and his union to the U.S. embassy. There were rumblings that he was a communist. Daniel gathered François—who had studied in the American heartland, at the University of Michigan—and set up a meeting at the embassy, eager to correct the libel being spread against his party. With Duvalier, ever quiet and mumbling, in tow, Daniel arrived to the private meeting with the U.S. chargé d'affaires, Horatio Mooers, in late 1946.

"Fignolé made clear MOP's anti-communist stance," a secret U.S. cable from the time states, "arguing that the party's only purpose was 'to bring help to the black masses.'"

Outside the embassy's walls, Daniel had already repeatedly denounced communism and Haiti's Communist Party in his speeches. He told his followers that communism was claustrophobic as a dogma and antidemocratic as a practice. What did communism say about the color prejudice that worsened his followers' poverty? Or about black solidarity? Communism, he believed, did not sufficiently factor in race nor adequately address racism in its social diagnosis or in its political solutions. Haiti's problem, he explained often, wasn't only to allot wealth more fairly. The country had to make education universal, to expand political participation—and to promote human dignity. Daniel loathed communism.

At the embassy meeting, Daniel "remarked that he welcomed U.S. interest in Haiti but resented the fact that officials since the occupation displayed mistrust in the capacity of the black majority by consistently allying themselves with the elite." Indeed, he, François, and MOP leaders hated imperialism because the U.S. government favored one caste at the expense of another.

"This is a politically inarticulate mass of disinherited Haitian blacks, illiterate, miserable, but loyal to their chief," wrote Jack West, an American operative in Port-au-Prince, to the U.S. secretary of state, in a confidential memo. "The MOP, as Fignolé's movement is called, is a racist organization which condemns mulattoes for all of Haiti's economic and political woes."

American operatives in the capital kept close tabs on Daniel. In a classified 1948 memo, the U.S. ambassador, at the request of his boss, Secretary of State George Marshall, profiled the "principal personalities" of Haitian politics:

"First and perhaps most important of these figures is the somewhat mystic figure Daniel FIGNOLÉ, professor of history by trade who entered politics about the time of the overthrow of the Lescot regime. He is a black and a champion of black supremacy. As such he is feared by the mulatto bourgeoisie. His political ideas, originally leftist, seem to have veered off to some form of neo-fascism."

The U.S. ambassador warned, "Left-wing doctrines are not considered menacing to the internal security of Haiti at present, although the elements mentioned above bear close and constant watching."

The more that workers exalted MOP, the more U.S. corporations targeted it, alongside the embassy.

THROUGHOUT 1947, U.S.-owned corporations and the milat plantation owners complained fiercely to the president that Daniel Fignolé and other union leaders were meddling in labor disputes. So that fall, Estimé passed a law that hamstrung unions in negotiating labor clashes. In response, Daniel organized general strikes against the president and the new law.

A few weeks before MOP's strike began, François made a flowery, showy speech to MOP's leadership, flattering the party and its principals. But just one month later, he declared that he planned to leave the party. He accepted a job in the administration of the president. Duvalier abandoned MOP just a year after its founding, a tender juncture in the union's early life.

Daniel, in public, refused to show signs of upset at his friend's betrayal. He dismissed François to the union's top leaders as "incoherent" and "unstable." Privately, though, Daniel correctly suspected that Duvalier was reading the tea leaves. Sussing out the power ladder, François calculated who in the president's administration was growing in influence and measured himself against them. He

decided that his career fortunes were better off by joining the president than by continuing in protest mode in solidarity with Daniel.

Daniel, in turn, decided that François couldn't be trusted—in his
party or in his home. He complained to Rodrigue and Carmen that
François's bumbling modesty was an act to conceal a mercenary self-
interest. His professional about-face dredged up the personal kinks
that had annoyed Daniel about François in the first place. Daniel
no longer trusted the Vodou-conjuring, Africa-touting, Marxist-
spouting, America-courting dark-skinned noiriste wed to an illegitimate, luxury-loving mulatta. The man was a big phony, Daniel
hissed to Carmen, even if he was Raymonde's godfather. What Daniel did not say was how much the betrayal wounded his pride: he
felt he had personally invested so much in seasoning François and
nurturing his political skills, only to see him walk.

To Daniel's chagrin, the breakup did become rather public. Newspapers reported François's exodus from MOP and Daniel's response
to the quitting. Then teledjol started churning gossip: each boss man
had severed the friendship like a rotting wart, cut his losses, and was
moving on.

DANIEL FOCUSED his efforts on fighting Estimé. Not long after he'd
taken office, Estimé had developed a wide popularity. Daniel's supporters had gotten over their shock at his election, set aside their
reservations; the president assured his critics that he'd work for the
black masses, pointing to Daniel's appointment as evidence.

But four years later, it wasn't just Daniel and MOP who despised
the man. The economy was in free fall. A severe drought ruined the
1949 crop, and the president's government was saddled with debt.
Even the mulatto elite, who had installed the president, complained
behind closed doors. The president, they groused among themselves, wasn't compliant enough. "Despite all the money they were
making in the post-war black market, along with the fabulous public
works contracts that the president had passed on to them, they were
not satisfied," Paquin wrote at the time.

Daniel scorched the president in the streets and on the airwaves. In turn, Estimé cracked down on him. One night in November 1949, a government worker, a fierce supporter of Daniel's, came cycling to the lakou, panting, with word that the police were on their way. Daniel crouched in the trunk of his car and Sonny drove him away. He narrowly escaped arrest by hiding in the embassy of Argentina, courtesy of his friend the ambassador. Nobody knew where he was, officially; hiding a fugitive was a diplomatic no-no for a supposed friend to Haiti.

Months later, Daniel launched a massive workers' strike against the president's regime. The Senate, the mulatto elite, the military, leftist intellectuals, students, Daniel's unions and followers—they all turned against the president. Opposition grew so heated that the president resigned on May 10, 1950, and fled to Paris.

Chapter 13

DANIELLE LEANED AGAINST THE KITCHEN WALL WAITING for the feast that Selavi would soon put on the table: pork griot, fried red snapper, heaps of rice and beans, and *sauce calalou*. On Christmas Eve in 1950, the Fignolé family wanted to take advantage of a rare occasion: Daniel's lingering good mood. Just months before, in October, he'd won his first election ever, as the congressman for Port-au-Prince; he was thrilled by his new platform, serving more than two hundred thousand voters. In November, Carmen had finally delivered him a son, whom he'd named exactly after himself, Pierre Eustache Daniel Fignolé. And then, weeks later, in early December, a new black president, General Paul Magloire, was inaugurated—a start to an era with appetizing promise.

Tonton Rodrigue arrived for dinner and Danielle ran from the kitchen to hug him. To accommodate their expanded flock, Daniel and Carmen had moved the family from their run-down lakou to 19 Rue du Peoples. It was a simple, un-enchanting house—some even said drab—on an unremarkable street in working-class Bel-Air.

Danielle preferred the larger home to their old place. It was a fresh-smelling roost of polished wood, glistening windows, and bright white bed linen, which Selavi laundered in vinegar. Also, its automobile, telephone, paintings, and carpets made it one of the fanciest homes in the workaday neighborhood.

Outside their new home hung a simple wooden sign: L'ÉCOLE FIGNOLÉ. As soon as they'd moved, Carmen had started a private school, to sustain her love of teaching and for the extra money.

Middle- to upper-middle-class families paid a premium to send their kids to L'École Fignolé, a primary school that ran from grade one to six. Carmen's school offered its students a solid education, Catholic grounding, and some social polish from Carmen—with the occasional math or history lesson thrown in from her renowned husband.

Danielle was in the first grade at her mother's school, though she received no special treatment from her stern parents. The school was on the ground floor, as were Daniel's office and printing press. The top floor was the private residence. On school days, Danielle headed downstairs to the classroom at seven and wasn't allowed back into the upstairs residence until six.

It was Carmen who afforded Daniel this congenial house, purchased with her family's money. The year he was elected congressman, Grand-mère Claire Mina had died, leaving her daughter an inheritance. Carmen decided to buy Daniel a nifty gift, a scarlet-red Ford. When it first arrived, neighbors crowded the carport to admire the 1950 classic four-door coupe, which had a wide, curvaceous front hood and a Victoria hardtop.

"How telling that his car should be red," one politician asserted to a local journalist, snickering at the supposed communist.

Asked by an American newspaper editor why his car was red, Daniel only shrugged. "There is nothing to the color," he said, a bit irritated. "It doesn't matter to me."

Still, Daniel delighted in driving his new toy. Zipping about to his appointments, he cut a dramatic figure across Port-au-Prince. He enjoyed the attention that the car brought him, even if it came with derision: his critics mocked him as a loaf-about intellectual sponging off his wealthy wife.

AWAY FROM PRYING EYES he had gathered in his peaceful living room with the family before sitting to Christmas dinner. It was then that a magnificent commotion erupted outside—the din of children's shrieks.

Shit you are! Shit you are!

Everyone ran out the back door into the alley. There stood 'Ti-Max—petit Max—covered in feces. Most of the neighbors shared an outhouse, three to four shacks per outdoor latrine, though the Fignolés had their own, a luxury. Selavi had taken a sturdy wooden box, cut a circle through its top, and placed the thing on top of a six-foot hole in the dirt. She measured the seat according to le professeur's grown butt, so that no adult, especially him, would be discomforted by a kiddie-size commode. All the neighbors made their latrine that way, a throne for a man, not a child, and so a child could easily slip through. When 'Ti-Max hadn't turned up for his Christmas supper, his cousin went looking for him in the alley outhouse, hauled him out of the hole and back through the communal courtyard. The kids pointed at him, doubled over laughing. *"Caca-ou-ye, caca-ou-ye."* From that moment, 'Ti-Max had a new nickname, ShitYouAre.

They all went back inside, still laughing. Danielle managed to claim her father's lap for herself—prime turf—something he ordinarily did not like or allow. But the moment's mirth had taken its hold. As he cradled Danielle, his mood bordered on joy. He reached for an envelope on the coffee table; the letter had been delivered the day before. Once he had the room's rapt attention, he put on his nonchalant voice to mention who had sent the letter: Léon Blum, the French socialist intellectual who had, in 1936, become the first Jewish prime minister of France. Rodrigue sat near the edge of his seat. Gigine listened in from a corner where Daniel couldn't see her, as he read the letter aloud. A tentative peace between the two had begun to settle.

After applause for the letter had ebbed to a hush, Selavi gingerly placed a record on the phonograph, careful to keep her fingers on the edge of the vinyl, so le professeur wouldn't scold her in front of everybody. Daniel, despite himself, joined the sing-along. He sang shyly, as if not wanting anyone to hear him. As he murmured Édith Piaf's words, his hard eyes went soft, a white stirring in his soul, sick with his love for France. After Piaf's torch songs came Aznavour.

Carmen knit quietly in a corner, biting her tongue. She had sat at the piano earlier to play Christmas hymns that they could all sing along to, but Daniel had cut her off.

Once the singing was over, Danielle stood in the corner, dressed as a slave in a costume that Gigine had sewn for her. She, Gigine, Raymonde, and Natacha performed a skit about Louverture's revolt.

United, let us march! Let there be no traitors in our ranks! Let us be masters of our soil!

"Eh, *ben*," said Rodrigue, peering over his glasses. "What a nationalist extravaganza." Daniel dug his chin into his collar to hide his smile, pleased by his dear friend's remark, by Rodrigue's appreciation for the staunch national pride lighting his new home.

There was a harmonized blackness, a dearth of mulatto features—aeroplaned nose bridges, green eyes—among Daniel's new neighbors. He delighted in living among them, the sort of people he loved most. His neighbor Franck mixed and poured cement; Fritz-Claude stacked shipments at the shoe factory; Fat Charles fixed cars alongside his cousin Pretty Charles, with his long eyelashes, in a little white's auto mechanic shop; and Toussaint drove taxis. Some of Daniel's neighbors had no work at all.

A decade before Daniel's arrival, Bel-Air had had a big inflow of new residents, when Generalissimo Rafael Trujillo had ordered the massacre and expulsion of thousands of black Haitians from the Dominican Republic. The city's property class took advantage of the newcomers by building cheap shacks in Bel-Air to rent to them. In the years since, the black intelligentsia had moved in too, out of choice and necessity. Albert, the doctor at the public hospital; Beethoven, the civil rights lawyer; Mirlande, the translator at the Venezuelan embassy, who had her unfinished novel tucked in her nightstand; Lillie, the director of the history museum; and Horace, the book editor at the blue-chip house. They stretched their modest paychecks working their rarefied jobs.

Daniel and Carmen knew that dark-skinned people such as they were upending the mulatto social elite. Their aging high school classmates, white looking—and even reddish bone—retained their formidable grip on the country's commerce and politics. But their social influence was leaking like a deflating tire. A cadre of black professionals was beginning to seize social ownership of the country, and Daniel and Carmen lived in the thick of this ascendant class. She received its brightest luminaries at her sprawling parties. They shook their hips to the Vodou djazz, which was all the rage, a mash of merengue, Vodou drumbeats, and big-band swing. The women spun with the melody in their *tarlatanes,* cinched-waist skirts that billowed into flowing hoops, preferably from the house of Dior.

Daniel's marriage to Carmen paid him back dividends—not only their rambling house and his scarlet Ford, but their joint life ascent. She was polishing his social edges, decorating his public image, implanting in him personal refinement that he otherwise did not enjoy. While he masterminded fiery labor strikes against Standard Fruit and the Bata shoe factory, she was all aristocratic manners and grace. She remembered your kids' names, where they went to school, your birthday, your spouse's birthday, where and when your kids had been christened, all their triumphs and illnesses. She remembered your favorite dishes, and when she had served them, and what everyone had been wearing. And when you were sick in bed, she cooked you a heaping pot of beef okra stew, tied it up in a cloth, and had her chauffeur, Sonny, deliver it with a touching note.

Daniel couldn't even tell you his own daughters' ages or birthdays.

SELAVI SNATCHED the small bronze bell on the dining room credenza and shook it with a scowl. How this ritual annoyed her, summoning everybody to le professeur's dinner table, a fussy prelude to the food she had cooked with grit. The adults, Danielle, and Raymonde sat around the mahogany table. Natacha had already fed the babies.

Tonton François was conspicuously absent from the Fignolé house that night. Daniel had cut ties with him after their falling out. Anyway, it had always rankled Daniel that while he could command the adoration of tens of thousands, the women under his roof often seemed to prefer the Duvaliers. He did not crave his children's affection, but still he had watched with envy as Tonton François played with Danielle. With François around, Daniel could not control the women's devotion. And he felt Simone had a snooty, imperious way about her, as if to compensate for her origins, which aggravated him, likely because her demeanor held up a pointed looking-glass reflecting his own.

Carmen had long known that Daniel's bile toward François and Simone was fermenting; the blowup hadn't surprised her. Neither man had ever loved the other nearly as much as he loved himself. As each man's profile grew, their delicate friendship could no longer sustain two massive egos.

Choop. Daniel sucked his teeth in scorn whenever he bumped into François and Simone at a party. And he had told Carmen that François was banned from 19 Avenue of the People, and the family forbidden to visit the Duvaliers. Danielle was stunned and confused by the order, but she knew her papa would beat her if she went across town to dally with her former playmates. Though when the Duvaliers' son, Jean-Claude, was born in 1951, Danielle and Carmen snuck past the professor out of the house to meet him. "Good Lord!" Danielle had shouted in the hospital. "What a huge head on such a tiny yellow baby!" Even as a child, she couldn't keep a good insult to herself.

But come Christmas Eve, the Duvaliers were home at the old lakou and the Fignolés were gathered with the friends most loyal to Daniel. Plates lay in front of the family. Raymonde spied on Danielle's plate a bone with lumps of pork hugging it. She reached. Danielle smacked her hand. Danielle loved to gnaw on the bits of pork still clinging to the bone. She saved them for last.

After dinner, Carmen told Danielle and Raymonde to go bathe and get ready for midnight mass. Daniel polished off his chocolate cake and sorbet grenadine, giving his thumb and pointer finger one last lick. Then he disappeared into his den and went back to work.

Chapter 14

GENERAL MAGLOIRE HAD BEEN INAUGURATED PRESIDENT not long before Selavi's glorious Christmas feast, on the morning of December 6, 1950—a moment Daniel was never to forget.

The country's business, political, and military elite put on their dandiest outfits and descended on the National Cathedral. The dignitaries took their seats on a VIP dais front and center. Then suddenly, a burst of applause rang out. The ovation was so rapturous that the dignitaries leapt to their feet. The elite clapped and clapped, under the impression that President Magloire had arrived.

But it was Daniel.

He smiled as he walked in, waving at the crowd. He patted audience members on their backs. He grinned and he grinned, talking to the people. No doubt, he had discreetly orchestrated his entrance, making sure his supporters were strategically sprinkled throughout the cathedral's nave and near its entrance. The spontaneity and vigor of his greeting startled the dignitaries.

The guest of honor soon arrived to a much-meeker reception.

The big whites laughed openly at the upstaged president: Daniel would be a handful for him to manage.

The two weren't strangers to each other. When Daniel lost his first race for parliament soon after the 1946 January Revolutions, it was Colonel Paul Magloire who had followed orders from his superiors and coordinated the milat and military junta's supposed election sweep, contriving Daniel's loss.

Tall, burly, barrel-chested, dark-skinned—Magloire was also

vain. He loved his custom-made military "uniforms," each costing up to a thousand dollars. His bespoke army outfits featured gold-braided epaulets, finely corded aiguillettes—ropes circling his right shoulder—spurred boots, and a plume jutting from his hat. One aide followed the general carrying his fat seven-inch cigars in a leather box. Another carted the gold-headed cane the general brandished like a scepter. Come nighttime, he traded his make-believe uniform for real formal wear. During his many balls at the palace, he'd wear white tie and coattails. He would elaborately ask each lady to dance on the gleaming ballroom floor in descending order of their husbands' rank. He bowed to them elaborately; they curtsied even more so. Other evenings, he played poker or bridge in the palace, then vanished into Port-au-Prince's smartest nightclubs. Spotting him out with his highball and cigar in hand, the elite did not expect that his florid vanity, his bon-vivant tastes, could be matched by a commensurate appetite for terror.

DANIEL WAS CLEARLY IN the president's sights, and Magloire would be quick to strike. Just before the New Year, on December 30, 1950, Magloire abolished MOP and the country's Socialist Party. The president claimed that both political parties would further "Haiti's collusion with Moscow." Complaining of "dangerous maneuvers" launched by Fignolé's political party, the Magloire regime shut down the party's newspapers too: *Chantiers, Notre Jeunesse,* and Carmen's dear *La Famille.* Daniel responded by renaming MOP as the Grand National Democratic Party.

He robustly promoted his party as "anti-communist" and "pro-labor." And he adamantly rebutted the president's accusations.

"Haiti must be anti-communist and truly democratic," Daniel wrote in his new journal. "Moscow-styled communism is certainly dangerous for the normal evolution of this little country."

He was not the only one to buck the president. Students had grown fed up with the government's meager-to-nonexistent support for their education. Their anger culminated in massive demonstra-

tions by January 1952, and Daniel galvanized his political base to
rally around them. Magloire responded by ordering his forces to
round up a small handful of the most visible student leaders and
ship them to distant prisons in the hinterlands.

Carmen watched warily from the side as her husband waged war
with still another president, leaving her to tend to their ever-growing
family. In February 1953, she gave birth to their sixth child, and second son. Daniel named him Bernard, his mother's maiden name.
As Bernard waddled toward his first Christmas, Daniel cofounded
the League for the Defense of Public Liberties, a group of twenty-
one public servants who opposed the president, working to fight his
growing despotism by promoting civil liberties: the right to assembly, the free functioning of political parties, and freedom of expression. True to character, Daniel established a journal, *Democratic
Haiti*, to champion the league's activities. Given his incendiary political activity and the volume of foot traffic into and out of his house—
members of his party and league—Daniel kept his office under lock
and key. He slipped a copy of the key only to Spenser Dominique,
his trusted valet and manservant, and to one other family member.
Daniel regularly changed which family member received the key, so
no one else could be certain who it was at any given time.

Daniel had a hunch that his home, his den, were in the president's
crosshairs.

DANIEL'S TWO ELDEST DAUGHTERS, then nine and eight years old,
were completing their math homework under Carmen's devoted
supervision. The babies had long since been put down to sleep, and
darkness had settled. Danielle fussed at the dreaded subject, knowing her grumbles would move no one. Finally, she and Raymonde
could shut their notebooks and scurry upstairs; they needed to
bathe and ready their hair for bed, partitioning their Afros into four
even shampoo-sheened, cocoa-buttered poofs.

Machine-gun fire sprayed 19 Avenue of the People.

At the first staccato blast, Danielle dropped to her hands and knees. Crawling, she and her mother collected the three babies, Leonie, three; Pierre, two; and newborn Bernard, and put them in the master bedroom—two underneath the bed, one under a night table. Raymonde and Marie were ordered to hide in their closet.

The shooting stopped. For a brief moment, calm. Seconds later, though, banging at the front door.

"Enough," a voice shouted. "Come here and we won't shoot."

Danielle and Carmen thought that they recognized the soldier's voice—he'd been there unarmed weeks ago, inquiring about Daniel.

"Go tell them he's not here!" her mother whispered to Danielle. Carmen stayed with the little ones so they wouldn't cry.

"Papa isn't home," Danielle dutifully reported to the policeman at the front door, staring, eyes wide, at the pack of soldiers crowded behind the officer.

"Where's your father?"

"I don't know. He went out," she said. "It's just me and my mother and my brothers and sisters here."

Magloire's soldiers had been looking for Daniel for months, ever since the general had banned his journal and Daniel continued to circulate it nonetheless. After a few visits from the police, Daniel had begun sleeping away from home. Sometimes he would disguise himself as a woman and go sleep at Rodrigue's house. Other times, he left with a couple of friends to guard him. As he walked out the front door, Danielle had seen the pistol he carried, hanging from his pants belt, hidden underneath his suit jacket. And one time, she had heard her father talking to Rodrigue about ditching them to take cover from the assaults. It's not cowardice to hide at your house as rivals blitz mine, her father had said. If I don't survive, the movement doesn't either. My life has priority over everyone else's.

THREE DAYS AFTER THE ATTACK, the house was bustling again. Carmen sat in the courtyard, playing her favorite card game, bési, in soothing company: Gigine and Jean; three apprentices from Daniel's journal; its typesetter, Edouard; a labor activist, Luc; and

Daniel's valet and assistant, Spenser. The moon shone on their crystal tumblers of rum as they flung their cards on the table, cracking salty jokes. Carmen remained sober, focused on her bids. Daniel's apprentices had volunteered to sleep at the house that night, and André Lafleur, a former MOP member, was camping in the courtyard too. They all enjoyed the free meals and shelter, and Carmen appreciated the comfort of more companionship. Daniel was hiding, in disguise, at Rodrigue's house again.

People were laughing and placing their bids when, around eleven o'clock, they heard the unmistakable clang of rifle butts banging the courtyard door. Roughly seventy military troops and police officers stormed in. Two police captains barked at the group to shut up and line up against the wall. Against Carmen's vehement protests, the troops hauled everyone off to the police station, except for her.

Just two hours later, she heard more pounding at the front door. It could only be more soldiers. She opened the door and scolded them for being so unruly. She was about to say more when she noticed Edouard, the typesetter, and Tonton Jean behind two police officers. The commanding officer shoved Edouard and Tonton Jean into the house and made a show of extracting a key from Jean's pocket. He ordered the two men to lead them to Daniel's den. Inside the lair, the officers found two printing presses, one large, one small. They took their sledgehammers and smashed them both. They carried their bounty off: the broken presses, a heap of greasy metal shards on the floor, the fusibles, and every ream of blank paper.

All the while, other soldiers guarded Carmen. They amused themselves by brandishing their revolvers and nightsticks in her face.

DANIEL FINALLY RETURNED HOME three days later. He talked politics with a friend in his living room until seven o'clock, then walked him to the door.

As soon as Daniel stepped onto the porch, dozens of police officers burst into the courtyard and surrounded him. They took away his pistol, helped themselves to his wristwatch, and handcuffed him. They shoved him into a waiting truck.

Daniel was tossed in the National Penitentiary and placed in solitary confinement.

Carmen and the children were forbidden from visiting him in prison. Locked away, he had no sanctuary from the heat, the mosquitoes, or the flies. He picked at fetid food, slept on the cement floor in his underpants, without pen, paper, or his beloved books, and was taunted by his prison guards.

Carmen had Sonny deliver several letters to the president of the National Assembly, demanding he intervene on her husband's behalf; after all, Daniel belonged to the parliament.

Daniel's activities were catching up to him, beyond his dissident league and journals. The president's circle was retaliating against Daniel for protesting two years earlier, in January 1952, against Magloire's education policies. "The most prominent student strike leaders were sent to distant provisional prisons," writes Matthew J. Smith. "Fignolé suffered most for his participation in the strike, as his house was stoned and set on fire by government-assembled thugs."

"I wear iron pants," President Magloire boasted in a now-famous 1954 address, directly taunting Daniel. The president stood on the steps of the National Palace, beside a gleaming oversize oil painting of himself. He said it was time to get tough and "repress some vagabonds," referring specifically to Daniel.

The president made good on his promise by arresting twenty more people after Daniel, including three other opposition leaders: two senators and another congressman. Daniel's colleague Senator Marcel Hérard barely managed to escape the police the same night Daniel was arrested in his courtyard: Hérard had workmen deliver him rolled up in a carpet to the safety of the Mexican embassy.

Not long after Daniel's arrest, a magistrate, a police officer, and two deputies arrived at the Fignolés' door, demanding to be let in to investigate. They wrote up bogus notes and hauled away three Underwood typewriters—two in excellent condition from the dining room table, and the third from a storeroom.

After two months and many phone calls, Carmen and the children were still banned from visiting Daniel. The president's magistrate refused Carmen's demands, claiming that secrecy and the prisoner's solitary confinement were necessary to the "integrity" of the government's ongoing investigation. Accusing him of "treason" and "undermining" the state, the country's police chief, Marcaisse Prosper, soon announced that the government had undeniable "proof" that the professor's league was sponsored by international communists, that arms were found in its leaders' houses, and that the league had planned to incite an islandwide revolution. Needless to say, the government never shared its "evidence" with the accused nor made it public.

"For his part, Fignolé entered the National Penitentiary with great dignity, his dark suit somewhat frayed and dust-covered," the leading international news correspondent for the *Haiti Sun*, Bernard Diederich, wrote at the time. "It was not difficult to feel a pang of sympathy for the 'Deputy of the People.' Former President Estimé had also feared Fignolé and his magnetic populist hold on the capital's poor, and he found it necessary to outlaw the charismatic leader's party. Now it was Magloire's turn to fear Fignolé."

THE PRESIDENT'S CAMPAIGN of repression sent thousands into hiding, Duvalier among them. Duvalier was still loyal to Magloire's predecessor, Estimé, having served in his Department of Labor. Magloire had made clear he would imprison Duvalier if given the chance. And so, the doctor dropped out of public view just before Magloire's crackdown. The Duvalier family remained in their old gingerbread house on Ruelle Roy, but François moved from safe house to safe house, as his family and confidants tried to conceal his whereabouts. His seventy-year-old father was once arrested for refusing to reveal where his son was hiding.

Separated from his house and family, Duvalier had to depend on friends for lodging, money, food. Doing so, he became untethered, demoralized, embittered. He began squirreling away guns wherever he could, in furniture drawers, beneath his pillow, under his formal waistcoat, everywhere. And he'd spend hours sitting naked on a rock, working his spells. Increasingly he identified as Baron Samedi, his Vodou persona, and turned to his paranoia and spiritual rituals for familiarity and comfort.

Duvalier's hardship in hiding intensified his sense of lifelong persecution, kindled his blistering ambition, and launched his spiteful skill for self-preservation. The experience bred in him a malignant strain of narcissism, a metastasizing desire to shield himself through power. He was learning to jettison his Hippocratic oath and to flip the Golden Rule: do unto others before they do unto you.

"What Duvalier became during his years of dodging detection in Port-au-Prince was far more striking than what he did—he shed his past as a dedicated country doctor and engagé scholar to become a politician obsessed with greatness, history, and power," writes his authoritative biographer, Elizabeth Abbott. "Former friends, and they were legion, claimed he studied his copy of Machiavelli's *The Prince* to tatters."

DANIEL LANGUISHED in the penitentiary for over three months. Finally, when the Fourth Session of the Thirty-Sixth Legislature opened on April 12, 1954, the president took the occasion to release him. Magloire had ordered each house of parliament to draw up groveling letters begging him for clemency on their colleague Daniel's behalf. Noting his graciousness and benevolence in heeding their pleas, he agreed, certain that he had taught his tormentor an unforgettable, humiliating lesson.

But Daniel did not absorb a lesson in obedience. Instead, the violent crackdown was a turning point. It convinced Daniel how deeply he'd gotten under the general's skin. Back at his perch at 19 Avenue of the People, he immediately resumed his political activities, his heart firmly fixed on achieving a dream he now believed within reach: the presidency.

Chapter 15

LIFE AT 19 AVENUE OF THE PEOPLE WAS BEGINNING TO FEEL unbearable to ten-year-old Danielle. The Molotov cocktails, the gunfire, the blitzkrieg arrests—they terrified her and her siblings. Carmen begged Daniel to move the growing family and L'École Fignolé to a more elegant neighborhood. The commotion was making the students' parents skittish, and Carmen worried it would soon scare them away. Of course, Carmen worried also about her family's safety; but the president would harass them no matter where they went, so they might as well live somewhere posher.

In 1955, Daniel, Carmen, and the children decamped from creaking 19 Avenue of the People to a grand two-story home in Carrefour Feuilles, which they rented for three hundred dollars a month from an enterprising landlord, the Reverend Bernard Lacombe, a Haitian pastor at a Pentecostal missionary church based in Tennessee. The house sat right behind a den of sin, the famed Hôtel Oloffson. Daniel laughed at the wicked irony. Luring all manner of Bohemians, celebrities, and ne'er-do-wells, the antique hotel was dubbed the Greenwich Village of the Tropics. Even Danielle knew that famous foreigners rollicked there, though she didn't know much about them: Graham Greene, Sir John Gielgud, Truman Capote, Marian Anderson. Noël Coward held court spectacularly at the hotel bar, while discreetly trolling for local boys.

In the years that the family had lived in Bel-Air, the number of tourists to Haiti had doubled. With its pristine beaches and supposed Vodou mystique, the island was a destination to rival Jamaica and Cuba. Movie moguls, starlets, bandleaders, writers: the world's jet set descended on the island, lured by its special blend of Parisian charm and popping African flavor. The city was a lullaby of colonial glamour enlivened by horns, drums, primary colors. Carrefour Feuilles, in particular, was loved for its chic lounges and dance floors, where the Dominicanas would teach the Haitian boys the newest merengue.

The family had barely settled into their new home when Carmen went into labor again. She gave birth in June to their seventh child, and fifth girl. Le professeur called her Carmen Daniel Fignolé; she was the third of his children whose name he modeled after his own.

Danielle, meanwhile, had recently graduated from sixth grade at her mother's primary school, and her papa wanted to put her in a public junior high school, in keeping with his egalitarian principles. Carmen would have none of it. She insisted that Danielle attend Collège du Sacré Coeur, fudging her arguments to Daniel about the school's superiority. The private school, Carmen knew, was not measurably better than the city's best public schools academically, but she wanted to infuse her girl's schooling with a stiff dose of Catholicism.

The decision to leave Bel-Air for softer pastures and to put Danielle in an exclusive private school: these were the very few battles in which Carmen ever bested Daniel.

AROUND THE TIME WHEN Danielle started at Sacré Coeur, her sister Marie was treated by the new neighbors to a gift: a chicken with a sweet, innocent face. Her open beak made her look as if she were smiling gaily. Her plumage fanned out delicately and voluminously at her neck, like reams of tissue paper. Marie fell immediately in love. Natacha bought her a bit of red yarn so that she could gently tether her darling to a tree in the courtyard. The chicken loved to be close to her. After a month together, the chicken would cackle softly whenever she saw Marie, in the hopes the girl would play with her, toss her some corn.

Not long after, Marie got into trouble at school, panicked, and blamed Raymonde. Marie was willowy and sickly, as her father had been, while Raymonde was thick boned, like her mother's people. Raymonde's eyes, direct and beady, sat above her pug nose: she was a squat girl with a combative face. Even when she was happy, she looked like she was spoiling for a fight. Adults often assumed she was up to no good. The teacher believed Marie's lie over Raymonde's protests and reported Raymonde to her parents. Le professeur and Carmen respected immediately the integrity of teachers, so the girls knew what was coming. That night, Daniel whipped Raymonde before sending her to bed without supper.

"When he was tired of beating me, the protocol was for me to kneel on the polished parquet floor, in the corner of the living room," Raymonde would say much later in life. "I faced the wall, until he signaled that I could go. My family would leave me there, in the dark, having missed dinner. I had listened to them making jokes about me, mostly my father and my wicked sister Danielle, his cheerleader."

Raymonde thought about nothing other than how to get revenge. Returning from school the next day, traipsing through the courtyard, an idea came to her. She decided to pluck a silken feather from Marie's cherished chicken and taunt her sister with it. She yanked a feather from the chicken's beautiful coat. Startled, the chicken nabbed at her. Raymonde yanked again, but the plume would not come loose. Plucking a live chicken was surprisingly difficult, much more so than she had imagined. She finally managed. But taking just the one feather from the bird wasn't even noticeable.

So Raymonde came up with a new plan to teach Marie a lesson: she would burn several feathers off the chicken. She went to the woodstove and fetched a carton of long-stem matches. She put a lit match to a feather and the whole chicken caught. It ignited into a squawking ball of flames. Soon the yarn snapped and the flaming animal went flying through the courtyard shrieking for its life. The faster it flew, the quicker it burned. By the time everyone rushed outside to see what the fracas was about, the bird's body lay lifeless on the ground. Marie fell to her knees sobbing and collected her baby's charred feathers.

Raymonde was immobilized into a kind of fascinated silence. She was tempted to lie, but she was still holding the two burnt matchsticks in her hand; she knew she was in for another beating.

It was out of the question for Daniel or Carmen to waste food; whole neighborhoods of people in the city were on the precipice of hunger. So Selavi stewed Marie's dead pet that very night with a full-bodied tomato sauce and served it up with rice, beans, and legumes. Scooting her fork across her plate, Raymonde took a good look at Marie and held her gaze. She smacked her gums, licked her bottom lip, bit into her drumstick, and smiled at her sister.

THE FIGNOLÉ CHILDREN TEASED and scuffled with one another while fighting for their father's attention. He abetted their frictions, pitting this one against that, favoring one over the other—Danielle above all. The oldest and most diligent, Danielle earned the best marks even as she took the most difficult classes. On rare nights, she was allowed to sit close to her father as he read her *les grands philosophes*—Voltaire, Rousseau, Diderot. About to hit puberty, she was growing into her switchblade personality—spunky, an independent thinker, and a shameless people pleaser. She was learning to inflate and shrink herself, like a canny balloon, to accommodate her father's mercurial moods. She could show off when his good humor fancied the grandeur, the sharp mind, the big personality, which he savored in his own image. And when his mood was foul, she knew to keep her mouth shut.

Raymonde, meanwhile, was not one to edit herself. Thoughts, copious and unvarnished, flowed out of her mouth. While Raymonde was not her father's favorite, she was certainly Natacha's. The more neglected of the family's two maids, Natacha nursed an affinity for Raymonde, took her side when she could. She treated Raymonde to long walks along the flower gardens in the Champ de Mars, would listen patiently to her colorful school stories, while Danielle would

The professor lounges at home; Danielle preens for the camera,
as close to her indifferent father as she can get. In the background
(*left to right*) are Bernard, Carmen, Marie, Leonie, Pierre, an unidentified
woman, and Raymonde.

go with Selavi to visit the furniture artisans selling their rich mahogany wares along the city's waterfront, luring *les blancs,* who were
arriving in boatloads and planeloads from Miami by the day.

As often as they fought, though, the three eldest sisters, Danielle,
Raymonde, and Marie, kept one another close. They put on plays
for one another, confided in one another, even as they ratted on one
another in school and took revenge on one another in the courtyard. Some weekends they'd watch the men boomba racing in native
dugouts at Kyona Beach. Others, they went to the beach on the sea-
facing side of the island, plowing their toes through the eskers of
egg-white sand. They could see their ankles soaking in the warm
water, it was that diamond clear.

Life was a whiplash of wonder and terror. The girls relished the
fragrant parks, the humming markets, the beauty overlooking the
harbor, and yet they never stood near their windows after dusk for
fear of bullets. Their papa had been banned from traveling into the
provinces and from speaking on the radio. He had to stop receiv-

ing mail at home and stop writing to his socialist and noiriste allies around the world. The secret police opened his mail and paid a visit to the house if they read anything they didn't like. President Magloire's desperation to hold on to power had only grown, and the threat to Daniel along with it.

"Last night, between two and half-past two, the crackle of a gun startled my wife and me. The numerous holes left on the door giving access to the living room, the broken windows of two doors in the direction of our bed, near which is the cradle of a three-month-old baby, the shards that can still be seen in the living room, on the parquet, on the chairs in the den, say more than anything I could express in this letter," Daniel wrote to Adolphin Telson, Port-au-Prince's chief of police, on October 11, 1955. "Lead is found under the chairs in the living room. The cries of my wife and six children called for help from the neighbors who, after the discharge of guns, kindly protected us with their presence near the walls of the fence of the property where I live."

No one, especially not secret agents, doubted the threat to le professeur's life. "Fignolé risks having his throat cut, literally not figuratively," a Haitian informant told the U.S. embassy in a classified memo.

None of them, though, were paying much attention to the threat posed to Daniel's family.

JUST MONTHS AFTER DANIEL was released from prison, a natural disaster struck. Hurricane Hazel's gale winds and flash floods destroyed cities and villages throughout the country. Roughly one thousand people died and a hundred thousand lost their homes. The devastation amplified the hardship in the provinces and sent even more people fleeing to the capital. By the mid-1950s, at least half the population of Port-au-Prince had been born in the provinces. It was precisely that ballooning, migrant, dark-skinned population—politically ignored, economically exploited, and bursting at the seams—who made up the heart and muscle of Daniel's steamroller.

The president, to few people's surprise, neglected to expand services and amenities alongside the capital's boom. Grifters in the president's good graces enjoyed luxury; the working and middle classes suffered worsening squalor. Shantytowns, mostly ringing the city's wharf, made up over 60 percent of the capital's housing. Fewer than 2 percent of Haitians enjoyed running water in their homes. Telephones had become a luxury found only in government offices and the private homes of the elite. Public services—especially schools and hospitals, which Daniel had worked so hard to improve in the 1940s—were now a shambles. Life for Daniel's followers became unbearably crowded and dangerous.

But nobody begrudged Daniel his tailored suits or his finicky, undulating French. To the contrary: his luxuries, his refinement, served as a beacon of aspiration. His followers saw him as a man who'd come from nothing and now seemed to have everything. And his neighbors saw firsthand his professional integrity. Daniel attached grave importance to the financial rectitude of all leaders in his movement. He did not dip into the union coffers that he oversaw, and his sharp sense of ethics earned him the absolute confidence of the dozens of unions he led. Even U.S. diplomats in Port-au-Prince made grudging, though unequivocal, reference to his ethics in their clandestine reports.

"Fignolé has a reputation for honesty, though there is no doubt he is a demagogue," one U.S. embassy official wrote to Washington in a classified 1954 memo.

As Daniel fought on behalf of working people, whose average income idled at roughly sixty-five dollars per year, the president and his cronies grew wealthier. Economic desperation led to an increase in murders in the capital. "Society has become a jungle where the knife is king. We kill to live or we kill [ourselves] to escape the suffering," lamented an editorial in a Port-au-Prince newspaper.

"Reports of the early end of the Magloire Administration are becoming as persistent as the beat of the Voodoo Drums in the hills," said a confidential embassy memo to Washington. Students, the press, the clergy, the labor unions, the legislature: Magloire had angered them all, leaving himself no organized allies but the military and business elites. And they were growing restless too. Unable to quell opposing strikes and demonstrations, Magloire quit and fled for Jamaica on December 12, 1956. A military caretaker government assumed power until it could hold elections, which were scheduled for the following spring.

Daniel put his hat in the ring.

Chapter 16

BY THE FIRST DAYS OF MAY 1957, THE CAMPAIGN WAS IN full swing. Daniel arrived at Port-de-Paix, a remote, threadbare town on the northern coast, where he'd been invited by locals to make a speech. He had accepted the tantalizing invitation, eager to expand his candidacy beyond the capital into the backcountry.

He strolled down the main street ahead of his talk that clear, warm afternoon. The townspeople, though, were less congenial than the elements. Men edged to their stoops as he walked by, as if to guard their storefronts and homes. Women stared stonily at him until he was out of their sight. Only then did it occur to him: His speaking invitation was a caustic joke courtesy of his rival Duvalier, who was also vying for the presidency. The town was smack in Duvalier's political turf.

As Daniel walked, a growing throng of villagers followed. He kept his stride, ignoring the pelting stares. When he reached a church at the end of the main street, he knelt before the Virgin Mary. Then he rose and faced the crowd.

He flung his arms wide in a messianic manner.

"Port-de-Paix," he declared. "Now I can talk to you."

He began by mocking one of his mulatto campaign rivals, then paused to let the tension smolder. Sweat dripped from his furrowed brow. His smooth ebony fist clenched a blazing-blue handkerchief, which he dabbed at his face. With his other hand, he stabbed the air with his forefinger, each thrust punctuating his words. He stroked the microphone and wrinkled his brow, then lit into his true rival.

"Duuuu-vaahhlllll," Daniel rumbled. "That man cannot be trusted."

Such was le professeur's epithet for his enemy: always Duval, never François or Duvalier. He rolled out the vowels and consonants to make the man's name sound ridiculous, sinister. Duval had been a corrupt civil servant, he declared. Duval had squashed the rights of ordinary people as a lackey to past presidents.

Daniel thrust his right index finger high into the air, then sent it crashing down. "À bas Duvalier!" he thundered.

"À bas Duvalier!" the crowd exploded. "Down with Duvalier!"

Daniel threw his arm high into the air, stiff straight, then hurled it down again. "À bas Duvalier!" he shouted.

"À bas Duvalier!" the crowd repeated, even hissing and sucking their teeth.

He shot his arm up high again, then slammed it down once more. "À bas Duvalier!"

After each volcanic call, he dropped his trunk a little lower, until, finally, he was artfully bent double at the hip.

"Down, down, down, down, down!" the crowd shouted.

Disgust crescendoed with each roar of their refrain. Daniel paused to acknowledge and stoke his admirers' fury. He chopped the air with his right arm to silence the anger he'd stirred.

Then he eased into a hopeful tenor—his aspirations for his presidency, pregnant with possibility, and his belief in the country's women, who had gained the right to vote just the month before. Women must finally claim their rightful places in advancing the world's first black republic, Daniel declared. He riffed on his own home and hearth. "Danielle! Raymonde! Marie! Leonie! Carmen!" He patted their imaginary heads and smiled broadly. "Shall I make them deputies in my administration?" The people laughed. A vote for Fignolé, he swore, meant a vote for better educating their daughters.

What may have sounded like a fifteen-minute campaign primer was in fact a two-hour discourse—a reverberant meditation on suffering and hope across the country. Satisfied with his brimstone,

Daniel threw his head back and flung out his arms again. Then he bowed his head into his chest, eyes half-closed, to thank the throngs.

NINETEEN MEN HAD STEPPED forward to run for president, but only three were real contenders: Senator Louis Déjoie, a wealthy mulatto industrialist, Duvalier, and Daniel.

To become president, a candidate was required by law to be a property owner. Comically, none of the three front-runners met the requirement. Senator Déjoie rented a fabulous villa in Babiole, an exclusive section in the hills overlooking Port-au-Prince. And Duvalier was renting a ramshackle house close to the National Palace. As for Daniel, his family lived in a house-school, whose rent payments were made possible mostly from his wife's business, a cutting embarrassment for a prideful man climbing the patriarchy.

The senator, a direct descendant of the Marquis d'Ennery, whom the Crown had appointed to rule the colony in the 1770s as governor-general, was the wealthiest of the bunch. *A grand blanc,* Déjoie had traveled the world and spoke fluent English. He was sixty-one years old and a bit of an Omar Sharif look-alike: with his sensuous smile, fine mustache, and wavy, jet-black hair, he was in the habit of throwing lavish parties for journalists and European expatriates. The international and national press were quite familiar with the bonvivant senator, as they were the spirited professor.

Duvalier, meanwhile, was a question mark. Newspapers regularly misspelled his name. Where Daniel and Déjoie had run in multiple elections, Duvalier, at fifty years old, was a rookie candidate.

Duvalier began the campaign as the underdog. A soft-spoken man, he keenly understood that he could not match Daniel's political pyrotechnics, so he ventured a more fitting approach. He purposefully ran a duller campaign than his old friend's. Rather than focus on big rallies, he held court with small groups of people and beseeched their votes. He appeared with his family on the campaign trail: Simone, primly dressed like a schoolmarm, his four plump children, and his short, dark, harmless-looking father. It wasn't hard

François and Simone Duvalier in 1957

for Duvalier to endear himself to disenfranchised Haitians: he had inoculated tens of thousands during his highly effective anti-yaws vaccination campaign of 1943. His efforts had earned him national acclaim and a personal reservoir of goodwill across the provinces. That's why they called him Papa Doc, a nickname that lovingly whispered the fatherly authority he so coveted.

Neither Duvalier nor Daniel offered a detailed platform; each knew the election hinged more on personality than policy. The general's presidency had come to reek of gaudiness, theft, and blood, so Duvalier put forth the opposite: naivete, personal integrity, and a wholesome sense of purpose. Dressing in natty, understated suits, complemented by a bow tie and simple hat, Duvalier presented himself as the earnest, simple ruler he believed Haitians craved: a humble, plainspoken worker bee. His camp was gambling that the country no longer wanted political drama or outsize personalities such as Daniel, but a quiet patriarch people could rely on.

Duvalier's vaccination campaign had not only burnished his reputation among the rural people; he had made himself conversant with them. He had learned, better than most national politicians, their everyday tics, their unspoken disquiets, the particular and mighty place that Vodou held in their lives. His intuitive grasp of poor black people was as cunning, as deep, as Daniel's.

Daniel understood he had to campaign hard to overcome that advantage and directed his bluntest attacks against his former friend. "It will be a national catastrophe if Duvalier were to win the election," Daniel said in a speech. "If Duvalier seizes power, he will not give it back easily." In his signature condescension, Daniel called Duvalier "a profoundly stupid little man." The press was titillated. Daniel—who often mistook articulateness for intelligence—fervently held that the short, tongue-tied doctor lacked the intellect and stature to lead the world's first black republic.

In turn, Duvalier mocked his enemy's vanity and eloquence. *"Kok tro fin pa bat,"* he repeated often, in his smoky bass. "A pretty rooster can't fight." More pointedly, he painted Daniel as a radical communist hostile to the United States. His campaign circulated a leaflet, "The Fignolé of Yesterday," featuring a funny photo of the young professor dressed as Chairman Mao. Daniel, in the 1930s, had been hamming it up for students in his Chinese tunic.

The charge rankled Daniel, especially since Duvalier had personally accompanied him to the U.S. embassy to make it known that MOP was not a communist party. And Daniel had been explicitly fashioning himself a "national democrat," not a radical, for years.

AFTER DUVALIER TRIED to screw him in Port-de-Paix, Daniel flipped the trick in his face. Daniel made even more speeches deep in Duvalier's territories, and they were turning in his favor. Daniel was transforming, as his old friend was, from idealistic thinker to brass-knuckles tactician, harnessing his gift of speech to conjure spellbinding political theater. For his part, Duvalier, with his Baron Samedi persona, was performing a subtler theater, rooted in quietude and mysticism and Africa, which could be just as bewitching.

The race was tight. With universal suffrage enacted, the mulatto vote had shrunk to just 10 percent. Remote towns such as Port-de-Paix were all-important; the vote in the provinces outnumbered the vote in the capital four to one. The three front-runners clawed toward power, enacting that old Haitian crab syndrome, as one local journalist deftly observed. Whenever one candidate seemed to be gaining, he was dragged back into the basket with the other crabs.

While Daniel's rivals jostled for advantage among wealthy land-owners, industrialists, merchants, the Catholic Church, military leaders, and Washington, he owned the campaign where black workers were concerned.

"Mr. Fignolé emerged a hero to the working classes," *The New York Times* reported. "He has exceptional powers as an orator and has traveled deeper into the provinces than any of the other candidates to date."

His followers coated billboards, bus stops, and storefronts with his image. His face glistened on posters plastered to the locomotives snaking across the country. Dockworkers chalked his campaign slogans along the wharves: FIGNOLÉ POUR PRESIDENT!

Daniel's followers outside the family's hilltop house,
Carrefour Feuilles, 1957

On a typical Saturday and Sunday, Daniel traveled to the provinces to campaign to teeming crowds, then hurried back to the capital to deliver his nightly broadcast on Radio Caraibes, a prominent network.

By the time he made it home, he said little. He'd return after midnight when the household was already fast asleep. Danielle hardly saw her papa during the campaign, though his voice rang everywhere.

AS THE CONTEST HEATED UP, a temporary civilian government was supposedly running the country. But voters worried increasingly that a power-hungry military might try to wrest power from the interim civilian leaders. On Flag Day, May 18, street protests erupted, and the military opened fire on a crowd carrying the country's flag in front of the National Cathedral. That didn't stop the dissent. Across the country, demonstrations grew angrier.

In an attempt to quell the people's worry and fury, the temporary civilian government fired the top general, Léon Cantave, for "inefficiency and insubordination." The civilian leaders then named Colonel Pierre Armand as his replacement. But the fired general wouldn't budge: He bunkered himself and his loyal troops in the nation's military garrison, Dessalines Barracks, refusing to be dislodged. He then retaliated by dissolving the civilian government.

Nonetheless, Colonel Armand had the Air Corps, Artillery, Coast Guard, Fire Brigade, and police force on his side. He set up 75 mm artillery field pieces and on May 25 shelled the barracks, showering Cantave's bunker with shrapnel and bombs.

A vintage World War II C-47 cargo plane swooped over the barracks, hovered low, opened its hatch, and sent a two-hundred-pound bomb barreling toward earth. The explosive hit the roof, then tumbled to the dirt. An officer had forgotten to ignite it.

Daniel, Duvalier, Déjoie, and their top aides were meeting—unbeknownst to the colonel—in the general's office at the time, trying to resolve the standoff. Shards of glass flew. The unfused bomb, the artillery shells, showered them in debris. A few shouted for mercy, others darted under the table. Daniel barely flinched, nor did Duvalier.

"There was a headlong rush for under-the-table positions of safety," a journalist present reported. "Duvalier however was not among those who panicked. Later, a lieutenant found Duvalier coolly strolling across the barracks' grounds toward the Palace. Duvalier appeared at the moment to be insensible to danger." He was as unflappable as Daniel.

Duvalier's calm was calculated. He and his allies recognized that he would likely lose the race, so they'd set about sabotaging Daniel by courting members of the military and the clergy. Military leaders wanted Duvalier as president because they thought him subdued, a little doltish—certainly the least objectionable, most pliable, among their options. To bolster his campaign, his allies in the military had been working with him to fan violence and undercut the temporary civilian government. A rich Duvalier supporter had even pitched in forty-six thousand dollars just days earlier to bribe soldiers to remain loyal to General Cantave and to fund the bunkered general's weapons.

Daniel, meanwhile, had made a secret pact with Déjoie to gang up against Duvalier. Daniel wanted to neutralize the military's support for Duvalier, whom Daniel thought to be his strongest rival. Déjoie, for his part, calculated that ridding a tarnished Duvalier from the contest would free him to go one-on-one against Daniel, "a radical black apologist," whom the clergy and foreign embassies hated. Déjoie thought that if he could expose Duvalier and the military's corrupt collusion, he could eliminate him from the campaign.

That morning, in a display of his own force, Daniel had activated his steamroller, a pointed reminder to his rivals of his power and popularity. While the military leaders were preoccupied with infighting, he instructed his followers to flood the streets. They thundered through the capital shouting, *"À bas le gouvènman!"*—"Down with the government!" *"Long ap viv Fignolé!"*—"Long live Fignolé!" They upended cars, leaving them stripped like picked carcasses, and smashed several radio stations and shops belonging to high-level Duvalier supporters. Police fired on them.

Later in the day, as military and police gunfire raged around the bunker, Daniel deserted Déjoie to meet with Duvalier and military leaders in secret. The men returned to the barracks to negotiate an end to the conflict, an eyewitness to the events journalist would later report. The day's standoff had killed seventeen Haitians and wounded scores more, including civilians caught in the cross fire.

Daniel seized the moment. I am the only leader acceptable to most ordinary voters, he claimed to the men around the table, the only one who can be trusted with this power. Once you stanch the violence, he added, a peaceful, proper election can be held. Until then, the country needs a clear leader, not an unwieldly committee. Who among you can stomach the deaths of more innocent people?

By the end of the day, General Cantave and the civilian committee called a truce. As dusk approached, at roughly six o'clock, the two warring army leaders agreed to resign and the temporary civilian government agreed to be annulled. They announced that a newly appointed president would lead the country until clean elections could be held: Professor Daniel Fignolé.

All three candidates supported the compromise publicly, even as they set about their private agendas. Three conflicting, if self-serving, interpretations of national law and political tactics sprouted— the unprecedented situation made all somewhat credible. Senator Déjoie believed that Daniel's tenure would constitutionally bar him from running for "reelection" in the following contest; Daniel estimated that holding the office would give him a crisp advantage in the future official election; Duvalier calculated that a hasty, neither-nor, sort-of presidency would politically hamstring Daniel, his only real competition; and the military elite seemed to agree that undermining Daniel would play in Duvalier's favor.

When the compromise was announced, Daniel went to Bel-Air, host to so many Sunday Clubs, his beloved former neighborhood and current stronghold, to put his confused, but happy, supporters at ease.

"Even if you see my head on a bayonet, remain calm and don't leave your homes," he said, standing on a crate. "I promise you I'll be fine. Anything else you hear will be nothing but a trap."

"Chita, chita, chita," he told them. *"Chita sou yon blòk glas."* "Sit, sit, sit—sit on a block of ice."

"I am your president," he said later that night in a radio address. "Go home without saying a word."

His public rejoiced.

Duvalier, in his yellow-brick house, was reportedly rejoicing too.

Chapter 17

O N ONE OF THOSE BLUE-CLEAR SKY SUNDAY MORNINGS, MAY 26, 1957, the day after his meeting at the barracks, Daniel and Carmen rode together to the National Palace for his inauguration. He soaked in the roars and car horns from the back seat of the black government sedan. They'd set out from their house in Carrefour Feuilles shortly before noon and were headed downtown. People spilled from balconies, roofs, buildings, and shanties all along the way, flowing like two great rivers on either side of the major roads. Carmen waved to the throngs softly. Daniel thrust a clenched fist out his window and pumped it in triumph.

Danielle, Raymonde, Marie, and Leonie rode behind their parents, in a car driven by Sonny. That morning, Danielle had paid no mind to Selavi's nagging and chose her dress herself: her favorite, a cotton top with a skirt made of crinkling crepe. In her neatest

Elated crowd dashes to the National Palace to witness and celebrate Fignolé's inauguration

hairdo, sparkling with blue and red cloth ribbons, she studied the sea of faces on the cavalcade. She thought about the times her papa had brought her along to campaign with him—only the instances when he'd felt sure the events would be calm. Some voters had recognized her from her papa's previous campaigns. They'd smothered her cheeks in kisses and said things like "Well, my dear! You're not that different from '46, '50, or '55!" Papa had been running for one political office or another since practically the day she'd been born. He'd wanted to give her a once-in-a-lifetime tutorial on how democracy worked; this car ride felt like the culmination of that lesson.

The morning's commotion made her cry. Her whole life, they'd been threatened. She knew how to hug the floor in seconds. She knew how to lie to police at the front door. But now, those threats seemed to recede in the rearview mirror. It looked as if the whole country were cheering for her father.

When her parents' car slowed in front of the palace, a pack of men, women, and children rushed toward it, slapping the doors, clapping the fenders in rhythmic beats. *"Daniel!"* they shouted. More hands smacked the sedan. *"Daniel!"* Soldiers cleared a space so that the couple could get out of the car, and as soon as they did, the crowd lurched toward them.

Carmen might have preferred a gentler, more discreet arrival. Humbler. But Daniel had insisted on this raucous spectacle. He wanted to show himself in person, reassure the people of his presence, convince them that their victory was true, that they could now see and trust their new leader and let go of the despair that had held the country in its grip for too long, culminating in the previous day's carnage. He was not alone in thinking this. An editorial in the country's leading newspaper, *Le Nouvelliste,* asserted, "It would have been a crime not to give the people the man they were demanding."

At the palace entrance, the once-warring generals snapped to attention, their upper arms crisply raised, then honored Daniel with a twenty-one-gun salute. After the last shot, the two generals shook hands as if to unite the country in brotherhood. The gesture was met with loud applause.

Daniel and Carmen at his presidential inauguration,
May 26, 1957

Daniel had insisted that the palace's front gates be flung open that day so that the masses outside could celebrate close to him. He and Carmen stood on the terrace and waved to the crowd on the front lawn. He was in his best pin-striped trousers, long coattails, and a cravat. Carmen wore an elegant dress topped off with a matching wide-brimmed hat. Four columns stood guard behind them, leading to a portico and a domed pavilion. The palace had a few small, manicured gardens decorated with statues—women in togas, lads strumming harps—and ivy-covered gazebos.

Danielle, wedged between her sisters, watched the inauguration indoors, from behind her tante Gigine. Danielle could see out the window to the lawn and noticed a man, skin dark like hers, rolling on the grass on his back, smiling so wide he looked as if he were leading Carnival. He wore a white guayabera and plain black pants. Next to him was a woman in a yellow floral karabela dress and a matching head wrap, clapping and dancing to a kompa beat in her head. The man leapt to his feet, took the woman in his arms, and twirled her. It occurred to Danielle that her father belonged to this man and this woman, to these people celebrating across the lawn, more than he could ever belong to her. No matter that she was his favorite, she felt that she was prouder of him than he could ever be of her.

After the short inauguration ceremony, Daniel walked down the portico steps to join his people. He was quickly swallowed by a sea of green-and-red MOP flags.

DAYS LATER, in accordance with tradition, the president was to be honored at a Te Deum, a ceremony of hymns chanted in Latin by the Catholic clergy.

The public put on its finest garments and lined the streets leading to the National Cathedral, Basilique de Notre Dame. The crowd was ten thousand people strong, the press estimated, the same number that had attended his inauguration. Many people sang softly. *Thee, O God, we praise.* They gently waved palm branches as they walked to the monument.

"Their dignity brought tears to the eyes," wrote Carlo Desinor, a longtime journalist. "To have suffered so much and to be capable of forgiveness seemed incredible."

But the serenity evaporated when motorcycle sirens announced the president and First Lady's approach to the cathedral. Celebrants rushed forward to greet the couple. A commotion broke out.

The president walked to the basilica door, where church elders stopped him at the threshold. Priests refused to chant the Te Deum. The president fixed them with an acid stare and a matching smirk.

"*Yo pa vle-m isit?*"—"You don't want me here?"

He was speaking folksy Kreyòl, not high Latin.

He suspected that the Catholic establishment, which openly supported his opponents and fraternized with the elite, was snubbing him.

The bishop of Port-au-Prince, Monsignor Rémy Augustin, told the press the next day that the president had not been slighted: "The clergy willingly agreed to sing the Te Deum in honor of Daniel Fignolé. The attitude of the crowds forced us, physically, to give up the idea. The crowd was so dense and noisy that it was actually impossible for the choir or the sounds of the organ to be heard playing religious songs for the occasion. It was a mistake to think that the clergy were playing politics. We do not have the right to do so."

That was just fine so far as my grandfather was concerned—it was meaningless superstition, anyway. He turned his motorcade right around and circled back to the palace, his crowds in tow.

G'mère was just heartbroken.

DANIEL THREW HIMSELF into the work of the presidency. Not long after the rooster's crow, as light began to settle, a bodyguard and a few aides would escort him from home to the palace, where he worked a twelve-hour day. While his family spent many hours there too that first week, Carmen insisted that they continue living in their rented house. Big shots, could-a-beens, wannabes, spies: the palace's hornet's nest of intrigue, she worried, would ruin family life.

In his first official order as president, Daniel named Antonio Kébreau as the new army chief, promoting him from colonel to brigadier general. Daniel installed his cabinet—nine blacks and four mulattoes—and set to work kick-starting his economic program: improving agricultural production, advancing industrialization, and developing the country's transportation network. He was angling to tackle unemployment and to make good on his campaign promise of tripling the minimum wage from sixty cents a day to two dollars. And he'd already decreed two weeks of paid vacation for all workers and abolished the harsh irrigation tax that had been levied on small farmers.

Six months of election crisis had walloped the economy, leaving Daniel little room to maneuver. The country's gold and dollar reserves had plummeted by half, from $11.3 million the previous year to just $5.8 million at the time of his inauguration. Worse, Daniel faced a gross public debt of $65 million, a staggering amount for any leader with a $35 million annual budget.

The debt that Daniel had to grapple with did not result from his predecessors' long-term mismanagement or corruption alone. Twenty years after Haiti's founding in 1804, France had sent a platoon of warships bearing five hundred cannons pointed at the island's coastlines. King Charles X demanded "reparations" for the colonizer, ordering Haitians to pay their former enslavers for lost property, including the enslaved people, or face a military blockade and invasion. The extortion was bitterly dubbed the "independence debt."

The European power sent more warships to ensure the "debt" was paid. Since the Haitian government didn't have the money, the French kindly supplied the government high-interest loans, courtesy of generous French banks and wealthy French families, including the Rothschilds. The new mulatto president, Jean-Pierre Boyer, was in a bind. The light-skinned ruling class wasn't thrilled over this independence debt; its families did not want their plantations and businesses confiscated, or even slightly diminished, their lush assets and profits accordingly taxed. So Boyer, who'd been educated in Paris, foisted the payment onto the backs of the masses. From the debt's inception in 1825 until 1957, when Daniel sat in the presidential study, an average of 19 percent of the country's annual revenue was sent to France every year, to pay off the initial sum, plus interest. Some years the debt ate up more than 40 percent of Haiti's yearly income.

Beyond the pressing purse-string matters, Daniel had dreams for the country, as bold as they were unprecedented. He went on surprise visits to government offices, hospitals, prisons, and army outposts at all hours to examine the bureaucracies that ordinary people wrestled with. After inspecting the National Penitentiary, where he'd been a prisoner two years before, he berated wardens for jailing minors in the same cells as adults and demanded his justice minister fix the wrong. He also ordered his cabinet to start round-the-clock police patrols of the capital's business district; businessmen, incensed by the last year's turmoil, had requested the protection.

Even as he drilled down on the country's immediate problems, a larger question loomed for Daniel: How could he help transform the idea of democracy in Haiti into a working success? He hosted a high-level symposium to discuss the question and held a press conference at its launch on June 6. There, he reread his executive mandate ordering the full safety of political parties and of commerce.

Several of his prominent rivals, including Duvalier, refused to attend his symposium; they believed, privately, that the nation was too dumb and impulsive for democracy. "Some argue that the Haitians are unprepared for democracy because they are so poor and so illiterate," Fignolé would later say. "However, illiteracy does not mean ignorance or lack of intelligence. The Haitian peasant is fundamentally intelligent. Within his own sphere, he is not ignorant."

Daniel was relying on the people to safeguard his principles—and even to protect his life. Upon taking office, he put out a not-so-coded appeal to the people to help his administration succeed:

"We ask you, People, to remain calm, but also to watch all that threatens the Government of the Leader that you have chosen freely." It was a devious twist on the facts: technically, the population had not chosen him. "We ask you, People, to respect lives and property, but also to open your eyes on all conspiracies, all actions prejudicial to the internal and external security of the state."

He'd spent the last decade looking out for the working people and was now asking them to do so for him.

Their bond was tightening.

"M. Fignolé's popularity seems to have increased hourly since his inauguration last Sunday," *The New York Times* reported. "His every public appearance has touched off ecstatic demonstrations by thousands of workers and peasants."

At the fruit stands, in the barbershops, on the loading docks, working people gossiped that Daniel would stay in power for a quarter of a century—at least.

Chapter 18

D ANIEL'S AMERICAN COUNTERPART WAS AN EARLY RISER
too: Dwight David "Ike" Eisenhower woke at the crack of
dawn. He was convinced that serious men did their best thinking
in the morning, so his aides scheduled his important meetings at
the earliest possible hour. Apart from accommodating his circadian
rhythms, the president's penchant for early meetings helped him
clear his desk by late afternoon to scoot off for some golf at the Burning Tree Country Club.

At six o'clock on Monday, May 27, 1957, Eisenhower padded out of
his bedroom quietly so as not to disturb Mamie. Over a light breakfast, delivered to him by a butler, he read the morning papers. That
morning, a day after Daniel Fignolé's inauguration, the international
press was reporting on his rise to the presidency and his boisterous
installment in the palace.

At 8:03, Eisenhower arrived to the Oval Office. At nine o'clock
sharp, he began presiding over a meeting of the National Security
Council in the Cabinet Room of the West Wing. In order of pres-
tige and influence on the president, the room included Secretary of
State John Foster Dulles, Secretary of Defense Charles E. Wilson,
CIA director Allen Dulles (brother to John Foster), Assistant to the
President for National Security Affairs Robert Cutler, Staff Secretary
and Defense Liaison Officer Brigadier General Andrew Goodpaster,
Treasury Secretary George M. Humphrey, and Vice President Rich-
ard Nixon.

The CIA director kicked off the meeting with a briefing on Haiti.

The situation had taken a "dramatic" and "somewhat disturbing turn overnight," Allen Dulles said. He reported that the new president was a "rabble-rouser, though not exactly a Communist," then argued that Fignolé had "a strong leftist orientation" and "was not especially friendly to the United States." Dulles warned that the situation required careful observation. "We'd hate to have another Guatemala on our hands," he said, referring to Operation PBSuccess, the 1954 CIA-led coup that had toppled Jacobo Árbenz, Guatemala's democratically elected president. Árbenz, like Fignolé, had run afoul of the major U.S. corporations in his country as a labor reformer.

The CIA was feeling cocksure. Along with booting the popular Árbenz from office in Guatemala, it had successfully executed Operation Ajax the year before, its secret action ousting Mohammad Mosaddegh, Iran's popular and freely elected prime minister, replacing him with a military strongman. Iran's new pro-U.S. government soon reached an agreement with largely U.S. and British companies "to restore the flow of Iranian oil to world markets in substantial quantities." With NATO gaining its footing and acting as a bulwark against Soviet expansion into Western Europe, America's battle against communism was shifting from Europe to the so-called third world: Guatemala, the Middle East, Indochina, and soon Cuba. Eisenhower and his cabinet believed that the Soviet Union was trying to exploit poverty to take over these regions. He'd made the grand struggle for "freedom"—preventing poorer nations from falling into communist hands—the theme of his second inaugural address, delivered just months before, and of his entire second term.

After Dulles finished his Haiti briefing, the president nodded. "I understand this fellow is being hailed by the mob," said Eisenhower. Dulles confirmed the "correctness" of the press accounts Eisenhower had been reading. For their part, the Dulles brothers did not have a neutral stance on Haiti, nor was the U.S. occupation of the country ancient history for them; their uncle Robert had presided over the occupation as Woodrow Wilson's secretary of state.

President Eisenhower adjourned the meeting at 10:50. The only decision the group made then, which would soon become public, was Eisenhower's refusal to recognize Daniel Fignolé as the new president of Haiti.

Later that night, Frederick Hassler, president of the Haitian American Sugar Company (HASCO), telephoned Haiti's ambassador to Washington to express his anger: "The number one enemy of HASCO," Hassler said, had been made president of Haiti. Fignolé had become the sugar company's "number one enemy" when he'd handily been elected president of HASCO's workers' union in February 1946, then led them on a strike that secured better pay and working conditions that very month.

Within days, Hassler also telephoned the State Department and the U.S. ambassador in Port-au-Prince to sound off again.

Other prominent men rushed to weigh in on the presidency too. Roy Tasco Davis, who had served as U.S. ambassador to Haiti from 1953 to April 1957, wrote to State Department officials that same week, noting that Daniel's rise to power was "the worst thing that could have happened." Davis described Fignolé as "probably non-Communist, but a fellow traveler." Fignolé had been responsible for all the labor trouble suffered by American firms in Haiti, Davis maintained, including HASCO's. Daniel would probably be conciliatory on the surface, Davis predicted, but "could not be trusted." Had he not retired already, the former ambassador revealed, he would have done so immediately after the man's inauguration—he would not wish to stay on duty "to deal with a person like Fignolé."

EISENHOWER, LIKE DANIEL, had an extreme work ethic; their similarities ended there. Eisenhower garbled his syntax and mixed up his words. Daniel spoke with precise eloquence. Eisenhower—a social animal—constantly surrounded himself with loved ones and friends. Daniel, prickly to his core, loved crowds, not individuals. Eisenhower did not have a philosophical or intellectual bone in his body, but nursed a formidable analytical mind, an unparalleled ability to distill problems, to organize solutions, to execute plans. Daniel enjoyed a glittering conceptual brilliance—for math, history, law, ideas—with little social intelligence or operational skill. Eisenhower instinctively sided with the powerful and elite consensus. Daniel's gut, his childhood, his intellect, led him to side with the downtrodden and oppositional thinking.

Eisenhower was putting more faith in covert operations than any U.S. president before him. He'd been supreme commander of the Allied forces in Europe during World War II and had seen first-hand how effective the American intelligence operations had been. The CIA, besides, offered the president an alluring quick fix to his international headaches—secret operations freed him from knotty strings such as Congress, the American public, international law, and world opinion.

Though he had meticulously helped plan the grandest military operation in world history, Eisenhower never participated, as president, in the planning of would-be coups. He left that to his deputies. And he set a firm rule: leave no document that could implicate him in a coup. But in the privacy of the Oval Office, or over cocktails, he exercised strong, wide-ranging control over the CIA. When Eisenhower ordered a covert operation there was no hemming, no hawing, no doubts, no second thoughts. "Do it," the general would say, "and don't bother me with any details."

At 5:37 that Monday evening, Eisenhower ended his official day. He left the Oval Office and retreated to the White House private quarters for an off-the-record discussion with congressional Republicans.

EIGHTEEN DAYS AFTER the White House meeting, General Kébreau gave all rank-and-file soldiers, most of whom were considered steadfast loyalists to President Fignolé, the night off. He invited the young troops to an American-cowboy double feature at the barracks. Its movie hall had just been renovated, with plush new seating and air-conditioning. The soldiers were told that they could not bring their firearms into the newly refurbished theater, to check them at the entrance. After the two movies ended, the soldiers were rounded up, put onto military trucks, and sent to the provinces.

That same day, the Eisenhower administration issued Daniel and Carmen Fignolé "temporary alien" visas in a secret maneuver and through strictly classified channels. The day of the coup, Haiti's top military officers went to the U.S. embassy in Port-au-Prince to finalize the two nonimmigrant visas. By granting a sitting president and First Lady visas without their request, knowledge, or consent, and by issuing those visas directly to a third party, General Kébreau, shortly before he kidnapped the president at gunpoint, the U.S. government had effectively hatched a coup.

Chapter 19

DANIEL AND CARMEN LANDED IN NEW YORK AT ELEVEN o'clock at night, June 15, 1957, more than twenty-four grueling hours after the ordeal had begun. Once General Kébreau had forced them onto a Haitian military plane that landed in Miami, the two boarded a commercial flight on Rasters Airlines to New York.

International press swarmed Daniel at the arrival lounge. Never having set foot in the so-called Western world, he took in the foreign surroundings—sharp, metallic, sterile.

"Mr. President! Mr. President!" the newsmen yelled. They asked Daniel what had happened to him in Haiti, what he thought about his predicament, whether he intended to remain in America, and if so, how.

"I literally don't have a penny in my pockets. I had to borrow one hundred dollars from the Haitian embassy in Miami. For now, I don't even know how I will eat," Daniel said to a Canadian journalist. "But I am comforted by the idea that my people have not abandoned me."

And then, through an interpreter, he told *The New York Times* reporter, "I now consider myself an exile. It is up to a representative of my government to find me and the First Lady quarters to rest."

Daniel thought carefully as he spoke, refusing, out of calculation, to describe the coup.

Standing by his side, Carmen watched, silent. No one said a word to her.

A small delegation of Haitian officials, including Haiti's ambassador to the United Nations and the Haitian consul in New York, were waiting for the ex-president at the airport. Daniel and the ex–First Lady would be chaperoned to new quarters they'd never heard of, the Cameron Hotel on West Eighty-Sixth Street at Central Park West. When the horde of newsmen ran out of questions, the Haitian officials escorted the couple into an unfamiliar car. The diplomats had been appointed by General Magloire, Daniel's predecessor and once jailer. He wondered to himself how deep their loyalties to Magloire or the current junta ran.

HAITIAN OFFICERS DESCENDED on the Fignolé home not long after Carmen and Daniel's plane took off from Môle-Saint-Nicolas. Shouting filled the house as soon as Natacha opened the door. Six soldiers barreled past her into the foyer.

One shoved her to the floor and yelled, "Bring them all downstairs!"

She tried to stall. "Who?"

"The children."

Natacha, weeping, went from bedroom to bedroom, telling the children to get dressed. Danielle's fingers felt numb as she fumbled to put her clothes on. Their house had been tear-gassed before, it had been strafed with gunfire more than once, but no soldiers had ever called after her or threatened to take any of the children away.

Now all seven of them gathered on the front terrace, and the soldiers shouted at them to climb into the back of a waiting truck. The machine guns strapped to their chests seemed as alive to Danielle as their twisted, veiny faces. She watched her siblings get into the truck bed and followed once they'd all climbed in. Piled atop the cool metal flatbed, the children, guarded by soldiers, could see out into the night through a slit in the canvas. Danielle watched as Port-au-Prince passed her by. The truck drove down Rue Capois and then took a left at Rue St-Honoré, and she felt a small relaxation in her throat: it looked as if they were headed to the palace, to Papa's office.

Finally, the truck tires came to a stop on gravel. Soldiers leapt out of the front and the back and shoved the children down to the ground. Danielle saw that they'd parked not in the front of the palace, where she'd go to see her papa, but behind, at the entrance to the Dessalines Barracks.

The soldiers shouted at the children to stand in an orderly line, then led them into the barracks, through the hallways, and down to the basement. It was stifling, so hot and airless, Danielle felt as if she needed to keep her mouth open just so she could breathe. The stale air made the space feel tighter, as if it were closing in on her. She looked at her sisters and brothers, whose eyes were big, swollen. They were all crying.

She wondered where her parents were. Somewhere in this barracks too? Could she call out to them? She wanted them, half expected them to walk through that metal door and save her, her younger siblings. She started to cry too and a soldier slapped her across the forehead to make her stop. She tried to ignore the awful suspicion growing within her—that her father's power no longer mattered, that these men did not care about her papa. She and her siblings were alone and all they could do was quietly beg to be taken home. Her tears wet her dress. Two of the soldiers laughed.

The soldiers were led by Colonel Beauvoir, who had colluded with Duvalier. They knew that killing Daniel on Haitian soil could provoke their own undoing, so they'd planned to murder the children in that dark basement instead. Now they hesitated. The second-oldest girl, Raymonde, was Duvalier's goddaughter, after all. And all the children belonged to Carmen, who was a beloved hostess, who had lovingly taught an entire generation of middle-class children, who was so well liked among many families, including the high placed. Had the sobbing children belonged only to Daniel, the soldiers would have slit their throats and not given it a second thought. For Carmen's sake, and as a courtesy to Duvalier, they let the children live.

Instead, the soldiers left the boys in the dark and took the screaming girls, one by one, into a closet and raped them.

Chapter 20

―――――

S DAWN BROKE THE NEXT DAY, SOFT AND HUSKY, A MAN named Bernier St. Jean, a devoted Fignolist, knocked on the front door of a small home in Mont Joli, a congenial Port-au-Prince neighborhood. The house belonged to his friend Bernard Diederich, a New Zealander who edited the *Haiti Sun*. Bernard lumbered out of his bedroom in his pajamas, cursing the disruption to his Saturday-morning sleep. He opened the door. Tears flooded Bernier's cheeks and sobs cut short his breath. "They have taken Daniel," he said.

How Bernier had found out, no one may ever know. But his words traveled in a flash. Teledjol went into high gear.

GIGINE AND JEAN WOKE UP that day as if it were any Saturday morning. Gigine asked her husband, Jean, to feed their two children, Jean-Jean, five, and Ginette, two, so that she could go to market to pick up fresh vegetables, visit the artisans, maybe linger and buy a tortoiseshell bracelet for Jean-Jean, or perhaps treat herself to a mac-ramé basket. Soon, though, came the unexpected. At ten thirty, the chief of the army, General Antonio Kébreau, issued a short, plain statement by radio: the army had taken over the government. He declared a "state of emergency" throughout the republic until a new election could be held and said nothing of the president's status or whereabouts.

He made no mention either of Carmen or the children.

Gigine heard the news and immediately jumped in a taxi to go see her sister. Her mind churned, agitated and bewildered, wondering how and why Daniel could have been ousted. At least she'd be there soon to comfort Carmen, Danielle, the little ones.

She was shocked by what she found when she pulled up to the house. Soldiers had sealed off the place and refused to let her in. They wouldn't tell her where Carmen and the children were. She went to look for Natacha, who she knew minded the babies weekday nights. No luck. No one answered Natacha's door.

New clues soon came. At eight that evening, General Kébreau broadcast on national radio a letter that he said Professor Daniel Fignolé had written to him. "At a moment when civil war threatened to lead the country into an abyss, I tried very hard to bring back a peaceful climate," a news announcer read. "In the presence of difficulties of all kinds in trying to accomplish this noble task, I see myself obliged to submit to the Chief of Staff of the Army my resignation. In uttering my sincerest wishes for the happiness of my beloved country, I ask you to accept my distinguished salutations on behalf of the Fatherland."

Gigine turned the volume down in disgust. What she heard sounded nothing like Daniel.

As soon as the broadcast ended, the general put the country on a hard-line curfew. Businesses and shops were shuttered. Taxis, trolleys, and flights were halted. Radio signals were disabled, as was the phone service.

The frightening silence birthed dark rumors. Daniel was jailed in Fort Dimanche. Daniel was in the gruesome fortress awaiting execution.

Tempers simmered a full day; by night, they were set to explode.

People seized the streets, singing, chanting. *"Ki kote li ye? Ki kote li ye?"*—"Where is he?" they shouted. "Where is he?"

The streets shook with *ténèbre,* an angry worship, a feverish cry. Speakers called out, *"Ban nou tounen Fignolé nou."* People replied, *"Ban nou tounen Fignolé nou."* The air trembled. Call, response, call, response. "Give us back our Fignolé!" They broke the steel-pole streetlamps block after block for cover, plunging the city into darkness.

I imagine it's what Haiti's early slave revolts must have sounded like, ringing covertly from the slave quarters to the big house. Furtive, hurt, threatening. Pitch-perfect unison of voices in pitch-black. Hands clapping, feet stomping, thousands marched toward the National Penitentiary to carry Daniel back with them, living or dead. Dark streets packed with bodies. Pots, pans dinged steel telephone poles.

Army trucks, loaded with troops, rolled into the tin-hut slums and the working-class neighborhoods. The people launched their defense. Men cut car tires to improvise oversize slingshots from the slashed rubber. They climbed telephone poles and catapulted rocks at the trucks and at government buildings. "Give us back our Fignolé!"

Armed with torchlights and Winchester rifles, soldiers shot point-blank into the crowds. Bursts of machine-gun fire tore into the people. They defended themselves, as best they could, hurling rocks. "Where is your mercy? Stop firing on us." They took up their slain brethren's nighttime chants of mourning, desperate pleas for the dead. "Where is your mercy?" Many thought Fignolé was now among the executed.

Methodically and systematically, the army arrested the defiant, blanketing the working-poor wards of the city, cleansing the ténè-bre, zone by zone, neighborhood by neighborhood, street by street, shoving men and women into trucks at gunpoint and carting them off to jail. Anyone they didn't arrest, they shot.

The terrified fled for safety, leaping over corpses, running in their neighbors' blood. Soldiers shot them too. They trained their guns on anyone still moving. Albert Salas, a medic and longtime friend of Daniel and Carmen's, set into the night with his bag of supplies, scrambling to save lives. From street to street, he pried bullets from tissue, crocheted wounds, and watched their former neighbors die.

Gigine and Jean heard the gunfire and turned off all the lights to camouflage their home, 47 Rue de la Révolution, thick in the middle of Bel-Air. They sat frozen in their living room, far from any windows. They heard the police's sirens, darkness sharpening the shriek, heard cries in the night, listening in sympathy, hoping for any news about Carmen, the kids. Gigine prayed the noise would not frighten Jean-Jean and Ginette, sleeping in their bedroom. The hours felt like a grim nightmare, as though an entire bloody year were unfolding.

Finally, the wails and the clanging started to quiet. Vanquished protesters were tossed into ditches in a dark, out-of-sight place. The ditches had been dug in advance.

Bernard Diederich could hear the *ténèbre*, locked down under curfew, all the way from his house in Mont Joli, many miles away. "I heard the most terrible collective sound," he reported soon after. "The sound echoed chillingly through that hot, humid summer night. The crackle of gunfire was interspersed with those mournful, desperate cries. For months afterwards I could still hear that terrible vocal crescendo, the death of Fignolé's vaunted human steamroller, the end of an entire movement and their hopes."

Most of the murdered came from the poorer wards, Saint-Martin, La Saline, Bel-Air. Most received no funeral. Loved ones were too afraid to claim them from the morgues, afraid to encounter vengeful troops. Morgue counts said at least 467 of Daniel's supporters were massacred in the *ténèbre*. Historians put the number as high as three thousand. No one can know exactly: the army loaded corpses onto lorries, then flung them into unmarked graves, the bodies unaccounted for.

"One would have to ask the city's poor population, whose only crime was to love a man, how they find a serious reason to stay living," a major newspaper, *La Foie Sociale*, asked. "We must question that night, tear away its secrets, plunge the depths of its cemeteries where men, women and children were given a primitive burial."

THE NEXT MORNING, Daniel's remaining supporters clogged the major roads leading out of the capital, making an exodus to the countryside for safety. Sullen stares, blank expressions, shell shock.

Port-au-Prince fell back into a macabre silence.

Gigine sat at home, nursing her coffee. Were Carmen and the children alive? If so, where? She wondered over her untouched plantain porridge whether Daniel's closest aides, cabinet members, and MOP officials had been arrested or shot. Her agony cut her appetite.

From her kitchen table she could no longer hear a thing, except Jean shuffling around with the children. The sirens, the trucks, the rifle shots, the cries: gone. She put on her plainest dress, one that wouldn't draw any attention, and eased her way into the streets. She pieced together bits of news, was devastated to learn from her neighbors that so many people close to them had been slain. Who? she asked. They couldn't say. How many? No answers.

She went home again and considered what to do next. Gigine had grown into a woman with a formidable anger and keen wits far beyond her twenty-seven years. She decided to entrust her babies with a neighbor, so she could secure the safety of her beloved sister's. She set out on foot, looking for Natacha one more time.

Rounding the corners, she kept a close watch over her shoulders. The military was on patrol all over. "Every day trains of people are led down the streets by the soldiery," a journalist wrote in *The Nation*. "Soldiers have been terrorizing, by illegal search and arrest, the followers of Fignolé."

Gigine soon found Natacha, who'd finally felt safe returning to her own home, two days after the soldiers had taken the children. Natacha was alive and unharmed—physically. She told Gigine every detail that she could remember, crying through the account. By the time Gigine returned home, she was still shaking, exhausted. She held Natacha's account close to her chest.

Major newspapers around the world had begun to report the coup, their pages hitting newsstands from Washington to Caracas to Barcelona, not long after Daniel had landed and granted interviews at the airport in New York. International papers and radio, through their own sources, were reporting also that Daniel's entire cabinet, along with MOP's twenty most senior leaders, had been imprisoned. But the press had no idea of his children's whereabouts any more than he did.

It took several days for word to make its way to Bel-Air that Daniel and Carmen had been ousted to America. Gigine shared her incomplete relief with Jean: at least those two were alive.

Soon she realized that Daniel's contacts were the least productive, most dangerous source for information on the children. She couldn't trust what precious few connections Daniel had in the army or among the police. Anyway, she figured, any soldier loyal to Daniel had been murdered or arrested. With no one else to turn to, Gigine sought help from the only other uniforms in the country that had almost as much power as the military: the Catholics.

Having attended mass every Sunday for the past two decades, Carmen was on a first-name basis with every Catholic person in the city with any standing, including Archbishop Poirier. And Danielle was a junior high student at the Collège du Sacré Coeur. Gigine knew the highest male clerics would not entangle themselves in assisting a "resigned" president's family and risk angering the military. So she turned to the nuns. One, in particular, la Révérende Mère Marie Nathalie, had loved Carmen for decades. She'd first met Carmen when she was a sister at the boarding school Carmen had attended as a girl. Gigine enlisted her and two more sisters from her order, Marie Edouard and Marie Antoine, to help look for the children.

Together they reasoned that it was highly unlikely that any soldier, especially if he had a wife, would hold the children hostage in his home. They wouldn't want to subject their household to such trouble, to such bad spiritual energy, to such haunting. If the children were alive, it would defy Vodou nature, or Catholic sensibility, or a woman's common sense, that they be held hostage in a private home. That left public buildings. City Hall? The National Penitentiary? The palace? Dessalines Barracks?

They turned the city upside down looking for the children.

THE CHILDREN HAD BEEN prisoners for ten days when Tante Gigine and the nuns finally found them in the barracks and wrested them free. By then, the army had destroyed the steamroller and consolidated its power. The children were no longer of use to them as pawns, alive or dead.

When Gigine helped the children into the holy sister's car, Danielle nearly vomited. She was dizzy from the pain. Confused by what the soldiers had done to her. She stared at the sisters. Her maman loved her Catholic community and told her that religion was a relief from life's pain. But her papa had told her that religion was a sedative, a soothing charade to keep black people as gentle and obedient as children. Now she didn't know what to believe. She looked at the dark habits framing the white faces and tears rolled down her cheeks.

As soon as they walked through her door, Tante Gigine sat the children around her kitchen table and fed them. She explained that their parents were now in America, that they'd been forced there by soldiers. She told the kids that they must leave the country immediately to join them.

Danielle wanted to see Maman and Papa, but she was scared. She didn't know in what state she would find them, and she was terrified that they would be as badly changed as she was. Part of her was relieved she could leave Haiti, which she'd come to feel was a horrible place, but what if the next place was worse? She felt dazed with hatred for the soldiers who had taken them, paralyzed by pain. She wondered if she would ever have her life back. Her self back.

She was exhausted. She had to have faith that Tante Gigine and the nuns would protect her, would somehow make things right. The military still had the airport on lockdown, so Gigine and the nuns decided to pay Toussaint, a broke taximan, fervent supporter and former Bel-Air neighbor of Daniel's, to take them all secretly in a plain car to the Dominican Republic. Gigine felt the man was savvy, having lived there right before the generalissimo had expelled Haitian workers such as him. But even having secured his guidance, she was terrified that something would happen to the children on the poorly marked journey, as they defied martial law. She trembled at the risk she was putting her own children in by saving her sister's.

Still, when the time came, Gigine helped the children into Toussaint's taxi and climbed in after them.

WHEN THEY ARRIVED at the Dominican capital, plane tickets awaited the children at Ciudad Trujillo airport. I tracked down the official passenger list of their Pan Am flight; it doesn't reveal who paid the commercial carrier for the seven tickets. It is highly unlikely that Gigine, in her midtwenties, had that kind of money. Every senior MOP leader had been imprisoned or murdered. No midlevel union manager with those kinds of resources would risk bringing attention to himself by assisting Fignolé's children. Certainly their parents couldn't have bought the tickets.

Perhaps it could have been the nuns or a member of Carmen's Catholic parish. I suspect it was Eisenhower's administration that bought the tickets, or possibly it was François Duvalier who, in a

Family portrait, 1957

pang of mixed loathing and affection for the family, paid for the fares. The truth will always be a mystery.

Gigine dressed the children in clean, matching outfits—all white—before the flight. The girls had neat ribbons tied in their hair and cinched at their waists.

Just as they were about to board—two weeks after they and their parents had been kidnapped—somebody took a photograph of them with their Tante Gigine.

Family portrait. The term implies pride, warmth, rootedness, cheer. But this portrait captures my family in harrowing flight. Tante Gigine wears a spotless white dress and stares fiercely into the camera, an avenged mother lioness. Some of my aunts and uncles frown in confusion; others stare with worry.

If you look into my mother's eyes, all you see is a black void.

Chapter 21

———

THE CHILDREN LANDED AT IDLEWILD AIRPORT. DANIELLE
recognized her maman's figure immediately at the arrival gate,
well before she could make out her face, her small, comforting silhouette holding her purse on her forearm. Danielle hugged her
mother and held her—longer than she realized she needed. A car
driven by some Haitian man she'd never met drove them away from
the airport and onto a highway, sprawling like a massive mechanical
spider. She had no idea where they were going.

Daniel and Carmen were still staying at the Hotel Cameron. When
Carmen returned with the children, they all filed into the suite, and
Danielle peered out of a window into a massive park below. Besides
the plane ride from Santo Domingo, her first, she had never stood
so high in the air.

Carmen spent the next few days helping the children settle. Danielle found it difficult to sleep. She was tired, and the telephone rang
nonstop with journalists calling for Papa. She could hear his voice
swell into the mouthpiece. "I am the president of the republic," he
yelled to one reporter. "What I would like to do is to return home.
Haiti is now under the dictatorial power of the army. It is corrupt
from one end to the other."

Daniel had been in war mode since the moment he'd arrived to
the hotel, fifteen days earlier. He had installed himself in the suite's
living room and granted interviews to ABC Radio and *The New
York Times*. He told the paper that he'd been ousted through "pure
gangsterism," then denounced the Haitian generals for the rumors

they had spread—that he didn't care about his followers, that he had voluntarily resigned, "overwhelmed by the difficulty of my job." He related his account of that night. "One of my own pupils came to arrest me when I was presiding over a cabinet meeting," he said to ABC Radio with indignation.

Daniel demanded quiet from the family at all times. He said he needed to concentrate on his interviews. A television sat in the center of the living room in their new suite. He ordered that it be turned off or on mute. No one could understand the English that clanged from the box anyway. To preserve the silence engulfing the place, to prevent being yelled at, Danielle shrank herself. She said next to nothing. Her jaw tightened, fastening into a kind of ache. She listened to her father answer questions about what was happening to him, but he didn't seem terribly interested in what had happened to her. She had to hold on to her pain like a secret.

Every sound amplified in Danielle's ears. When her maman unzipped a suitcase, or Raymonde flushed the toilet, or Pierre accidentally slammed a door, the noise struck her with force—she froze. When she had to go to the bathroom, she held it for as long as she could, to avoid making noise herself. She shuffled past her father with no words, and he past her. As she quietly watched him pace the suite, she felt her resentment follow him like a fog. Her carefully maintained silence suffocated her, sharpening the pain she felt in her jaw. A child looks up to her father to protect her and he had failed. Why wouldn't he talk about that?

I do not know what my mother did or did not tell her parents about the rapes. It was only in 2017, sitting in my kitchen in Brooklyn, that she opened up to me about them, in a rare, unguarded moment. She ripped herself a tranche of paper towels and wiped her tears. "He never believed me after what I told him. I pushed the secrets way deep down. Otherwise the information would make me choke," Mommy said. "I'll never forgive him."

Here is a formidable woman who had never, not once, cried in front of me. Her breath panted in the telling, her sobs hoarse and uncontrolled. The sound of six decades of pent-up rage.

• • •

EXACTLY ONE WEEK after landing in New York, Daniel wrote to
President Eisenhower. Written in French, the terse three-paragraph
letter was translated by State Department officials once it arrived
to the White House. In his elaborate decorum, Daniel tried to hold
Eisenhower accountable for his family's safety while they were in
America. The letter, from one president to another, was written on
the Cameron's fine letterhead. Embossed on the bottom, with raised
purple engraving, is its motto: "The best home away from home is a
good hotel."

Soon they didn't even have that. As Danielle tried to adjust to
her altered life, the family was upended again. Carmen packed what
few possessions they had, and they moved from the Hotel Cameron
to larger, cheaper quarters at the Raleigh, an inelegant "apartment
hotel" on West Seventy-Second Street at Columbus Avenue. Daniel
begrudgingly agreed to the dingier place, resigned to saving money.
Their surroundings didn't matter anyway, he told the family: any day
now they'd be checking out and returning home.

Shortly after, Daniel received a visit from a Monsieur Maurice,
who had emigrated to America from Haiti years before. He lived
in Brooklyn, where he strung together odd jobs to support himself: driver, translator, all-around fixer to newcomers. He was a lifelong supporter of Daniel's and had been sent to greet the family by
a mutual ally. He brought with him gifts for le professeur, a book,
newspapers, and copies of the major magazines. Daniel asked him
to read aloud a short article from *Time*.

"Lunging too fast for power," Maurice read, "Mr. Fignolé post-
poned the presidential elections originally set for June 16. Then he
maneuvered to get himself a full six-year term without an election.
Fanatic Daniel Fignolé suffered the disability of excessive ambition.
Now he went meekly into exile."

Daniel knew that the false information was some foreign stringer
mindlessly reporting what he'd been told by officials. And still,

remembering the guns trained at his back, it was the word "meekly" that galled him most.

He raised a thick eyebrow over his deep-set eyes and cocked his head as though he needed to hear better. He didn't like having his failures debated in public, certainly not in this cramped room. Maurice gave a small, embarrassed frown, but Daniel was insistent. Read. That. To. Me. Again. A caustic pause between each word.

Once he'd heard it a second time, Daniel shut down the conversation. He went to sit in his favorite chair and stared out the window at the endless skyline, flicker-lit Manhattan etching his face. He recalled and reanalyzed the details of his last days in Port-au-Prince again and again, lost in his own reflection.

Life in the suite was unraveling in a blur. Dank and boiling, the August air carried a stench, the alien TV blinkered. Each muggy day went like the last, with little to do but wait. The family trained themselves in the condition of waiting. For what, nobody was sure.

Carmen, meanwhile, did her best to busy herself bathing the babies, laundering everyone's clothes in the sweltering bathroom. Just like the children, she tiptoed around Daniel, who was growing angrier by the day. Moving about, doing chores, she realized how badly he had miscalculated the terrain, then acted in bone stupidity.

I'm ministering to the nation, he'd told the family the morning of the inauguration, I've outflanked my rivals. But in the Raleigh hotel, everyone understood the truth: Daniel had vaulted into Duvalier's mousetrap. Now her children were being made to pay.

EVENTUALLY THE CALLS from journalists tapered to a trickle. The summer days were winnowing and Daniel's new people, a group of expat sycophants who hovered about him, broke the news. A fresh recall election, scheduled for that September, would pit Duvalier against Déjoie. Daniel bristled to hear how both men were angling to woo his supporters. Duvalier was touting a "clothing relief crusade for the poor," while Déjoie distributed free rum at jukebox dances.

Daniel knew his supporters would see through the antics, but there was nothing he could do. How could he campaign from a hotel in another country for a job he had supposedly forfeited?

Danielle watched as these strange men, so enamored with her father, paraded through the family quarters. They brought her papa news articles from around the world, and advice—solicited and unsolicited—on what he must do next. They praised him, and every time they opened their mouths with flattery, Carmen assumed a request for a favor was coming. Eventually she realized that not all of them were leeches, nor rubberneckers itching to see a man at the pit of his mighty fall. Some of them were true patriots, devastated to see her husband languishing in a hotel. They had risked arrest, their careers, during the January '46 Revolutions and come to New York at some point to flee persecution, or to seek opportunity. They still cared dearly about their country. And Daniel reassured them all emphatically: he and his family were on guard, ready to board a flight right back to Haiti at a moment's notice.

Unbeknownst to the family, the U.S. government seemed to agree with his hopes. "It would appear that Mr. Fignolé will probably not take up permanent residence in the United States, but will eventually return to Haiti," a State Department official wrote to the commissioner of the Immigration and Naturalization Service (INS), the week after his arrival, in a confidential letter. "It is the opinion of the Department of State that Mr. Fignolé should be admitted into the United States for a temporary stay."

Once his new followers had left, Daniel returned to his chair, unbothered and alone, rehashing in his mind, over and again, new details about that night. After kidnapping him, he'd learned, soldiers had returned to seal off the house. And ransacked it. Breaking into his den, they discovered the stash of more than forty thousand gourdes. The army dispatched its own lawyer, who announced to the public that he was itemizing the objects in the failed president's house for safekeeping. Then the top military officers inspected "the official ledger"—and stole everything on it.

When President Magloire had fled Haiti, the foreign press estimated his family assets at five million dollars—a true looting. When Daniel and Carmen were expelled, they had the assets of any comfortable Haitian couple: roughly ten thousand dollars in cash. Never dreaming of dipping their hands in the national till, they lived the modest life of an honest civil servant and a successful businesswoman.

Their cash and belongings would never be recovered.

Chapter 22

C OME SEPTEMBER, DANIEL'S NIGHTMARE WAS BROADCAST in papers around the world for all to see: Duvalier was announced president after winning a sham election. Daniel's face crumpled in fury as he read the news. "How can Haiti have free elections," he growled to an *Ebony* reporter, "when candidates are in exile?"

In theory, every polling station had monitors from the major political parties. "But in practice, ballot boxes were stuffed, stolen, and miscounted," Elizabeth Abbott has noted.

The U.S. government was quite familiar with Duvalier and rather liked his odds. "Although the defeated candidates can always cry foul, it appears to the Embassy that a rigged election in favor of Duvalier, if skillfully and discreetly managed, would have a fair chance of sticking," a then-classified dispatch said. Indeed, not long after the vote, Duvalier arrested hundreds of people who contested the election, including a journalist, Pierre-Edouard Bellande, whose first infraction was having refused to campaign for him.

An embittered Daniel talks to *Ebony* magazine, 765 St. Johns Place, early 1958

When François and Simone moved into the National Palace, Carmen understood: nobody was flying back to Haiti anytime soon. What to do with the family? They couldn't afford to keep racking up hotel bills in Manhattan.

Monsieur Maurice offered to rent the couple an apartment at a good price, in a place called Brooklyn. While it was less luxurious than the Upper West Side, it had other Haitians and even a small teledjol. Carmen thanked him profusely; Daniel agreed with a scowl. He insisted that the move was temporary.

They arrived to their new home in Crown Heights, 765 St. Johns Place. No one in the family had seen anything like it, a long building called a row house, with four floors, two apartments on each. When Danielle stepped through the door, her tongue bunched up. The one-bedroom apartment was one-fifth the size of their house back home.

Daniel and Carmen shared the bedroom with baby Carmen. Her maman laid a dresser drawer on its floor and put towels in it to make a crib. They hung a curtain across the living room to create

Carmen cooks for the family in a staged photo
for *Ebony* magazine, 765 St. Johns Place, early 1958

another small bedroom, where Danielle, Raymonde, Marie, and Leonie slept. Most nights, Bernard and Pierre lined up two chairs in the kitchen or in the hallway, padded them with a blanket, and lay down to sleep.

Danielle was often sent out to run the family's errands, with Pierre and Bernard in tow. Crown Heights was a salty, down-to-earth, workaday place, nothing like their leafy neighborhood behind the glamorous Hôtel Oloffson. The area was three-quarters white and one-quarter black and Puerto Rican. Since the 1920s, black Americans had slowly been streaming into the neighborhood from the Jim Crow South; they landed in Crown Heights either because they couldn't afford Harlem or had no interest in Manhattan. Of the white folks, half were Jewish, the rest mostly Italian American. When their home was built, in 1931, Monsieur Maurice explained to them, devout Jews had been moving to the neighborhood. Sabbath forbade the newcomers from handling elevators, so the building was constructed with stairs only. Up and down, the Fignolés climbed, down and up, to their fourth-floor walk-up.

A local supporter helped Carmen enroll the children in the local public schools—Danielle in seventh grade. None of the siblings had their own clothes or anything that really fit. Even though Danielle was bigger than Raymonde, and Raymonde bigger than Marie, and Marie bigger than Leonie, they rotated four dresses among themselves to go to school. The dresses were loose fitting; the smaller girls had to wear a rope or a cloth tied around the waist so the dress wouldn't look too funny. Each night, they'd scrub away any stains from the day so someone else could wear the dress next. Pierre and Bernard, two years apart, shared secondhand clothes and shoes too.

NOT LONG AFTER they'd arrived in Brooklyn, Carmen was finally able to take Danielle to Kings County Hospital. They were seeking medical treatment to help heal the damage the soldiers had done to her reproductive organs.

When they returned home from the infirmary, Danielle did her best to hide how depressed she felt. She missed her friends and teachers at her private school back home. She wondered if they missed her. She missed her old clothes and books and the gold earrings and necklace that her tante Gigine had given her. She missed her maman's house-school.

When will I see Tante Gigine again? Danielle prodded her mother. Her maman tried to soothe her but had no answer. She missed Gigine herself.

Daniel didn't pay any mind. When he heard Danielle crying in the bathroom that evening, he banged on the door for her to hurry, so he could relieve himself and get back to work, his long-distance campaign to lead Haiti again.

His disciples had followed him to their new home. Some months after they'd moved in, a man came by, pretending not to notice the ironing board heaped with diapers in the makeshift, shrunken living room. Danielle could see two fingers on his left hand trembling as he opened his mouth. Through backdoor channels, he had learned that so-and-so had been sent to Fort Dimanche, Duvalier's political prison. Somebody else had gone missing in an alley in Port-au-Prince. Yet another person had been hunted down and shot to death by Papa Doc's henchmen.

Daniel's former students, union members, political advisers, and cabinet officers: to Daniel, every victim had a face to his name. The painful update that afternoon served Daniel a reminder of what they already knew: if he returned to Haiti, Duvalier would have him executed without a second thought.

Another night, the family was startled to hear knocking on the front door. Daniel cracked it open and became even more astounded to discover a face he recognized instantly—Lyonel Paquin. Daniel had no idea how Lyonel had come to find him in Crown Heights.

Lyonel had to stifle his own surprise—all those children milling about in circumstances that shocked him, "a pitiful apartment, cold and damp," he would later write. "The furniture was shabby and sparse. The walls had an indefinable dirty pink color—and water was oozing from them."

Daniel gestured his hand toward a chair for Lyonel to sit, then sat down himself, his spine a perfect erect line.

"What brings you here?" asked Daniel, as if the decor and backdrop were the National Palace.

The resistance in Haiti wanted to draft a formal document announcing to the world a coalition opposing Duvalier, Lyonel explained. Just weeks before, Lyonel's house had been ransacked by Duvalier's police and he'd fled the country to save his life.

Daniel shifted a little in his chair. "Like all of you I am very impatient to know more concerning the details of Duvalier's rule. We shall see who shall profit from his crimes. Fignolé is watching!" In moments of drama, Lyonel knew, Daniel talked about himself in the third person. Now his eyes drilled into Lyonel. "The people of Fignolé are watching!"

After a dramatic pause, Daniel added, "The minute I set foot in Haiti, nobody can prevent me from resuming my presidency. History still owes me a mandate of six years less nineteen days."

Lyonel let out a small cough and tried not to stare at the leaking walls.

DANIEL'S GUESTS BLEW THROUGH the family's living room like an unannounced storm to flatter him and plot how to restore his presidency.

When he was alone, he wrote.

It was difficult for him to read; there was no French library nearby. The army had stolen all his belongings, but he was most bereft without his books. No matter how overpopulated the apartment, he looked so lonely to Danielle without his books. America felt like a prison without an exact sentence, the apartment a cell, even if her father held the keys to its locks.

At home, Daniel was not free. Everyone in the family knew but didn't say: Papa was working on deadline. The longer Duvalier kept power, the less likely Daniel's return. He was living in Brooklyn on borrowed time.

Donning his suit, tie, and fedora, Daniel made the rounds to the newsstands in the late mornings, picking up his daily assortment of international, national, and local papers—not only to disappear into the news but also to study English. And late at night, hands jammed into his pants pockets, he prowled Nostrand Avenue, its sidewalks dark and empty, managing his thoughts.

When 1957 had rolled in, Daniel had been the dean of Haiti's intelligentsia, the chieftain of its populist politics, the steward of a movement's dreams. When 1957 rolled out, he was just another Negro deep in Brooklyn.

Chapter 23

————

LITTLE CARMEN THREW HERSELF TO THE GROUND, POUNDING her chubby fists.

"Maman, I'm hungry!" the three-year-old sobbed. "Is anybody going to feed me?"

Her mother scurried to the kitchen and asked everyone to sit. The family had not sung hymns, had not been to mass, that Christmas Eve 1958, as the elder Carmen would've liked. She stood over the eight children and Daniel and ladled soup into their bowls. But lacking any solid ingredients—meat, noodles, vegetables—it was not soup so much as chicken broth.

Watching the meager portions get passed around the table, one of the kids made a sideways remark: "What a wonderful holiday feast."

"Who said that?" Daniel hissed, his eyes stern and barren.

Nobody spoke.

"Who said that?" he repeated.

Leonie pointed at Marie. Raymonde pointed at Danielle.

Daniel took his paper napkin from the lopsided, wobbling table and calmly wiped his lips. He decided, for whatever reason, that the sarcastic mutter had come from Raymonde.

"Pierre, go get my belt," he said, his tone sharp, commanding. Poor Haitians loved that arresting voice, but his children had grown to dread it.

As the oldest male child, it often fell to Pierre to fetch whichever weapon their father asked for to unleash a beating—a shoe heel, a metal cooking spoon, a whip, whatever caught his mood. He loved the exclamation point of having a child go retrieve the instrument of their sibling's punishment.

Pierre brought the belt and Daniel whipped Raymonde on her naked backside so hard that the metal buckle came loose.

"I had taught what was left of my brain, my mind, my heart, my body, and my soul not to register that pain anymore," Raymonde remembered later in life. "I would just stand there, staring him down, wishing he would beat me to death, wondering how he would explain my passing and my injuries. Would you believe that I loved and admired him? It made me so sad that he did not love me."

Her Christmas beating, Raymonde realized with relief and sadness, wasn't as vicious as Bernard's had been the week before. Daniel had sent Bernard down the street to buy *The New York Times*. Bernard got a piece of candy for himself on the way home, the little candies with the hole in the middle, like a wheel. The kids all did that. When he got back to the apartment, he hid the candy behind the front door for later. Daniel had seen him do the same thing the week before, so this time he lay in wait. He let Bernard hide the candy, then retrieved the contraband and held it up for all to see. He beat Bernard with electrical cords to make an example out of him.

"Daddy, Daddy, please don't kill me," Bernard begged, as Raymonde recalled. "I'll never do it again, Daddy. Punish me any other way you want, but this hurts too much. Daddy, I love you. Please love me." Bernard fell to the floor with a sickening thud.

Raymonde thought she wanted to die anyway, so why not defend Bernard? If she failed, they'd go to heaven together. There could be no other hell for them after living like this. She threw herself over him and blocked the blows while their mother, who had just given birth to their baby sister Joelle the month before, crouched in a corner. Seeing Raymonde flail, Carmen stood and tried to wedge her body between her dear Bernard and his father.

Later that Christmas Eve, Raymonde found her mother outside, sitting at the top of the stoop in her nightgown, soaked in blood. She was sobbing like a child. Raymonde half carried her inside and removed her bloody nightgown, wiped her body with a wet, soapy towel. The blood had frozen and gelled on the stoop. Raymonde had to use laundry soap with a bit of Clorox to get it off.

This was one of the rare instances, Raymonde claimed, in which Danielle got involved. "Seeing our mother in blood, that bitch started to help me. The only funny thing in this whole hellish scenario was that, for the very first time, Danielle was helping me and actually working Christmas night when Maman was beaten."

The children had grown used to listening to their maman's smothered cries as Daniel shook and hit her behind the closed bedroom door, to seeing her stricken as badly as Bernard and Raymonde had been. "I had witnessed my mother getting attacked savagely in the middle of one night, those times I was fighting my bed-wetting. Can you imagine how I felt watching that?" Raymonde recalled. "She started screaming too, thinking of her newborn, as she was bleeding all over the floor. I knew in my heart that there would be no police, no ambulance, no Natacha, my other mother."

The family lived catch as catch can while Daniel lived in his daydreams. An errant comment, a late arrival, a broken dish—at the slightest mistake, he'd raise his right hand and smack his children on the face. He struck them so hard they learned instinctively to cover their faces as he began to swing. And as if his beatings and their tears and their squirming stomachs were not enough, Daniel sometimes made them kneel on a pile of rocks before going to bed. He thought their stinging knees would stiffen their spines.

When he wasn't pelting them with blows, Daniel mostly didn't speak, except to address the small constellation of advisers who shuffled through the apartment, supposedly helping him win back his presidency, among them Monsieur Maurice. Ever since he'd helped them rent the place, Maurice would come by and let himself in; Daniel and Carmen were often out. He told the children he was there to help their father, but then he'd take little Carmen into the bedroom and shut the door. It was only many years later that Danielle learned what Monsieur Maurice had done to her sister.

•   •   •

DANIEL ESCAPED THE SUFFERING he produced as often as he could. Every Sunday, he'd put on his suit and leave 765 St. Johns Place with scarcely a word. He headed to the local barbershop, a different kind of Sunday Club. He played checkers and talked, as some men waited to get their Afros trimmed by Monsieur Saveur, the Haitian barber, and others lined up for their chance to meet their legend and maybe even beat him in a match.

Carmen and Raymonde, meanwhile, would put on their Sunday best—ironed secondhand dresses, hats, and purses—and board the subway for church. One week, Carmen fell ill on the fast, jerking train. *"Raymonde,"* she blurted, *"votre bourse!"* Confused, Raymonde dutifully handed over her purse. Carmen vomited discreetly into it, gracefully snapped the clasp, dabbed her lips with a tissue, and handed the purse back to Raymonde. *"Tenez!"*—"Here, take it." Carmen sat the rest of the ride, her back a perfect straight line. As I grew up, the Haitian aunties, especially Auntie Ray, loved telling this story with a ribald laugh, not just for its gross-out comedy but for what it said about Carmen. On the convulsing F line, Carmen addressed her daughter in formal third-person French, retched, then resumed her poise, as if nothing had happened.

Sunday was Carmen's one day off, and she spent it at mass. The other six days a week she worked "in service," as the neighbors said, trying to be polite—meaning as a "domestic." She hovered over stoves frying, inhaled ammonia mopping floors, lugged bags of laundry, kneeled beside washboards scrubbing clothes, hung garments on clotheslines, and hunched over ironing boards pressing finery.

Eventually the work became too much. Carmen was depleted from her collection of jobs and bosses, never mind caring for her own eight children. She said to hell with her and Daniel's Haitian pride and did something that deeply hurt: she put the family on welfare. Sending a Haitian neighbor a pot of bad stew or getting caught waiting for the bus in her domestic's clothes would embarrass, but only temporarily. Going on welfare, though, was a humiliation that could never be taken back, a particular and lasting stigma. Where our identity is concerned, my family has always believed you can't unring a bell.

CARMEN, CONSUMED BY HER WORK, and Daniel, preoccupied by his politics, counted on Danielle and Raymonde for a lot. And life in that one-bedroom apartment was quickly creating enmity between the girls. Their harmless rivalry kindled into a pyre of disgust. Natacha had once provided the two sisters succor, a valve that relieved pressure from their mutual banal grudges. But that release was gone. Nestled in comfort in Carrefour Feuilles, neither girl had ugly concerns about her future. Now both wondered how the family would eat, whether they could finish school. Coming and going from the apartment, cluttered with papers and dishes, they felt the stakes of their lives had never been so low or high: nothing and everything seemed on the line. They each felt tempted to say to hell with it all. And yet they ingested brute pressure not to let the family down. They inflicted that defeatist despair, that tight strain, onto each other.

Raymonde felt that she was made to tend to everyone's needs alone—even though she was the second eldest. Danielle, she fumed, had turned away from them.

"Where the fuck was my sister?" Raymonde later asked. "I had to take care of all our brothers and sisters, so the bitch didn't have to dirty her hands. Danielle did not have a heart. She only enjoyed watching me get beaten and was hoping to see me break. She never got that satisfaction."

Even on holidays, Raymonde and Danielle kept to a routine that was more adult grind than teenage enchantment. Getting Pierre and Bernard dressed, scrubbing the only toilet, buffing the linoleum kitchen floor: Every time Danielle had to set aside her book, or Raymonde had to put away her paintbrushes, to slog through a chore, each pointed her finger at the other. Each convinced herself that she was receiving more drudgery and contempt, less sympathy, from their parents. Raymonde claimed that on the mornings that the apartment smelled of urine from her bed-wetting, she had to endure the jokes that her father and Danielle made at her expense.

"It was a battle of wits with my father," Raymonde recalled, "him trying to break my spirit, as well as my body. He did not know that he had already killed my spirit many years before. So, like Natacha had taught me to pray to Jesus, I did so. But I did not ask for the things she told me to pray for. Instead I would always ask Jesus to let me sleep forever. I was unable to pray for my father."

Raymonde, when she could find quieter moments, dreamed of becoming a fashion designer, while Danielle wanted to be a historian or a journalist, not unlike her father. She enjoyed juggling difficult, conflicting ideas and had a great capacity for remembering different events and figures. She earned high marks, while Raymonde had middling grades, which surprised no one: Raymonde did not cotton to her schoolwork. She loved to paint and draw and had a creative flair, also, for telling a colorful tale.

As an adult, Auntie Ray always spoiled me with sweet words, then unloaded her bitter resentment about her childhood, in particular toward her father and my mother. So much of their parents' emotional energy was funneled into Danny's future, Auntie Ray seethed, at the other children's expense, especially hers. I visited Auntie Ray for three hours, right before the COVID lockdown. By then she was diabetic and severely arthritic, entirely alone in a Florida nursing home. She complained to me that Danny was able to save herself only by throwing her under the bus. Auntie Ray told me in detail about the Brooklyn whippings, though my mother never does. One sister talked; the other repressed it all—a telling note of comparison on their strategies to survive. Raymonde was always a tender, messy creature, one moment issuing a sweet, generous laugh, the next vomiting a lifetime of bile. Daniel had never liked children who complained or made their emotions known. And so, a lineage emerged, grandfather, mother, me: we've always favored people who can master their feelings, discipline their words.

Danielle, for her part, was growing into an observant teenager who'd learned when to speak and when to keep her mouth shut in order to broker herself some peace. She never whined. Most nights, she tried her best to get used to the neighbors shouting in the hall-ways, to feet stomping across the floorboards, to the mice running behind the walls. Her ears were filled with these bothersome noises, persistent, subtle reminders of the privilege she had lost. Silence, especially her father's, had unnerved her in their Port-au-Prince home. Now it was a prize.

Chapter 24

WHILE MOST OF THE CITY RESTED IN A HOLIDAY TORPOR, Daniel was greeted by knocking on his door early New Year's Day 1959.

"Hello, distinguished visitors," he said, opening it with a solemn bow.

Lyonel Paquin, and eight other Haitian expatriates, trudged in. Daniel swept his arm across the air inviting the men to sit. Lyonel, Daniel's former student and fellow exile, looked at him wearily. Whenever Daniel greeted him ceremoniously, it was bad news—a sign of Daniel's imperious mood. Lyonel had come for a political meeting, not to christen a ship. Their purpose was to form a worldwide coalition to liberate Haiti. The men intended first to solicit members to join their far-reaching alliance, then to define its mission, and finally to make an action plan to rid Haiti of Duvalier.

Daniel complimented the men on their timing. Nineteen fifty-nine, he declared, would be the decisive year in which revolt would upend the Americas. "The events in Cuba are proof that the hour had come for authentic revolutionaries, authentic patriots, and authentic Haitians," he said, leaning into their faces. "The people of Fignolé are ready for action. My people in Port-au-Prince are waiting for me to step down from the airplane."

He took a pause, then started to lecture the men on the history of the labor movement in Haiti. Hearing Daniel refer to himself as "President Fignolé," one man elbowed Lyonel. Every time Daniel referred to himself in third person, they knew, it could cost them an hour. Since Lyonel knew Daniel better than the others, the men had tasked him with trying to rein in his monologues. Still, Daniel prattled on until, suddenly, he noticed a guest snoring, bundled in his overcoat; the apartment had no heating. Daniel swatted the slumbering man's shoulder, accusing him of "a lack of respect for a President of Haiti."

Lyonel, despite all the work he'd done with Daniel, had never been his fan. Over the years, Lyonel had wanted Clement Jumelle—a dull, politically moderate, well-educated black economist—to be president, especially during the 1957 crisis. Daniel had "docilely made himself a footstool to the little doctor," Lyonel would later write. In assuming the presidency, he added, Daniel had succumbed "to the temptation of power for his own benefit like Eve in the earthly paradise who ate the fruit of the forbidden tree for the ruin of her and her descendants."

Still, the men came over every weeknight for some time to work on their coalition. Danielle and Raymonde darted in and out of the kitchen, dishes piled high in the sink, serving watered-down instant coffee to them, then clearing away their plastic cups. Carmen was always away cleaning another family's home.

The apartment hummed with the men's voices. Sometimes they lurched toward progress; others, they bickered. Standing over the dining room table, which was also a kitchen counter and folding board for clothes, Dr. Roger Rigaud, an exile living in Harlem, spent a few hours one night insisting to Daniel that, in some cases, a semicolon could be used in lieu of a period. Daniel, furious, insisted the sentence needed a period, not a semicolon.

A month after the nine men had first arrived, they completed their "Constitution for the Haitian Democratic Front." After Daniel signed it, he asked Carmen to have the document laminated. They all toasted one another in plastic cups, and that week Daniel announced their broad alliance in newspapers worldwide. The coalition encompassed exiled Haitians everywhere, anonymous and famous. It included supporters of every political figure from the last presidential campaign, especially betrayed onetime backers of

Duvalier. In addition to dissident Haitians, the group enlisted advocates from around the world. Soon enough, Dr. Rigaud would secure financial backing for the coalition from the president of Venezuela, the governor of Puerto Rico, and other influential anti-communists across Latin America who loathed Duvalier.

Daniel longed to celebrate the launch of the coalition with a big event. His accomplices took action. One Sunday not long after the alliance's announcement, Haitians from every corner of the city packed into a church in Brooklyn to fete their united opposition. A speaker walked to the pulpit and recited the name of every person known to have been tortured or killed by Duvalier's police. Every guest could think of a family member or close friend. "Oh, God, have pity for him," the crowd chanted in unison after each name. Sobs rang from the pews.

"Then Fignolé came to the lectern," Lyonel recalled. "The multitude roared its joy. That moment, he was more than a remarkable orator. He was an extension of Haiti. He was more than a man. He was a symbol. To see him, to listen, on that cold Sunday afternoon in Brooklyn, was to recall the nostalgic epoch when all Haitians were free."

Chapter 25

A YEAR AFTER THE FAMILY HAD SET FOOT IN AMERICA, Danielle enrolled at Girls' High, one of the city's most esteemed public schools. For months after they'd moved to St. Johns Place, Danielle would go out of her way to walk by the building and marvel at its imposing Gothic facade, cobbled ornately from gray stone. Accomplished women had passed through its halls before her, though she didn't recognize their names: Shirley Chisholm, Lena Horne, Rita Hayworth. It would be a place finally to call her own and it was just a ten-minute walk from home, in Bedford-Stuyvesant.

The racially integrated school drew girls from all over the city. Danielle's classmates were Italian American, Puerto Rican, black American, Jewish, and Eastern European immigrants, but she had little time to make friends with any of them, between her part-time job and time spent caring for her sisters and brothers. She was also guarded with her peers, since few girls in her school relied on food stamps as she did.

Whenever she got a free moment after school, Danielle pored over her books. She hated chemistry and zoology, though she loved history and literature and psychology. Her English was improving in giant strides. Ms. Weinstein, Mr. Goodman, Mr. Yacker, Dr. Cohen: her teachers fell in love with her, and she loved them in return. The knockabout, refugee faculty was seething with memories from the Holocaust and other repressed griefs. Danielle felt that they truly understood her, and she them. *I know where you've come from even though I've never exactly been.* All that learning, their quiet everyday kindness, was something of a balm.

At school, time sailed by. In spring 1961, she was poised to complete her courses at Girls' High with honors. Mr. Yacker and Dr. Cohen took her aside to discuss her future education. She longed to attend a Sarah Lawrence, a Vassar, a Smith, but couldn't fathom how. How would she get to any of those places? Who would pay her tuition? What would she wear? She would have to buy elegant dresses, white gloves, jewelry, and books to attend a college such as those. She barely had the twenty cents for a subway token to work.

One thing was for sure: even if the Seven Sisters were out of reach, Danielle wasn't going to stick around 765 St. Johns Place any longer than she had to. She wanted to get out of Brooklyn, to flee that prison hovel as fast and as far as she could. She wanted finer, sunnier things for herself than to dwell with the living dead—that monstrous, workaholic ghost.

She chose to enroll at Hunter College, part of the City University of New York, the best option she could afford. The place had a dual reputation: estimable, all-girls college for the white middle class and a ladder extended to the city's yearning bootstrap masses of immigrant youth, a kind of Harvard for the poor.

In true spirit, her papa was a no-show at her high school graduation. And Maman had to work.

Danielle went to the ceremony by herself, and after it ended, she counted the money from her small earnings from all her jobs. Then she walked across the bridge to the midtown movie palace and, all alone, treated herself to a matinee showing of *Spartacus*.

My mother's senior portrait at Girls' High reveals little, or even nothing, about how much she'd endured. Just her hopes. She stood out in a class where the vast majority listed their ambition as "homemaker," "clerk," "typist," "secretary," and "nurse."

Chapter 26

IT MAY NOT HAVE BEEN SMITH OR VASSAR, BUT HUNTER College still jarred Danielle. Most mornings, she plundered her closet to put together an outfit, which might have looked smart at Girls' High but was less so on a campus straddling Park Avenue and Sixty-Eighth Street. Her cut-rate glasses were horn-rimmed; they made her look like a brown house cat. Most of the other girls took their cues from fashion magazines and snickered quietly at Danielle's ensembles: a turtleneck bunched under a sleeveless corduroy dress, a wide belt cinching a matronly skirt that matched too closely to her blouse. She carried the gust of someone fresh off the boat, that new-immigrant striving, a too obvious determination to get things right.

She took notice of her white classmates, some of whom had more time and money on their hands than she. They took long lunches in the cafeteria, inhaling deep drags from their Tareytons between spurts of gossip and dainty forkfuls of food, and napped on the leather sofas in the student lounge afterward. They driveled on about boys and *Lover Come Back*, Doris Day's new romantic comedy. They seemed both impossibly glamorous and frighteningly basic—entrancing because of their smartly tailored minidresses and slender cigarettes, and banal because their girlish antics would never size up to the intrigue, the history, that she had experienced as the daughter of a president. But the allure, the stature she'd accrued in Port-au-Prince, had no currency at Hunter.

• • •

BY THE FALL OF HER sophomore year, 1962, she started to settle in. She'd made a best friend, Joan, who had also come from the Caribbean. Together they commuted from Brooklyn to Hunter, where they decided to pledge Zeta Phi Beta, a black sorority. Joan, the pledge sisters—they all called her Danny.

Come pledge night, Danny spent hours at home getting ready. She set her bangs in large wire-mesh rollers, then brushed and smoothed the rest of her hair, teased it, and piled it into a beehive: the idea was to look easy, natural, but with a bit of sass. She wore a long-sleeve black cocktail dress, which she'd sewn with her mother the week before. Her hemline had to be ladylike, her mother reminded her, a few centimeters below her knees. Readying herself, Danny swayed her hips and sang as sensually as she could to her favorite song, "Don't Make Me Over," by Dionne Warwick. Before she headed out the door, she took her horn-rimmed glasses off and left them at home, even though she could barely see.

Danny and her Zeta sisters, Pledge Night 1963

Once she and Joan arrived, they circulated in the student lounge with the other sophomore pledges. Nervous spitfire chatter spilled from their lips, their smiles too eager, while the upper-class women in the room mingled easily. They owned this roost. They quizzed the younger ones: What do you study? Where do you live? What do you dance to? Danny eyeballed the other girls' outfits, all more expensive than hers.

She'd studied hard her first year at Hunter, but aside from Joan had made few friends. Most of the women surrounding her had grown up in Manhattan and arrived at Hunter with friends at their sides. Danielle had no time to assemble a friend group from scratch. Besides her studies, she helped her mother at home and worked a part-time clerical job in the dean's office, and, of course, she traveled back and forth to campus daily, an hour each way on the subway. The sisterhood, she felt, would give her an organized, ready-made social life.

As she stood by a bay window, an older Zeta approached and asked her why she was pledging. It was Barbara, the dean of pledges. Danielle put on a smile. "I want to excel academically among women like me," she said, "demonstrate my concern for the human condition, and especially to elevate my gender and race." She'd stolen those lines from the sorority's mission statement, which she'd found on an old brochure. Her answer did, though, have truth to it: she was riveted by social science and determined to work her way into a profession that would allow her to help women and girls.

She kept to herself that she was taking as many French classes as she could, to guarantee herself some A's, which went a long way toward balancing out the D's she was earning in chemistry and physical education.

No matter the subject, Danny was always the only black girl in the classroom. There were times, though, when she didn't mind standing out. Her history professor had pulled her aside and confided that he saw leadership qualities in her, that she spoke up in class with rare conviction, carried herself with confidence, exuded a palpable certainty of her plans to help the world. She just had to figure out how.

She and Joan had decided to pledge Zeta because the sorority boasted high GPAs and a sense of purpose, though they'd heard from their friend Jeanne, who was born and raised in Manhattan, that the Zetas weren't known for being the prettiest flowers in the nursery. The Alpha men joked that the Zetas were "beastly," and the Omegas called them "Zeta dogs." To see a black college woman swing her long, silky hair about her high cheekbones or gaze lovingly at her golden skin was to see a perfect candidate for the city's more fashionable black sororities, Delta Sigma Theta and Alpha Kappa Alpha. Jeanne had explained to Danny that she and Joan were both "too chocolate" even to be considered for admission to Delta or AKA. Those two prize sororities threw the loudest, most sought-after parties and kept the darker, more bookish women at bay. And neither Joan nor Danny had money, nor did they come from highbrow American-born families, ideally from New Orleans, DC, Atlanta, or Manhattan—the profile necessary to become Alpha or Delta princesses.

It was the Zetas who offered Danny refuge. She and her Zeta sisters hustled together to the movies, to card parties, and to Danny's favorite, rent parties, which were always thrown on the fly. The hostess would cook up a heap of food, which she'd bought in bulk, dust off her leftover liquor, then charge a few dollars at the door to raise cash to pay her family's rent. The women would carry on and dance to the Miracles, the Chiffons, the Supremes, and gossip about how they'd parlay their Zeta sisterhood into securing eligible beaux, or at the very least, dates to escort them to the Greek house parties. The Omegas, they knew, were wild partyers. The Kappas were pretty boys and smooth talkers, with medium complexions and wavy hair perpetually slicked close to their scalps; they'd turn up to parties as if they'd just rolled in from Motown. The Alphas were the manly men, husband material who'd ripen into leading black politicians and businessmen. And the Sigmas were the serious ones, completely devoted to their studies, just like the Zetas.

· · ·

WHILE DANNY STEEPED HERSELF in Zeta life, her mother contended with raising the children. One morning, waiting her turn for the bathroom, Danny noticed Carmen's reflection in the bathroom mirror: creases bunched alongside her maman's eyes, rough patches surfaced on her hands, her hair coarsened at the fringes. Her mother had left Haiti a true ingenue, its young First Lady. But now her face, her hands, her flesh—Danny could see that her mother was starting to look old.

A much-younger woman had, meanwhile, started occupying her father's head.

When they were still living at 19 Avenue of the People, it turned out, Daniel had begun corresponding with a Haitian medical student living in Canada named Georgette Legerme. Georgette was passionate about Fignolism, peppering le professeur with questions and good wishes in her letters. And now, having graduated with a degree in pathology, she'd left Canada for New York City. Once she'd gotten there, in the early 1960s, she'd gotten back in touch with Daniel—nobody in my family is sure exactly when. What is certain, though, is that soon enough Georgette, in her midthirties, and Daniel, in his midforties, were secretly spending hours on end together.

As Danny was studying and paying her way through college, and the family was still on public assistance, Daniel picked up and left. He proposed to Georgette and they jetted off to Puerto Rico to enjoy a brief honeymoon of sorts: theirs was a marriage in name only. Carmen, in her devout Catholicism, refused to grant Daniel a divorce.

Daniel loved Georgette, and, likely, her naked, tireless devotion to his political pursuits. In mind, body, and soul, she said, she was his disciple. She gave up her medical career to become his right-hand woman. From their new home in Brooklyn, the couple closely monitored events in Haiti—how Papa Doc disguised his security forces as journalists to terrorize the people, how he imprisoned his army supporters, including General Kébreau, how the cells of Fort Dimanche were swelling beyond capacity, how Duvalier was sinking even deeper into his Vodou madness. The couple revived *Construc-*

tion, one of Daniel's old MOP newspapers, with Georgette taking charge as editor and administrator. She became the single custodian of Daniel's public image, even as she sullied his private one. Learning that François was informed that he had deserted Carmen and the children caused a true embarrassment for Daniel.

Soon, though, Danny had stepsisters; Georgette gave birth to two daughters with Daniel. I imagine Carmen, acidly amused, learning that his mistress had delivered him girls only. Georgette took to homeschooling their daughters, eager to control their education and panicked over their safety. Some days, Georgette believed other exiled figures wanted to assassinate her husband or harm their children. She and Daniel fed each other's paranoia, saw enemies everywhere. Georgette and the daughters would remain lifelong strangers to Danny.

Watching her father abandon her and the family, particularly during those perilous years, enraged my mother as badly as the sexual assault she'd suffered. A main reason she banished her father from her life and refused to speak of him to me, I believe, is that he betrayed her so flagrantly. He exiled her from his life and made her ashamed. Divorce was uncommon then. Her mother's single parenthood carried a stench of failure just as the food stamps had. She had endured so much violence because of her father, and at his hands— had she stood by him in vain through all that bloodshed?

DURING DANIELLE'S SENIOR YEAR at Hunter, in 1964, Duvalier declared himself president for life—a rhetorical exercise, as he'd already taken total control of the state. While the Tonton François she'd loved as a child had been so modest, content in their simple, workaday lakou, he had since accrued, alongside power, a ravenous appetite for money. He imprisoned wealthy mulattoes and helped himself to their bank accounts. No financial scam or political revenge was too petty to interest him. His looting of the public treasury had become as open and crass as the widespread murders he ordered. He had exiled or killed most of his opponents, both suspected and confirmed. And he'd decreed it a crime to speak Daniel's name or to print his image.

The few Fignolés stuck in Haiti had gone into hiding. Daniel's brother Necker, by then in his thirties, still lived in Pestel. There, he, his wife, and their five small children were able to keep a low profile. But whenever Necker or one of the older children saw Papa Doc's soldiers in their village, they ducked for cover under the nearest shield, then remained vigilant for weeks. Evelyne, Necker's eldest child, told me that she's still traumatized by her years of hiding.

For the Brooklyn Fignolés, though, with Daniel out of the apartment, the distance between New York and Port-au-Prince widened. The mirage of returning home was fading. Danny wasn't the only one studying, working to better her days. Carmen took classes in bookkeeping. Not long after she got her certificate, she accepted a job as a bookkeeper-accountant for the city's Board of Education and proudly took the family off welfare. A fastidious planner and entrepreneur, Carmen was well suited to her new position and worked for the board for the next thirty years. She almost never mentioned her husband's name again.

Danny, for her part, was learning to shed ties with her father, to grow in an alien climate. Her new country peddled a chilling conformity, which made idols of white washing machines, white picket fences, and Rock Hudson. America didn't feel like a home to her; it felt like a big salesroom. She had once avidly listened to the family radio when it broadcast calypso and her father's thunderous voice. Now she listened to R&B.

She still loved Dionne Warwick, especially "Don't Make Me Over." Warwick had wanted to record a classic ballad but was told by two white male producers that her looks and voice needed "work," so they offered the opportunity to Jerry Butler. Warwick screamed at them, "Don't make me over, man!"—and stormed out of their office. Chastened by her protest, the contrite producers composed a new song for her, which became her breakthrough solo.

To see black-and-white footage of Warwick performing her song that year, walking onstage in a sequined gown, which could not camouflage her twenty-three-year-old innocence, the purity so visible in her waifish bare shoulders, the crystalline beauty of her taut skin, is to see a vulnerability and confidence that are heartbreaking, astonishing. Her voice, delicate and strong as a willow, pleads through her overbite:

> *Don't pick on the things I say, the things I do*
> *Just love me with all my faults,*
> *the way that I love you,*
> *I'm begging you,*
> *Don't make me over. . . .*

The footage is an uncanny mirror to how I picture Danny then. Singing along to her favorite song, it was as though Danny serenaded her twin. Here was a woman who toggled between her fragility and her star power, a woman who, in the face of an overbearing father, an overbearing past, an overbearing new country, was deciding which parts of herself to retain, which to make anew.

Chapter 27

DANNY GLANCED AT HERSELF IN THE HALLWAY MIRROR ONE last time. Satisfied that her face was right, she headed out of her small shared apartment in DC's U Street corridor and walked toward Howard University's Greene Stadium to see the university's booters play their rival in soccer.

Soon after graduating from Hunter in 1965, Danny boarded a bus south. She was enrolled at Howard, thanks to a scholarship, working toward a master's and PhD in linguistics and social science. She'd come to DC because she badly wanted some action. Dates, parties, theater, political activity—more than she could find in plodding Crown Heights. For that, she'd chosen her new neighborhood well. Sometimes called "black Broadway," her residential stretch near U Street was one of the most vibrant nerve centers for black culture in the nation.

Best of all, her new neighborhood was four hours away from her father, the farthest she'd ever lived from him.

Weekdays, she went to her classes, which she so loved, then trekked to her clerical job in the university's administration. A handful of afternoons, she crossed the quad and went to teach French to undergraduates. That Saturday, though, she was out to have fun. She entered the stadium stands and embraced her new friends cheek to cheek, women not unlike her, who'd pledged the big sororities, liked a rollicking dance party, and were keenly attuned to the protest politics upending the country.

The whistle blew, and Danny and her friends cheered on the

Bisons. As the men scuttled down the field, the women pretended to know the difference between the front line and the defense, between a punt and a free kick. Really, they were there to see and be seen, to trade gossip, to gather intel on who might be throwing the sauciest parties. As indifferent and clueless about the rules as the women were, they knew that the Bisons were an increasingly impressive squad. At most other Division I colleges, soccer was the preserve of upper-middle-class white men. The Bisons' coach, Ted Chambers, however, was pushing to elevate the sport at Howard and to rescue soccer, generally, from its upscale, all-white reputation. A Bermudian drove the defense that afternoon, and a Ghanaian, the season's lead scorer, tore toward the goal. Danny and her friends screamed after the handsome players handpicked by Chambers, children of immigrants from Latin America, the Caribbean, Africa.

It might have been that day, or another like it, that Danny, pretending to cheer on the Bisons, met Edouard Benjamin. He had begun playing soccer as a boy growing up in Guinea and mastered the game early. He was a tangle on the dirt, bare feet churning. The other boys chased him, unable to see the crazed look of determination on his face, and they wondered how his feet could hug the ball so close, how he could flit sideways, and backward, speeding up, slowing down, changing direction, as the others hacked away at his shins. He passed the ball, it was passed back to him, and he was off again, a dervish whirl of limbs gliding down the field. Just when they thought they had him, he looked toward the goal and cocked his short left leg backward and sent the ball cannoning. It whizzed through the goal, a lonely rock sitting for each post. As the goalie lay with his chubby cheek in the red dirt, Edouard's team leapt into the air, clutched one another. He could feel their spittle as they surrounded him, and a thick contentment enveloped him as he breathed in the pungent smell of the bauxite dirt, the aroma of fish and yams grilling on the squat outdoor woodstove nearby.

Years later, when he introduced himself to Danny, he mentioned, casually, that he had been the captain of the varsity soccer team at Yale.

Edouard was born in 1941, in Boffa, a small fishing village in the French colony of Guinea. With no more than five thousand people, Boffa sat on the western edge, not just of the colony, but of the entire continent, its horizon the Atlantic Ocean. The slave trade had come to this small port in the sixteenth century, and by the 1860s it was a major trading post for slaves. By the time Edouard was a child, men, glistening in sweat, would turn up to the village square, arms full of fish, swamp rice, palm oil, and bananas to trade. Boffa, in its purposefulness and character, was not all that different from Pestel.

When Edouard was a teenager, his parents sent him from their small village to the big city, Conakry, to study at the most prestigious high school in the colony, Lycée de Donka, which was modeled after the French lyceums. At the start of his junior year, October 1958, Guinea declared its independence from France—the first colony in Africa to do so. The nation won an iconic standing among African peoples because of its early, total, unqualified rejection of colonial rule, not unlike Haiti's. The French state responded with purposeful vengeance, not just to punish Guinea but to make an example out of her people, a warning to its other colonies should they

consider such insolence: "The French pulled out of Guinea over a two-month period, taking everything they could with them. They unscrewed lightbulbs, removed plans for sewage pipelines in the capital, and even burned medicines rather than leave them for the Guineans."

As Edouard graduated from high school, he was named the valedictorian of the republic. The proud, freshly formed government

His looks and bachelor ways aside, my father was what they called "serious" in those days—reliable in his word, poised in his mien, steady in his temperament. His position as captain of Yale's soccer team suited him.

made a point of identifying him as the top graduating senior in a land of supposedly inferior minds. He won scholarships to grand universities in France, England, Belgium. He wanted to go to France most, but his father—a kind, wise Anglican reverend of modest means—counseled against it. Reverend Martin Luther Benjamin was an Anglophile, with a poor opinion of France. He advised his boy to strike out for America. So Edouard packed a suitcase and left his parents and seven siblings behind.

When the scholar-athlete arrived at Yale, the place was on the cusp of big change. Some of his classmates wanted a classical gentleman's education, some got shit-faced at Mory's and were indifferent to education, and others yearned for a rigorous, modern training. Edouard did love reciting his Latin and reading the Greek epics, especially *The Odyssey,* but he devoured his political science and international relations courses. As knowledge in the hard sciences and technology was mushrooming beyond old imagination and the social sciences were becoming more specialized, the ideal of a sentimental education, a soft upper-class learning anchored in the classics, in the style of Eton and Oxford, was fading. As luck would have it, Edouard had impeccable timing: his personal transformation happened in sync with the university's. Yale was transforming from a glorified 1950s finishing school for the rich Anglo-American elite into a merit-conscious technical training ground that prepared boys to become leaders of an increasingly complex world.

Edouard's graduation from the university was an unwitting parallel to what Daniel had fought for in Haiti.

"The social revolution must consist in change of viewpoint among the elite," Daniel had said on the floor of Haiti's parliament in the fall of 1954, roughly a decade before Edouard and Danny met. "Or rather, the old traditional aristocracy should give way to an aristocracy of merit, of which all should have equal access."

LIKE DANNY, EDOUARD CAME to DC for graduate study; he was pursuing a master's in economics from American University. He no

Edouard's personal coming of age coincided with Yale's.
The university aspired to transform from a glorified finishing school
for the Anglo-American elite into a merit-conscious powerhouse
of modernized learning.

longer played collegiate soccer, though he couldn't resist watching
free matches, and Howard had the most successful squad in the city.

Both striving outsiders working to infiltrate the inside, Danny
and Edouard shared quite a bit else in common. Each came from
a big family. Each was the most studious of their many siblings,
though also socially extroverted. Each traveled far from home to
find intellectual adventure. Danny and Edouard were introduced by
a mutual friend at a pivotal inflection point in their young lives and
in the young lives of developing nations. Colonial administrations
were collapsing around the world, and a glimmer of optimism took
root among cosmopolitan and technocratic-minded young people
that they could help the millions emerging from bad rule.

Leaving her shared apartment in the heart of black Broadway,
Danny visited Edouard in Adams Morgan, which locals called "the
Greenwich Village of Washington." Adams Morgan lured all manner
of artists, social activists, Bohemians, and a cross section of immigrants to its four-block radius with bargain rents. Several countries
had recently won their independence, and their fledgling new embassies threw blowouts in Kalorama, the adjacent neighborhood.
The couple's weekends were a ganglion of sweaty parties pulsing with
sambas, merengues, and African jazz. Edouard and Danny listened

to music in the neighborhood lounges, shared late-night meals—barbecue chicken or cut-rate burgers at the House of Al, a popular delicatessen—and traveled to New York together to hear Nina Simone cast her moody spells at the Village Theatre, in a concert with Miriam Makeba.

While I can easily see the union of my parents' professional ambitions and political interests, their romantic kinship is more of a mystery to me. One time, I was kissing a boyfriend on a street corner in the East Village when it occurred to me: I had never seen my parents kiss. Not romantically. And I never would. Perhaps the thought occurred to me then because my boyfriend and I were the same age as my parents had been when they'd first met. So much of my parents' courtship, like my own romantic landscape, remains a family secret. I have no idea what went through their minds as they dated, no idea whether they wrote each other love letters, no idea about their attraction to each other, the skin that burned on their bones.

Full lips, squat nose, flashy smile. Alongside my father's macho, amiable face, his impeccable physique, and his vague aspect, his origins might have carried an allure for my mother.

Guinea held a rather special place in the imaginations of most Haitians. It was said in Haiti that the first African slaves in the New World had been taken captive from Guinea and that a Haitian's soul returns there after death, the ancestral home. Some Haitians believed that dying would send them back to *lan Guinée,* the physical nation of Guinea. Others thought *lan Guinée* was a metaphorical place, an afterlife where they could be free. One of Haiti's most celebrated novelists, Jacques Roumain, wrote a poem, translated by Langston Hughes, called "Guinea":

> *It is the long road to Guinea*
> *where our fathers wait for us patiently.*
> *There, there awaits you beside the water a quiet village,*
>   *and the hut of your fathers*
> *and the hard ancestral stone*
> *where your head will rest at last.*

Daniel did not share his fellow Haitians' fascination with Guinea. He had no patience for such folk wisdom. To him, black uplift meant bringing Enlightenment values and living wages to Guinea, not mythologizing it. In private, he dismissed Africans and their traditions as barbaric.

I suspect that Edouard's heritage held a contrarian attraction for my mother: her father had always told her to marry a black Haitian.

She had other ideas. Danny dropped out of her doctoral program after two years and married Edouard in 1967. She was twenty-three; he was twenty-six. Surrounded by her mother, siblings, and friends, they married first in New York City, in the fall, and then in December they had a second ceremony in Boffa, which was officiated by his father and followed by a massive home-cooked feast. Danny saved herself time and money by carting the same outfit across the Atlantic: a slim-fitting white cocktail dress with a short hem and three-quarter-length sleeves, all overlaid in lace.

Never has my mother told me why she decided to abandon her dream of a PhD or why she followed Edouard to Africa. At that certain point in a woman's life, in those days, she had to decide whether she'd strike out on her own or whether she'd hitch herself to a guy, because striking out on her own could be a very shaky enterprise, right? Danny had to figure out what to do. Whether she saw it or not, she'd grown up a kind of addict to novelty and turmoil. She had that fire burning inside her, a desire to follow the excitement, to lead a roving, worldly life, to help people. With Edouard, she'd found a handsome, erudite man, one who seemed as if he would reliably provide for their children but could also furnish her with adventure, wonder.

There is nothing that reveals more about my young mother, to my thinking, than her choice to marry Edouard, a blueberry-black, Ivy League–educated social scientist from the mythical *lan Guinée*. He was from the spiritual homeland of Haitians and so hearkened back to an older ideal, but was also modern and ambitious and educated—exactly what she was fixing to be.

Daniel skipped both wedding celebrations. Still, a nagging feeling, alongside his manners, compelled Edouard to pay his new wife's father a courtesy call. He briefly returned to the United States from Guinea and made the trek to Brooklyn. He knocked on the man's door. Daniel sat at one end of a long oak table and instructed Edouard to sit at the other. Looking across, Edouard felt they might as well have been bargaining across Lake Titicaca. He told his father-in-law about the wedding ceremonies and Daniel nodded his head. Then he narrowed his eyes and looked Edouard in his face.

"Young man, you married *way* out of your league."

Once he left the apartment, despite himself, Edouard had a laugh. My father always had a sense of humor about everything—even the so-called father-in-law who completely dismissed him.

Chapter 28

DANNY AND EDOUARD HAD A CHILD NOT LONG AFTER marrying—Marcelle, a rotund, fleshy baby. Soon after she was born, in 1967, Danny shipped Marcelle off to Haiti, to be raised by Tante Gigine. It is customary for busy mothers with precarious footing to hand over their children to close relatives to raise, just as Danny herself had been minded by Tante Gigine—at least, that's what Danny always insisted to us and to strangers. Marcelle was able to enter the country without being detected by the Duvalier regime because she carried Edouard's last name.

Barely a year after Marcelle was born came Edouard Jr., who resembled his father exactly, even as a newborn. As Marcelle grew up in Haiti, Danny and the two Edouards moved into an unassuming four-bedroom apartment in Addis Ababa, Ethiopia.

Edouard had accepted his first major job, serving as the second-in-command of the Organisation of African Unity (OAU), at its world headquarters in Addis. Newly independent African nations had formed the organization in 1963 to promote trade and economic growth among member states. The budding institution would represent Africa's interests to the world, much like NATO, the better to banish colonialism from the continent. Edouard was handpicked for his new job by his mentor Diallo Telli, also from Guinea, a brilliant diplomat as well as a voice for democracy around the world, who had helped found the historic organization. Danny found work teaching grade school, much as her young mother had, though at an international English-speaking academy.

The three had barely settled down when Danny's belly swelled again. All my life she's told me about how, in her ninth month of pregnancy, she flew from Addis to New York City, via Rome, arriving to America in the nick of time to give birth to triplets.

Not long after arriving to the small Brooklyn apartment that her mother and Raymonde shared, she rushed the short distance to Adelphi Hospital, a financially struggling sick bay in Fort Greene. She's told us how she lay without her husband in one of the facility's 146 beds, how the doctors slit a long incision the length of her abdomen, how they angled to pull the tangled bodies out. How she screamed, felt her trunk jerked and yanked. The babies were extracted from her womb in a nearly botched cesarean section.

I lay moments later in an intensive-care incubator. Doctors put me on a ventilator. My listless lungs had trouble breathing. Bleary in her hospital bed, Danny worried I would never come home with her. Then she trained her attention on her own survival. The eight-hour operation left a knobby strip of scarred flesh across her stomach.

Only two of us were born that late October night, just hours before Halloween. My mother would never discuss the exact cause of my triplet brother's death—one more tract in a plot of our secrets.

It was my beloved twin sister, Sara, and I who made it into this world.

Me and Sara

By six months old, Sara could swipe her bottle from the play table with a terrific grip of swift, chubby fingers, her eyes alit with wonder. She blabbered heartily. I was not so fortunate. My eyes stared ahead blankly, the white parts a jaundiced yellow. My arms faltered reaching for my bottle. My babble lagged. My mother worried over my wan expression and brought me back to the hospital.

In the sterile, silver-dull office, benumbed with machines, a doctor broke the news to her: your newborn has sickle cell anemia, a crippling disease that twists his red blood cells from robust balloons into mangled crescents. Round, bouncy red blood cells glide through the veins of most healthy people. His are deformed, so they get stuck in his blood vessels. The sickling, tangled cells lack oxygen, so his whole body does too. That oxygen starvation causes pain and tissue death. Sickle cell disease can stunt a child's growth, the doctor added, and increases the likelihood of kidney failure and strokes—if and when Richard grows.

My mother learned that one in four babies born with sickle cell anemia do not survive past two years old. The life expectancy for people with sickle cell anemia: forty years old.

Edouard and Danny each carried the gene that causes the disease. But he had no idea. Why would he? A prime athlete who had never gotten sick, let alone set foot in a doctor's office, Edouard would never have thought to test himself, even if he'd had occasion to. At any rate, there was no way to know before birth whether a child would definitely get the disease from a gene-carrying parent.

Sickle cell strikes mainly black people. Well into the 1990s, I saw signs wishing my extinction, placards waved by white supremacists celebrating my blood disorder as a form of eugenics: RACIAL PURITY—LONG LIVE SICKLE CELL ANEMIA. SICKLE CELL ANEMIA—THE GREAT WHITE HOPE.

The worldlier, more humane medical authorities singled out sickle cell anemia as a "neglected disease." They demanded screening to improve medical care for infants. But the rest of the medical establishment ignored the disease in its research, public ethics, and treatment. Medical research was rarely conducted on black populations, except as guinea pigs to improve medicine for white people. The health-care complex used the disease as a bludgeon, mostly. Thirty states required sickle cell tests for schoolchildren, marriage license applicants, and prisoners. Many demanded screening for the disease to discriminate when hiring and selling health insurance— who wanted to employ or insure someone whose life expectancy was forty? Often, doctors urged gene-carrying couples not to have children.

Back at home, Danny tried to ignore the feeling that she had delivered a boy living on borrowed time.

Ya'arburne, they say in Arabic: "May you bury me." It's the hope that you'll die before someone you are intensely attached to does, so you'll never feel the pain of having to let them go.

My whole life I have felt that way about my twin, Sara.

And I could always sense that's how my mother felt about me.

CLUTCHING SARA AND ME swaddled in blankets, my mother, at twenty-nine years old, returned to Addis to rejoin the family and to resume her teaching job. When Sara and I arrived in Addis as infants, Marcelle was five, still in Haiti, and Edouard Jr. was four. Edouard Jr. grimaced and screamed whenever he was fed couscous, hysterics that amused my parents so much they nicknamed him after the food; he's called Couscous to this day.

In August of that year, 1973, Edouard celebrated his thirty-second birthday. He closed out the evening in the living room, reading his favorite newsmagazine, *Jeune Afrique.* An article announced what he'd already feared: the president of Guinea, Sékou Touré, had issued a decree demanding the immediate return to Guinea of all Guineans around the world working for the Organisation of African Unity. Touré, Guinea's first president following its independence, had declared himself supreme leader in 1960 and had, soon after, begun executing his Permanent Plot to keep himself in power. From afar, Edouard had watched as Touré outlawed political parties, purged his opposition, and installed a police state.

Going to bed that night, Edouard decided to stall on the dictator's order.

A few nights later, his best friend in Addis, a lower-level Guinean diplomat at the OAU, didn't make it home for dinner. Massimo Soumare's wife told Danny about her husband's disappearance. The only logical explanation that either woman could think of: local Guineans had kidnapped him upon orders of the dictator. Danny rushed to the ambassador of the Ivory Coast, a friend, and asked for his help. Late the following evening, the ambassador took his pistol and made a surprise visit to the Guinean embassy. He'd had the good sense to inform the Ethiopian police in advance, who were sympathetic to the OAU and its mission; they stood guard outside the residence. The Ivorian ambassador demanded that the Guineans cough up Soumare, and as soon they did, the two sped off while the Ethiopian police looked on.

One week later, on August 17, 1973, Couscous was scurrying about playing games in the courtyard of his nursery school when the front office received a call: a woman announced, ever so politely, that she was en route to the school to pick him up. She instructed a teacher to ready the boy to go home with her. Africa thrived on villages and extended family raising children, so the call was not extraordinary. A nursery school aide—on a strange instinct, not custom, rule, or obligation—telephoned my mother to tell her that an auntie was on her way to fetch Couscous. Danny hung up with the nursery and called the Ethiopian police. By the time the sweet-voiced lady arrived, Ethiopian policemen, waving pistols, had snatched my brother from the playground and sped off to safety, Couscous wailing in the back seat.

Police shunted my brother behind the gates of the Ivorian ambassador's house, where he joined Soumare in hiding. Danielle begged her friend to keep her baby until further notice. Couscous was Danielle's only child born in Guinea. She understood that the dictator wanted to use him as human ransom to force our father to return.

Touré lit up in rage when he heard about the armed rescue of

Edouard's deputy and the bungled kidnapping of Edouard's son. He demanded that the Ethiopian government and all OAU staff members reveal Soumare's and Edouard Jr.'s whereabouts—immediately.

Touré's maneuvers jolted Pops. He accurately suspected what had yet to become public knowledge: Touré was torturing and killing his opponents. And he was arranging to extinguish his future rivals, especially competent, foreign-educated, pro-democracy ones such as Edouard.

Edouard sent an urgent telegram to the U.S. State Department asking for emergency evacuation—his life was in danger. The State Department official who received it walked into his colleague's office and said, "I just got a cable about this guy Edouard Benjamin. Wasn't he a friend of yours at Yale?" The man's colleague, Allen "Tupper" Brown, answered, "Yeah. He was a roommate and a good friend." The boss said, "Well, look at this. A cable from our embassy. Addis. A person there named Edouard Benjamin is asking for emergency evacuation."

U.S. diplomats concluded that Edouard was not overreacting. In a classified telegram, they bluntly told their boss, Secretary of State Henry Kissinger: "Embassy considers subject's apprehension to be realistic."

Pops nervously waited for a response to his telegram. Complications arose. In order to approve Edouard's visa to America, the State Department had to verify his identity. A lowly official at the U.S. embassy in Addis prepared to contact the Guinean government to do just that. When Washington caught wind, it sent its embassy a stern warning: "Alpha care should be exercised not to jeopardize subject." The government of Guinea "should not—I repeat, NOT—be informed of Benjamin's intention not to return to Guinea."

More hurdles surfaced: Edouard's visa required his birth certificate and two "police certificates," one from the United States and one from Guinea, proving that he had no criminal record in either country. My father had none of those documents in his possession. He had to stall a little longer; to evade further suspicion, he started telling colleagues how eager he was to return to Guinea, but only after his current posting had ended and after he'd taken a nice long vacation.

Touré was not fooled. He issued another order commanding Edouard to conclude his affairs at the OAU and return to Guinea "at once."

There was no doubt in my father's mind: if Touré captured him, he would be slaughtered. Edouard had first cropped up on Touré's radar at a pivotal moment in both men's lives, when Touré, then a young labor leader, guided the country to independence in 1958, and his budding government proudly celebrated Edouard as the top graduating high school senior in the new republic. In the fifteen years since, Edouard had built a reputation in high circles as one of the country's most daring thinkers and hardest workers. By virtue of being Telli's top protégé, Edouard was a marked man. A few years later, in fact, Telli, a former UN diplomat, a founder of the OAU, and a champion for global democracy, was tortured and starved to death in Camp Boiro, the dictator's gruesome gulag.

The danger to Edouard was so pressing and primary that he and Danny decided to try to evacuate him first, then worry about their eldest son.

On November 21, my father received bittersweet news: his U.S. visa had been approved. A confidential telegram stated, "In issuing the U.S. visa, State Department waives following document requirements for Benjamin: birth certificate and Guinean and U.S. police certificates. Subject is well and favorably known to Officers in the State Department, therefore, Department has no objection to waiver of police clearances."

Days later, Pops boarded his flight to America. Little did he know that his old Yale roommate, a decade after their graduation, was working at the State Department. He had no idea that Tupper Brown had vouched for his character, was rescuing him like a guardian angel.

What a tortured, double-edged escape: in securing passage to the United States, Pops left us behind. He was dodging a dictator's claws and making himself an exile from his homeland, a decision he could not reverse for the foreseeable future.

WEEKS AFTER POPS SENT his emergency telegram, my mother visited the U.S. embassy in person to ask for help.

"Following the attempted kidnapping of Soumare, Mrs. Benjamin decided it was advisable to leave Addis with her family as soon as possible, rather than follow her previous plan to depart at the end of the school year in June 1974. Her decision was prompted by the fear that her family might be in physical danger," a confidential telegram from the U.S. embassy to the State Department noted. "Mrs. Benjamin confided that it was she who informed the Ivorian Ambassador of Soumare's detention at the Guinean Embassy in Addis, and thus precipitated the former OAU staffer's rescue and escape."

Danielle had convincing reasons to fear for our lives. She worried that Touré knew that it was she who had initiated Soumare's escape and that she knew where Couscous and Soumare were hiding. She was certain: if Touré abducted Couscous and flew the boy back to Guinea, his father would be forced to the country too. There, both would be killed.

To save the family, Danielle had to secure a visa for herself and Couscous to get to America. She was still a Haitian national. On her paperwork at the U.S. embassy, she fudged some facts. "Mrs. Benjamin indicates she first entered U.S. as alien resident in 1969 following her marriage in Guinea in 1968," an internal U.S. embassy telegram states. The embassy did not research Danielle's audacious claim, counter her cunning evasion, but her father's dramatic history with the State Department was well documented, clearly verifiable in the archives. Her real history was hiding in plain sight.

She chose not to send Sara and me to the Ivorian ambassador's house to join Couscous in hiding. It was less likely, she calculated, that the Guinean dictator would kidnap American citizens. The U.S. embassy wasn't so confident: the last thing it wanted was the hassle of seeing two American infants kidnapped under its watch. So a U.S.

embassy official called the Ethiopian police and asked its Special Branch to provide plainclothes protection for us at our apartment building. The embassy official confided to the police that he had classified reasons to worry over the safety of two American infants in the capital.

Just after Christmas, on December 26, three Guineans approached my mother in a bank lobby. They had just arrived to Ethiopia. One was a judo expert. "Why, Mrs. Benjamin," he asked, "are you still here?" When she described this to the embassy officials hours later, she was still shaking.

The encounter hastened the Americans' decision. Danielle was granted an appointment for the very next day, December 27, at eleven thirty, to collect her and Couscous's visas at the U.S. embassy.

But at eleven thirty, she was nowhere to be seen. An hour later, she still hadn't shown up. Another hour passed. And another. By the time the clock struck three, the chief consul was pacing the building lobby, frantic. Had Guinean mercenaries abducted us from under the nose of the police? Had the Ethiopians bungled their jobs? Would he soon be managing a diplomatic nightmare? He collected a few U.S. security officers and drove to our apartment complex to track my mother down.

As soon as they arrived, the armed men searched the complex's surroundings. They found the two plainclothes Ethiopian police-men assigned to watch us lurking across the street. The policemen had no idea where we were. The chief consul located the building's stairwell and bounded up the steps. He banged on the front door, cupped his hand and ear to it, hoping Mrs. Benjamin would answer. No response. He pounded harder.

Finally, a young black woman cracked the door ajar. Red-faced, the American demanded, "Where is Danielle Benjamin? Open this door now!"

The bewildered young woman stared at the aggressive Westerner. Tears welled in her eyes.

"Mrs. Benjamin went out to lunch," our babysitter stammered.

The Americans shoved past her and stormed into the apartment.

Noticing the phone in the small living room, the boss called his assistant at the embassy to see if my mother had turned up in his absence. His assistant replied that she had; the vice consul had just given her the visas.

What possessed my mother to take a leisurely two-hour lunch at the very hour she had agreed to go to the U.S. embassy to pick up her critical exit papers? One cannot know all these decades later. I suspect that she was so late because she was overwhelmed with raising twin infants, even with a sitter. Or because wires got crossed and she misunderstood the time of the appointment. Or because, as per usual, she was running on Haitian time.

That night, Danielle phoned the U.S. embassy to tell the chief consul that she and her children were now staying with the Ivorian ambassador, who would take us to the airport the following morning at 6:10 to catch our secret flight to DC, via Paris. The chief consul got to the airport at 5:45 the next morning to make sure she'd keep her word—he was so eager to see us leave the country.

We all arrived with the ambassador and his wife—ten minutes late.

His pistol loaded to ward off any Guineans, the ambassador took us to check-in. After we got our boarding passes, Mommy nervously shepherded us through the airport's extreme security, which was put in place in the wake of a December 1972 hijacking. The incident was fresh on everyone's minds: six members of the Eritrean Liberation Front had been killed while attempting to hijack an Ethiopian Airlines flight. One of them had thrown a hand grenade during a mid-air gun battle, and an American professor had seized it and tossed it to an unpopulated section of the plane, where it had blown a hole through the side. Somehow the pilots had managed to land safely.

The plane had been bound for Paris; the very same flight we were about to board, exactly one year later.

ONCE WE LANDED IN AMERICA, officials at the State Department sent a confidential memo to Secretary Kissinger to detail the embassy's actions in Addis Ababa. They titled the memo "Protective Services: The Benjamin Family."

Since my mother studiously evades the questions I ask about our past, I've had to recover the facts of our survival, once again, from secret government cables. Our flight from Addis echoed my mother's flight from Port-au-Prince. Only this time, the children were saved, thanks to my mother, a stark contrast with her father's failure to protect her and her siblings.

Chapter 29

─────────

"PICK ME UP, MOMMY! I WANT TO SEE THE STARS."
I was a short, reedy runt, even for kindergarten. I couldn't see the sky from our suburban porch in Maryland. But my mother, who favored dark skirt suits, her eyes cool and laminated like stainless-steel bolts, wasn't one to wrinkle herself by lifting me in her arms.

Since my mother never learned to drive a car, she and I walked, rode buses, transferred to a Metro line or two, often walked again, to get to my doctor's office, or the Children's Hospital, or a blood clinic; she'd curse the unreliable bus lines all along the way. Early on that particular morning, though, I watched her, back slumping in her formidable skirt suit, as we stood underneath the bubble shelter waiting for the 47. Her limbs looked as depleted to me as my own. Her job at a signature women's civil rights organization, the National Council of Negro Women, tired her. My father, meanwhile, worked downtown as an economist, the reason we now lived in the greater DC area.

The bus finally arrived and we zigzagged our way around the bland, stupefying suburbs. I watched the interchangeable strip malls stream by, sitting numbly. The ride churned the breakfast in my stomach.

During some commutes, my mother talked on and on. She leaned in and divulged a secret tidbit—like her Christmas plans for the family or why she loved *Le Petit Prince*. I savored the moments she confided in me. But this morning her eyes pinched, her lips flared. The long commute was making her late for a meeting. What did you do to land us back at the doctor's? she demanded, stretching out her scolding, which had begun at the house. Grabbing hold of my arm, she bucked me up for the needles that would soon pierce my tiny veins. When you've been to hell and back, she hissed, nothing can ever destroy you. I frowned and shrugged my shoulders. We sat in a long hush. Loving conversations, loaded silences. I could hear the unspoken, her dread that she would outlive me.

Arriving at the doctor's office, we heaved our coats into the cloakroom. I studied the coffee-stained carpet and the other patients in the room, entertaining myself by trying to guess who was the sickest and which order they would be summoned in.

The dreary, fluorescent-lit overheated waiting room threatened to put me to sleep. Then I heard the nurse call my name to draw my blood in the exam bay. I was so accustomed to giving blood samples that I could doze off as the woman in blue stuck me with a needle. Sometimes my veins seized up, stiffened, in a kind of defensive posture, as though fighting to hoard my blood—they'd been pricked so often. I was hoping this wouldn't happen. The nurse poked the tender dip inside my elbow and nothing came out. She tried again at a spot nearby, then pricked that same spot on the other arm, rummaging the butterfly needle to find a vein. No avail. She asked me to make a fist and then stuck the needle into the tender part at the top. When that fist didn't yield blood, she tried two separate pricks into the other. Still, nothing. She summoned her boss for advice. On his order, she strapped me in the mechanical bed near a side wall and pushed the button to raise my feet and lower my head until I was lying upside down. When she stuck a needle in my jugular, my blood streamed into the vial only from gravity. I was used to my uncooperative blood. I watched the vial fill, in pain but not in a state of tears.

Once the draw was over, we returned to the waiting room.

When Dr. Hobart emerged from his office calling out for me, my back stiffened. Another wait was finally ending, but I could feel Mommy tense at what might follow. I sat in the doctor's office, cold in my cartoon underwear on his exam table. Mommy sat feet away in the visitor's chair across his desk. Peering through his thick glasses,

Dr. Hobart delivered grim reports on last week's blood results. Hematocrit count, hemoglobin, platelets. Then the severe commands. Today's sample could land me another doctor's visit, an intense round of antibiotics, or a stint in the hospital. I tuned it all out, gazed through Dr. Hobart, letting his words float over me.

Packing up our things in the waiting room afterward, Mommy scolded me with a series of concise, matter-of-fact instructions: Take your folic

My mother, cool, aloof, 1980s

acid. Drink two liters of water. Get lots of sleep. One of the things I love about my mother is that she never talked about my sickle cell anemia as a debility or a handicap. The disease never became a full-time identity nor an excuse for failure.

Mommy and I boarded the bus and returned home from Dr. Hobart's office, alone among strangers, bonded by our will toward my survival, estranged by things unnamed. Ours was an intense, closed universe, routine and yet worrisome, isolated from one another by the separate worlds pooling in our heads.

When you've been to hell and back, nothing will ever destroy you.

TWO YEARS LATER, when I was in second grade, my parents planted us in a four-floor house on Tuckerman Lane. Our new home sat in the kind of grand suburb, Potomac, Maryland, that would allow my mother to yank us out of Catholic school, where I'd been forced to wear a clip-on tie, and enroll us in the local public school, which was better than any private one. Marcelle was in seventh grade when we settled in; she'd rejoined the family when she turned seven.

By family agreement, Pops was always entrusted to decorate our homes. He draped Tuckerman Lane in a symphony of leather and cotton and linen. His eye, his taste, accorded the place such serenity, such joy: Tuckerman Lane would be no Guinea. He slept in elegant pajamas and put on smartly tailored suits, paired with understated designer neckties, to go to work. When I hugged him hello at the kitchen door at the end of his workday, I could smell a faint trace of his cologne, Impériale, which was created by Pierre-François-Pascal Guerlain in 1853, leading to his appointment as purveyor of fragrances to Emperor Napoléon III. How my dear father loved a beautiful world, well-ordered.

By eight, I'd already manifested my father's partiality to fine things, so I was forbidden from entering my parents' bedroom without their presence. There was too much nice stuff for me to wreck. But I couldn't resist. Mommy could always tell when I was snooping through their belongings, though—"Get out of there," she'd holler up at me, as soon as I'd snuck into their room.

At Tuckerman Lane, my mother strove to keep us children in our place. We were not to grow lazy, spoiled, as she worked overtime at her demanding job.

"Kids! Get here right now!" she'd yell bright and early on Saturday mornings. "It's time to clean the house."

As usual, the maid was on her way to come clean the house. But my mother did not want the maid to think we lived in a dirty house.

"Who is this crazy woman?" I wondered, upstairs in my jammies. "And why is she interrupting *Richie Rich*? Doesn't she know the maid is already on her way to clean this filthy house?"

When the maid did arrive, my mother would hover over her like a storm cloud to make sure she was cleaning the right way. The maid glanced behind her back, frightened by my mother. It was one immigrant woman hectoring another, which embarrassed me more than some stranger thinking we lived in a dirty house.

The mood at Tuckerman Lane could crack at any given moment. One night, Pops thumbed his newspaper peacefully in the family den at the end of a long workday. Mommy slammed the phone in the kitchen and started screaming. She'd just spoken to my violin teacher, and together they'd figured out that I'd been forging Mommy's signature on my practice log. She paused ironing our clothes for school and grabbed the nearest weapon, an extension cord plugged into the iron. She wrapped a loop around her knuckles and beat me with the cord, again and again.

My chest pulsed with my sobs.

"I'm sorry, Mommy," I pleaded. In no mood to get thrashed, I shot my voice a couple notches higher. She liked this. She liked to hear me good and scared.

She thrust her right index finger in my face and yelled, "Never, ever allow a white man the satisfaction of seeing your dignity stream down your cheeks."

I didn't know it then, but I see now, that she wasn't talking about Mr. Lerner, my violin teacher; she was referring to police officers, to professors, to would-be bosses, to my future.

"Stop crying or I'll give you something to really cry about!"

Before putting down the extension cord, Mommy threatened to beat me more if I cried, because crying itself was an infraction—the symptom and evidence of weakness.

ONE SUNDAY AFTERNOON, alone in the den daydreaming, I heard Mommy yelling. "Get your butt downstairs!" she shouted from her large bed. I knew that was my cue to go to the basement and sort the clothes before she washed them for the workweek. Hunched over our dirty laundry, I put her panties into the pile of delicates. Then I placed all the colored cottons with colored cottons, the white cottons on their own.

Once the laundry had been washed and dried, my mother hoofed downstairs to get me to fold it. Rifling through the piles of newly clean clothes, her face froze. I saw her notice a stray crimson sock. I had failed to separate it and now her white hand towels were pink.

In the dank, stuffy basement, the faint sound of Helen Reddy floating, my mother slipped off her Dr. Scholl's sandal. She held its top leather strap tight in her hand and lashed the chunky sole against my buttocks. I stared into her face. Then she swung the wooden heel against my hip.

My side bone stung. I could see it, the glimmer in her eyes, the small smile on the corners of her mouth. I could tell she was enjoying herself. Each whip was a win for her: If I cried, she would have the proof and pleasure of hurting me. If I didn't cry, she would have evidence that I was practicing her lesson in resilience.

Put out your hands, she ordered, then whacked the wooden clog on my upturned palms and the front of my thighs. I stared her down. I put a defiant smirk on my face, determined to escalate this grotesque power struggle.

I was going to deprive that woman the satisfaction of seeing me cry.

POPS WAS NOT USUALLY one to fly off the handle. "I'm doing this for your own good," he liked to say, on those very rare times that he beat me. As I'd put my pants back on, skin stinging, I partly believed him. Before he thrashed me, he'd explain, "This was my expectation. This is what you did. This is how your action fell short of my expectation. So, this is why I'm beating you."

His floggings were a rational, bourgeois affair.

I got beaten way more often than any of my siblings ever did. I had a habit of breaking the simplest rules, but I couldn't stop myself. I'd secretly open my hidden Christmas gifts, then retape the wrapping; push my twin sister down a flight of stairs; forge my parents' signatures. Still, everyone could see plainly: I was the most spoiled child on Tuckerman Lane. When they weren't slapping me, my parents fell over themselves catering to my desires. I knew how to push my mother's buttons and get what I wanted: a long meal at the Prime Rib, a good Halloween costume, a nice summer vacation. I'd come to realize that the less I complained when I was anemic, in sickle cell pain, the more I endeared myself to Mommy. Stoic silence brought me pity. She spoiled me because of her primal fears. I knew that this silent child, nose dripping, forever wheezing from a lingering pneumonia, could tilt the family's goodwill in his favor and take his mother emotionally hostage.

"DON'T TELL THE NEIGHBORS." That's what Mommy liked to say after she or my father attacked me. "They'll call Protective Services." It was a half joke, a running gag laced with acid. Outside, we presented well. Our neighbors—the Williamses to our right, the Smiths to our left—loved us. Curbside, we looked happy, successful. We matched the house. I had no one to trust with my secret, the unremitting drubbings, certainly not my friends.

Returning from a blood commute one afternoon, I flung open the front door, kicked off my Hush Puppies, and lay on the carpet in the den, daydreaming. The chocolate leather sofas, which Pops had just bought, caught my eye. I ran my hands along the tops of the cushions, the sides of the sofa.

There was an X-Acto knife lying nearby, from one of Marcelle's art projects.

I wondered whether that sharp, gleaming blade could puncture the tight skin of this wondrous new couch. I decided to experiment in a tiny spot, where no one would notice. I pressed the blade against the taut leather; it relented in a clean, beautiful tear. I heard a small whiz as the blade pierced the cloth. Who knew that a sharp blade against good leather cut so nice? I scooched on my knees to another part of the couch, to see if a fresh patch of leather would slice as crisply as the first. I wanted to hear once more, just once more, that soft sound, a small gust of air jetting from a brisk cut. I did it again. Then again. I kept slashing the couch, expecting a dull snag, but each new slice felt as exhilarating as the first.

I came out of my trance. There were tears across the cushions, small incisions at the armrests. No matter how long or short, every tear was like a clean, brisk wound on skin.

Later that night, the whole family heard something rare: my father screaming. He demanded that everyone get downstairs to the family den—immediately—and line up in the middle of the room. Once they arrived, my siblings' faces dropped. No one could miss all those cuts streaked across my father's new leather couches.

"Who did this?" he demanded.

I watched his lips quiver.

No one said a word.

"Who did this?" he shouted, louder.

Marcelle, Couscous, and Sara glared my way, impatient for this charade to end; we all knew only I was capable.

"Me." I made my voice shake, go small.

"Why? Why would you do that?"

My father's eyes blazed, but with a soft perplexity—how could anyone destroy the fine belongings he'd worked so hard to provide?

I dug my big toe into a square in the plaid carpet, staring at them both. I muttered something about how it all made such a perfect sound, it was all such a clean break. And after I made the first satisfying slice, the second came, and then I just couldn't stop myself—I had to keep cutting.

Pops's face froze in anger and bewilderment.

"Go to bed," he said to my siblings.

His muscled arms hung loosely by his sides, his hands compact explosives. He unwound his belt from his svelte suit trousers and lashed its long, stiff tongue on my outstretched palms, its silver Pierre Cardin logo shimmering at me. After several beatings, Pops demanded I lie on the leather love seat. I lowered my pajama bottoms, lying on my stomach. I yelped each time the belt crashed my backside. I was wailing by the end.

Pops looked me in the eye one last time, then calmly rearranged the belt back into his trouser loops. He left the room without another word. Lying on my stomach, I glared at his disappearing shadow, furious he'd given me such a whupping. Then, noticing the sliced-up sofas again, I wondered if perhaps he had shown me more mercy than I deserved.

•   •   •

POPS'S NEW LEATHER had cut so nicely, I thought, compared to what? Looking back, those crisp rips remind me of my skin, my body, the violation of both.

Stooped on hands and knees, collecting shreds of leather from the carpet, I had the feeling that some other monster was responsible for this mess. I hadn't meant to destruct his property; I'd meant to deconstruct my feelings. I was looking for something, though I didn't know it yet, information that would help me understand this world. The surface, the layers, what lay beneath.

Chapter 30

———

ROUSTING ME FROM SLEEP TO GET TO SCHOOL WAS AN ongoing ordeal for my mother. One morning in fourth grade, in April 1981, I rolled out of bed. Lumbering in a way that didn't feel typical, I went to the bathroom, then curled up in a ball to take a nap on the shaggy rug. I awoke to Mommy's banging outside the door. Staggering to my feet, I could only lean on the towel rack, slumped over, my body dragging me downward. My vision went black.

When I came to, I found my sisters, brother, and mother standing over me. I whispered, Everything is fine. Then get ready for school, Mommy answered. A child had to be on their way to the morgue to receive permission from my parents to miss school. She wiped a wet rag across my face and sent me off to Georgetown Hill Elementary.

When I came home at the end of the day, I shuffled to my parents' bedroom and climbed into their bed. I heard Marcelle talking to Mommy on the phone. My mother made Marcelle, by then thirteen years old, call her office every afternoon as soon as we'd all returned from school. Marcelle approached me to have a closer look. She could see a faint, impish vein barely pulsing on my neck. He doesn't look so good, she reported. Hearing this news, my mother came home. She could read my body; she knew I wasn't faking anything. She rushed me to the hospital in an ambulance.

The doctors rigged me up to an IV drip at Washington's Children's Hospital to treat my sickle cell crisis. They put me in the intensive care unit next to the terminal ward for the children with cancer.

I was battling a chest infection, receiving an on-and-off opiate drip to manage cancer-level pain, as well as blood transfusions.

I knew nothing of HIV. Nor did most of the public. Still, my mother had a sharp suspicion of governments and their agencies and hectored the doctors about the blood that had been assigned to me. When I was finally released from the hospital, she demanded that, going forward, I receive blood only from the young daughter of a patrician white family she knew of with a rambling horse farm in Virginia. I met the girl on her family homestead months later; she was innocent from history, sovereign from the public blood supply. Had my mother not insisted in knowing where my blood was coming from, had her embattled-refugee instincts not kicked in, I am certain I would be dead.

The bag hung over my head, the blood slipping through the drip chamber, the tubes, ever-more crimson, the catheter into my vein, the fleshy inner crook of my elbow. Tethered to the bleating machines, I smiled falsely, tried not to think about the pain that the very sight of me was putting on my sisters and brother, standing bedside.

I had nightmares that Sara would one day have to bury me. *Ya'arburne.*

I thought often of my dead brother.

There is a price to surviving a sibling.

OUT OF THE HOSPITAL, far from the nurses, I could forget the humiliation of feeling in need. My family tried to discard their fears, return home, where we wanted for nothing, financially. My parents were enjoying some shiny years, the kind where a couple's careers, their futures, look like an open road. Playing Battleship on Pops's fine, fine sofas, or sprawled alone, reading my encyclopedia on his plush carpets, I could never have imagined that the woman cooking me pot roast for dinner had once lived jammed into a one-bedroom apartment with nine others, wondering where her next meal might come from. Far from Tuckerman Lane, though, her sisters and brothers—Raymonde, Carmen, Marie, Leonie, Pierre, and Bernard—were living hand to mouth in crime-pocked Brooklyn. My mother, in her own way, had outsurvived her siblings.

There are two kinds of people who grow up under brutalizing circumstances. There's the casualty, who is destroyed by the events, unable to come out the other side, and the mercenary, who cuts and runs. If I stick around, the mercenary says, I'll go down with the family. If I stop to pull somebody out of the pit, I'll never climb out myself. Danny, to her extraordinary credit, is neither person. She did not succumb to the tides, nor did she sacrifice her sisters and brothers to save herself.

Danny may have escaped Brooklyn the first chance she had, but the moment she landed her first serious job, she began sending her siblings help.

I used to love to eavesdrop on Mommy, cupping my ear on her bedroom door while she dispensed hours of advice to this or that aunt or uncle. Even if it was a school night, even if we had yet to eat that pot roast, she'd stay on the phone hour after hour, trying to help her siblings.

Uncle Bernard was my favorite of the lot by far. He came to visit us during my Christmas break one year. Soon as he arrived, nylon duffel bag in hand, Mommy put him to work. She made him install exercise equipment for Pops in the basement, near the guest room. When he was permitted to rest, I crept on tippy-toe to his room, crouched by the wooden door, and listened to him render ballads on his trombone, the jazz ringing defiant and bold. His coal-black skin, straight nose, and high cheekbones gave him the look of a Slavic Miles Davis.

Uncle Bernard had a great stash of magazines. He'd show us kids his comic book collection, flaunting the superhero, sci-fi, and humor strips with equal gusto, but he got a vicious scolding from Danny when she discovered his porn rags in the basement bathroom. Uncle Bernard smelled of dirty socks, my father's whiskey, and brass. He dispensed his colorful jokes and I got lost in his outlandish stories. As he moseyed to the punch line, his eyes would pop out, his grin would go dizzy. He was part street-tough, part Romantic.

He lived a universe away from us, one that I did not know about, let alone visit, in a one-bedroom apartment on the third floor of Building #3336124 of the New York City Housing Authority, the Unity Plaza housing projects in East New York. He lived there with our Auntie Carmen, by then in her late twenties; Carmen's young son, Sean; and G'mère, whom the neighbors adored. Not long after the family moved in, the electricity in the whole building died during the 1977 New York City blackout. When G'mère entered the dark building, it was her neighbors who walked her groceries up the three flights and made sure she arrived to her apartment safely.

The subsidized shoebox had little room to maneuver. There was a small bedroom, a galley kitchen with a fire escape, one kitchen window looking out onto the center courtyard, and a lone bathroom. Most nights, G'mère and Sean slept in her queen bed; Aunt Carmen slept on a mattress on the bedroom floor; and Bernard slept in the living room. Whenever anyone reached to turn off the television, they were startled by a deep voice. "No, no," it would bellow. "Don't you touch that. I'm listening." Eyes shut, with a sly smile, Bernard announced that he had perfected the art of listening to TV. It was always *Star Trek, Space: 1999,* or some other sci-fi show. Bernard sprawled himself anywhere he could find a free spot; he'd always pleaded tired from his job at a sporting goods store.

Some weekends, he took Sean, about eight years old, to Coney Island for rides and hot dogs. Others, he prowled Brooklyn looking for the best places to take my other cousin Misha, a wiry teen, to listen to jazz. On his way home, he'd stop at the corner bodega near the subway station for a pint of Wild Irish Rose and gulp it down before either Carmen could see him.

G'mère still worked as a bookkeeper for the Board of Education. When she left the apartment for work in the mornings, Bernard would shut himself in her bedroom to sleep off his hangover. After work, she did all the food shopping, the laundry, and cooking for the household. Bernard was usually drunk on the couch, his Wild Irish Rose dangling from his loose grip.

Some evenings too G'mère would find Carmen nodding off on the toilet. G'mère knew her daughter was strung out on heroin. She'd shake her and try to put her to bed. Then G'mère would disappear behind her bedroom door and pour herself her Manischewitz or take a bedtime tea. She'd top that off with Stanback—a powdered aspirin—and a menthol Kool.

Carmen's boyfriend, or her dope dealer—her son doesn't remember which—banged her up one Saturday night. When she returned to the apartment bloodied, G'mère put her to bed. G'mère was soft-spoken, but when Bernard or Carmen's booze and drug hunts brought violence back to the apartment, G'mère had strict words for them. A sharp sentence or two and her grown children knew she was furious. There were times, though, when all she could do was distance herself: she could see them drunk on the couch but chose not to.

Soon "fry daddy"—cooked cocaine—came to Unity Plaza. News of the quicker, cheaper way of devouring cocaine spread. A bag of blow or PCP cost a small fortune, but residents paid as little as $2.50 for a hit of crack. Hustlers set to work selling the cheap, plentiful elixir, which hooked its claws into people's hungers, churning chaos. Their next-door neighbor was stabbed in his apartment. Dealers lurking in the lobby drafted kids, including Sean, to deliver crack throughout the building. One child plunged off the roof. A top-floor resident heard footsteps through her ceiling; then, looking out her kitchen window, she saw the child falling. His mother and grand-mother were summoned by police to the courtyard. When they saw their seven-year-old boy lying in the dirt, they screamed. They were all taken to Kings County Hospital. Nurses treated them for severe shock; the boy was pronounced dead. G'mère heard from the neighbors later that the child had been hurled off the roof for losing or stealing a delivery of crack.

Gunshots rang outside the family's apartment at night. G'mère

ordered Sean to sleep in the bathtub and never to stand near the
window after dark. The irony of bullets threatening her children in
Unity Plaza, just as they had in Port-au-Prince, surely was not lost
on her.

Better than Sean, I knew Philippe, Auntie Ray's son, who visited
us on Tuckerman Lane and played touch football with us in the
backyard. He called me Cher-cherd, short for "Richard." As I looked
toward the left, his perfectly lobbed football would bounce off my
chest from the right. "Cher-cherd!" he'd shout, laughing. "Where
you running to? McDonald's?" I adored Philippe. He always had a
joke, a kind word for me. His winsome smile featured a snaggled
front tooth, chipped I don't know how. I only knew the playful, teasing Philippe, the Philippe who had me aching in laughter, waiting
until grown-ups were just out of earshot before telling some rowdy
sex joke. Though brined in masculinity, he hadn't reached that point
in a black boy's life when Reagan's America would batter the sweet-
ness out of him.

But when he was fourteen, Philippe came home to Raymonde
and said, Mommy, I did a terrible thing. I met a man. Mommy,
he is so nice to me. He gives me something called crack. When I
take crack, I forget how life makes me feel. So I go again to him and
he gives me the crack for free. But yesterday the man said, Give me
the money. I said, What money? The money for the crack. I never
paid before. You gonna pay now. I don't have any money, said the
boy. Your mama pay rent, don't she? Yes. You know where she puts
her money, don't you? Yes. Philippe said, Mommy, I gave him money
for a hit of crack.

My aunt Ray told me she once told her therapist, My son is on
crack. Living on the streets. The therapist replied, You have to do
tough love. If he's hungry, don't feed him. He's dirty, don't let him
bathe. He's all wet, don't let him change. He needs to go to the bathroom, don't let him in the house. He never laid a hand on me, she
told the therapist. The worst thing he ever did was try to shove by
me to get into my apartment for money. We had a tussle at the door
and he left.

Philippe had turned to G'mère too. She gave him money, if she had it. Other times, seeing that crack furor fill his eyes, she and Bernard would shut the door in his face.

Philippe's father threw him out for stealing valuables to pawn on the streets to buy crack. He soon joined the city's army of homeless. He returned to his father's apartment when he wasn't home, banging on neighbors' doors. Could they help him get in his dad's apartment? He lived there too, he lied. They called the cops on him for trespassing and harassment. The arrests piled up, on top of his record for jumping the turnstile and other nuisance crimes.

By the time he'd turned seventeen, Philippe had seen the inside of a jail. He saw his cellmate get his face carved out with a razor blade.

Mommy, he said, I don't want to go to that place again.

JUST BEFORE THANKSGIVING 1983, an ambulance came blaring to Unity Plaza. By the time paramedics carted Uncle Bernard from his couch to the waiting vehicle, he was dead. He was just thirty.

To strangers in East New York, Bernard was another dead junkie. To G'mère, he was a tender boy, volatile with love and desires, who somehow never found the tools to cope with his life. G'mère cried inconsolably for Bernard, her youngest boy, with deep-rumbling compassion and self-blame. He had always been all the girls' favorite brother. The only time I ever remember seeing my mother cry as a boy was when she received the news that Uncle Bernard had died.

Uncle Bernard was stabbed to death, one cousin insisted to me over the years. Another cousin claimed he'd drunk himself to death after his wife left him. What wife? I wondered. One aunt swore he'd died from a crack overdose. It was cardiac arrest, another aunt said. Another vowed that he'd died during an epileptic seizure. My relatives have always been slippery with the truth. But Bernard's life was so precarious that all these claims are plausible.

There lay Bernard with his soft smile and untamed Afro cushioning his head, and the coffin's ruching, all silk, swallowing his shrunken dark body like a white-foam tide. The bill for the funeral fell to Danny. That she assumed this responsibility came to no one's surprise. By the time Bernard stopped breathing, this type of duty, that kind of bill, were automatically passed on to her. She was the well-thought-out one, the steady one, and why not—she was also the one who had the savings and the secretary and the suburbs mortgage. She was the one, just as she'd been the one to read to her siblings, or dress them, or feed them, or wallop them when their mother had been too busy, too tired, too deflated, to do so herself. So Danny was the one to pay for Bernard's coffin and cremation, roughly four hundred dollars, at the Green-Wood Crematory. Financially, it was just a rounding error on her tax returns. Emotionally, the figure was bloated in pain. Bernard's coffin contained the siblings' joys, rivalries, hurts. Who knows whether they ever forgave their parents the hand-me-down love, the secondhand clothes, the beatings, the lifelong preferential treatment some accuse Danny of having received. It's true my mother enjoyed a head start of attention from her father, from 1944 to 1946, when he had no other children and had yet to evaporate into his aloofness and fame.

Daniel, a subway ride away, did not bother to attend Bernard's funeral.

He was too busy buffing his luster across Little Haiti. He continued holding court wherever he could, spellbinding expatriates with live speeches, appearing on radio programs, firing off articles to international newspapers. The dissident press considered him Duvalier's chief rival abroad. Just months before Bernard's funeral, the eminent Haitian journalist Paul Clitandre called Daniel "the person arousing the most discussion amongst all political leaders in exile."

G'mère endured the fallout from her children's drink and drugs alone. It brought her sorrow as it brought her shame. Had she made so many sacrifices in her children's behalf for them to shoot dope or smoke fry daddy?

Bernard was but the first family casualty of the coup; more collateral damage followed. Three of Danny's siblings would suffer from severe mental illness. Just like Carmen, Uncle Daniel Jr. would get hooked on heroin. He left East New York, and Aunt Carmen followed, her crack addiction nipping at her heels. They landed in rural South Carolina to clean out.

Danny always sent her brothers and sisters money when they needed it. She opened her home to them. Aunt Leonie stayed at Tuckerman Lane for months on end with her two daughters when her Brooklyn apartment burned down. Aunt Marie, utterly broke, moved in with us, with her daughter, for an entire year, until she could find employment as a nurse's aide. One of Ray's sons, straight out of prison, moved in for half a year. In those years Tuckerman Lane to me had the feel of a homeless shelter, a sanctuary that my parents served up to strangers and relatives in dire straits. Danny was wildly, deeply generous, just as she was ruthlessly disciplined in not letting any of her siblings take her down with them.

It was around that time that she started a job helping orphans of war in Guatemala secure passage to the United States. Later, she set out to run UNICEF campaigns in Cameroon and Rwanda not long after the genocide, to protect young girls from sexual assault. At the time, I didn't know how her childhood had galvanized her into an advocate for children, especially girls who had suffered violence.

Suffering must never separate people, her father had once told his loyal union followers. It must unite them. As it turns out, he wasn't bonded by hardship personally. When things got tough, he walked.

I often wonder which of my family members are ready to sacrifice themselves for the others. Which would pick up and leave.

"Dignified, honorable fashion." That's how my grandfather entered the National Penitentiary. That's the front he presented to Eisenhower when he landed in America. That's how my mother staged herself at work. Meanwhile, shit was pelting the fan and our souls were bleeding.

Unspeakable things, unspoken.

Machine-gun nights, Dessalines Barracks, crack-dope heads: I knew nothing of this growing up.

It was not a story to pass on.

Chapter 31

"THIS AIN'T YOUR TRIBAL VILLAGE, AND YOU'RE NO AFRICAN chieftain," my mother loved to bark at my father.

We kids left my father's earshot and just laughed and laughed. Pops wore citrusy cologne and a good Saint Laurent suit, but we knew exactly what she meant: he liked to vanish himself from the tedious work of the household, then resurface to make big statements, dispense grand treats.

Like that August night in 1986, just before my first day of high school, when Pops walked through the front door. Exhausted after work, his lips were fixed, forehead flat, pupils afire. I knew his solemn look well. He gathered Mommy, Marcelle, Couscous, Sara, and me into the living room. I could tell before he opened his mouth that a real declaration was on its way.

He had just agreed to a job offer in Guinea, he said.

For how long? we asked. Indefinitely, he said.

Guinea had recently been liberated from a twenty-four-year horror; Touré had died. The new government was recruiting Pops to be minister of finance. He wanted to help the country tackle corruption, confront poverty, and lure honest global investment.

I looked at my mother to gauge her reaction. She squinted at him like he was a dense child. Then she interrupted. She said that he was a fool to give up this comfortable life on Tuckerman Lane and forfeit a stable salary and his upward career as an economist. She felt blindsided, she added.

The look of confidence and altruism melted from his face. He seemed to have expected unconditional support for his news.

He reminded Mommy that since leaving Yale, it had been his dream to return to serve his native country. He looked us all in the eye: If ever you're presented with a once-in-a-lifetime opportunity, he told us, don't waste it.

On most matters, my father could open his mind, listen to others. In that living room, though, he was not soliciting our feedback or anyone's consent; he was making an announcement. What Pops didn't say, still standing above us by the coffee table, was how much he missed his family in Guinea. Both his father and mother had died during his exile. Returning to attend either's funeral in their tribal village could have cost him his life.

The struggling small republic had no high schools or colleges to speak of; my siblings and I would have to stay put in America. To my surprise, Mommy did not. Over the next few weeks, she decided to follow her husband all the way to Africa, to leave us behind. I don't recall any discussion or explanation of her choice.

Nights and weekend afternoons, we crouched on the kitchen floor packing up my parents' belongings. My mother lorded over us, telling us exactly how the boxes should be packed. She yelled at Couscous for taping one shut wrong. Soon G'mère would arrive with her suitcases and settle into a second-floor bedroom. On October 6, 1986, before flying a continent away, Mommy would issue a notarized letter naming her mother as our caretaker and legal guardian.

IT WAS ONE OF THOSE coincidences that nobody could foresee, and whose jarring details no one talked about: the year Carmen left Brooklyn for Tuckerman Lane, Daniel returned to Haiti.

As he boarded his flight at JFK, Haitian Americans crowded the departure gate to cheer him on. He was easily recognizable to the well-wishers: he sported the same rough, alluring face he had for the last forty years. That afternoon of March 20, 1986, he met his admirers with supreme confidence—only his gait was rickety.

A month earlier, the Duvalier era had come to a crashing end. Jean-Claude "Baby Doc" Duvalier, dictator and only son of the late Papa Doc, saw his tenure disintegrate under a groundswell of mass anger after his security forces had opened fire on student protesters, killing three. Millions of Haitians had protested his viciousness and incompetence until Baby Doc saw no option but to flee. At one o'clock in the morning on February 7, 1986, a U.S. cargo plane waited on a runway at François Duvalier International Airport in Port-au-Prince to escort a humiliated man into exile.

The dictator-son and his luxury-loving mulatto wife had fleeced the nation of reportedly four hundred million dollars. During their combined reign of terror, lasting from my mother's departure at thirteen to my teenage years, the father-son dictators murdered roughly fifty thousand people and banished tens of thousands into exile.

Daniel and Haitians the world over finally felt they could return home safely.

MIST KISSED THE PLANE windows as my grandfather's flight hummed above the sea, circled the Dominican Republic, then dipped, swerving above his country's mountains. The slaves who had founded the nation named it after the indigenous word *hayti*, "mountainous." Dipping, softly dipping, the plane looped and looped around all those peaks.

Daniel sat in first class alone, except for the Haitian journalist who accompanied him to report the return.

Journalist: What do you expect when you land at the airport?

Professor: I did not travel in order to be cheered by crowds when I land. If the crowds turn up from Port-au-Prince and from many areas of the republic, for us in MOP, that would be normal.

Journalist: What do you think of this panoramic view?

Professor: It is moving. More than twenty-eight years of exile. I need to see it closer and think more deeply.

Journalist: It's a view from above. I think one needs to be in the interior of the country to see the difference between 1957 and 1986.

Daniel turned to gaze out of his porthole at the landscape. The cabin crew announced the plane would soon land.

"You're returning home after thirty years," the journalist said. "When we touch ground, do you think you will cry?"

Daniel startled at this curveball. Eyes watering, he smiled tightly. "It is not an impossibility."

A CROWD HAD WALKED and whooped its way from downtown to the airport. Large trucks and camionettes were crammed with young people. Some brought boom boxes to pulse calypso and bullhorns to broadcast their mirth. MOP sent its own delegation to greet Daniel. Merchants closed their shops to join the fray.

The plane screeched to a halt.

Daniel appeared at the top of the jet staircase and the crowd erupted. He paused for several beats as if to give his countrymen a better look at his visage. Carefully he ambled down the steps, stalling here and there to steady his aching limbs, to smile again at the people.

At the foot of the staircase an honor guard briskly saluted Daniel. He was led to the airport's dignitaries' lounge, where more press camped out. When Daniel was ousted, the country barely had any televisions. Now television camera lenses stared him down. Two reporters thrust TV microphones in his face.

Professor, what is your first impression being on Haitian soil again?

"It is very moving," he answered. "If you were in my shoes, you would understand the joy that I naturally feel to be standing on the soil of a country I have always loved so much. My one greatest love."

An elderly man watched Daniel's airport interview on television that night in a bar in Bel-Air, not so far from his idol's old home, 19 Avenue of the People. He ordered a beer and softly declared to other patrons, "Now I can die in peace. I've seen Daniel Eustache Fignolé again."

Having been banned for more than a quarter century, Daniel's face and voice blanketed Port-au-Prince. *The New York Times* called his homecoming "triumphant."

MOST OF THE COUNTRY didn't know the details of Daniel's health, though. Just before his return, he had spent many weeks convalescing. A complicated operation on his intestines had gone wrong. He was peeing blood.

So Daniel held court at Canape Vert Hospital in Port-au-Prince. His loyalists gathered in his room for political bull sessions. On one of his more passable afternoons, he stood on the hospital balcony and waved to the well-wishers crowded below. He lectured MOP senior officers, he pep-talked the rank and file. He doled out instructions for the party's future.

Closing his door behind them, his party leaders whispered, *"Mèt la se mouwi"*—"Master is dying."

Pills, tests, doctor-talks. Daniel juggled his medical regimen with his work. What was more pressing: cancer or nation?

He cursed the fatigue that his prostate cancer inflicted on his flesh. *"Gade jan m'ap domi, yon neg tankou mwe nki ta ka soud pye-l,"* he said. *"Gade jan m'ap. Domi Ki bagay sa-a?"*—"Look how I am sleeping. A man like me who should be on his feet. What kind of mess is this?"

Imprisoned on bedrest, what Daniel remembered, I now imagine, were the mix-match shadows of his life.

There is Maman being lowered into earth, dearly beloved.

There is master dictating to the hungry schoolboy the hard-pointed dictates of mastering French.

There is le professeur brandishing master's bloodied tongue.

Thus spoke the Uncles.

There is the Vodou doctor in his gingerbread house.

There are the nuns spiriting his children to the Pan Am clipper.

There is Carmen's Catholic catechism, Credo in Deum. "I believe in God."

There are Danielle and Raymonde and Marie and Leonie and Pierre and Bernard and Carmen and Joelle.

Children don't know their parents' ordeals.

CATHOLIC PRIESTS CAME TO my mother's slumbering father to deliver his last rites, on August 26, five months after he returned home. The next day he was gone.

DANIELLE RECEIVED THE NEWS as she was packing for Africa. I don't remember any discussion about Daniel's death. I don't remember her crying as she had for Bernard. I remember only, vaguely, her telling us she had to fly to Port-au-Prince to attend her father's funeral. As his eldest child, she was tasked with leading his state funeral procession on August 29, 1986. The official convoy snaked through the capital for miles, and my mother walked beside her father's horse-drawn casket. Feeling obliged by protocol and duty,

Crowds pay tribute to Fignolé during his funeral
procession, Port-au-Prince, 1986

she walked in dignified, honorable fashion. Privately, she seethed at having to offer a celebratory public face for her deadbeat father.

"My one greatest love." That's what he had called the country. Not his wife, not his children.

DANIELLE'S FATHER and her husband returned home from their exiles at the same time. She was chasing a kinder, more cheerful, more sophisticated version of her father to Africa.

Pops as minister of finance, Republic of Guinea

I think of Tante Gigine's lament about Daniel when I think about Pops: "Your grandfather was obsessed with politics—to the point of mental derangement." Just as Daniel had, my father devoted his waking hours in Guinea to undoing colonialism. It was his one greatest love.

Chapter 32

————

OUR PARENTS AN OCEAN AWAY, SARA AND I SLOGGED through four years at Churchill High School. The school was so monochrome it inspired Darren Star, an alumnus from the late 1970s, to create *Beverly Hills 90210*. Star had originally called the pilot *Potomac 20854*, but industry execs convinced him to set the show in Beverly Hills instead. When I was told to read a passage from *Othello* in Honors English or asked a question about the Emancipation Proclamation in AP History, a disgust stirred my stomach. I wanted to go mute. So many exercises, so many sideways remarks, reminding me again and again that I was the sole black person in the classroom.

"Do you comb that?" a kid sitting behind me in class asked, swiping me on the back of my head. Another rummaged his hands through my Afro, sniffed his fingertips for traces of my hair product, then wrinkled his straight nose. Even the bus driver had words for me. "You know," he muttered once, "your head's so thick and nappy, if you combed it, the teeth would bleed."

The place gave me whiplash: My classmates' parents and grandparents included liberal Supreme Court justices, congresspeople, TV news anchors. My peers, teachers, neighbors: politically they were liberal, but spiritually the place was Reaganesque. The students in the Democratic Club outnumbered their Republican rivals by about five to one. Kids joined Greenpeace and signed Amnesty International petitions. And yet fathers wore popped collars under Lacoste sweaters. Mothers turned up in red blazers with power shoulder pads. My classmates drove Mercedes and Range Rovers and bragged about snorting good blow. In Health Ed, some students recited Nancy Reagan's "War on Drugs" prattle in earnest reverence, others as a sarcastic punch line. Parents cooed over their tax cuts, but the only thing that trickled down was their aerobics craze. Exercise transformed from a pastime into an industry. Nike went from personal shoe to late-capitalist ethos. No pain, no gain, shouted Jane Fonda. Girls took notice, vomiting out their meals in a race to look the thinnest. Just Say No. Just Do It. In the gyms, the classrooms, the offices, management controls subjected each body unit to exacting regimes of productivity. Reaganomics was a soulless juggernaut working to whip white people into a delirium of competition and to dismantle black lives.

Meanwhile, the Reagan administration had started to send the Coast Guard to intercept Haitians fleeing at sea. They were seeking safety, a chance at a new life, after the Duvalier regime crumbled. America detained and deported Haitians intercepted in Florida, while Cuban refugees were permitted to stay. The administration and the public associated the growing AIDS crisis with Haiti; in 1987 the federal government enacted a law barring anyone with HIV from entering the country, targeting Haitian migrants especially.

From the gutted factories of Gary to the streets of East New York to the shores of Florida—so many people were deemed disposable, incompatible with Reagan's America.

I had no clue whether G'mère was following the country's hard-line rejection of Haitian immigrants. We never discussed politics.

G'mère was stooped and sixty-four when she moved in with us. She had her uniform of sorts: a black Haitian turban affixed to her head, with all-black trousers and shirts. Since the moment Daniel died, she had resolved to mourn his life, wearing black every remaining day of her own.

When I came home from school, she might be simmering herself chicken wings in a saucepan. Late nights the house smelled of garlic as she boiled cloves to eat plain before bed. I winced when she bit into raw onion and coughed when I entered her bedroom, piles of butts overflowing in her plastic ashtrays. The walls turned a dark yellow from the menthol Kools that she chain-smoked alone in there. She left the door open when she wasn't smoking and watched old black-and-white movies on her tiny television. Some nights I sat next to her and told her about my day at school. She regaled me with stories about movies she'd seen or magazines she'd read, and I pretended not to notice the tobacco stench.

EXCEPT FOR G'MÈRE, there was no question that everyone at Tuckerman Lane had to work—our parents, even a continent away, couldn't abide laziness. Besides, we wanted some spending money in our pockets. A few days a week, I walked to the nearby strip mall for my job at Popeyes, where I battered smelly chicken parts, mopped floors, manned the register. Just two storefronts away from me, Sara worked as a salesgirl at Dressbarn, a clothes store for plus-size women. One weekend, she went to retrieve clothing from the dressing room and nearly vomited when she entered. A customer had pissed all over the fitting room. Sara had to toss the urine-drenched clothes away and scour the carpet fresh. Meanwhile, Marcelle and Couscous worked at Sears, Roebuck, she in the jewelry department, he in automotive. The four of us would share our war stories and stinging rebukes and bit comedies that visited us at our jobs.

Still, I never really felt in those days that we were a family. I felt like a child, shuffling between school and my part-time job, while G'mère smoked and watched her movies. G'mère helped raise us, as best she could, but I resented my mother for abandoning me for Africa, more so than I did my father. While I missed my father's company—his easy jokes, his delightful, smart conversation—I needed my mother. She was the one who knew where my vaccination records were, which emergency rooms to trust, whether my doctors' bills were paid. She'd left me to take care of my sickle cell anemia by myself.

My adrenaline surged whenever a letter from her appeared in our tall metal mailbox. Bright Guinean stamps popped on the fraying,

Danielle doing her humanitarian work
in West Africa, unspecified date

travel-worn envelope. I lit up at the sight of her familiar penmanship arriving from all those miles away—arcs and circles looping cleanly into a decorative flourish.

As Pops worked to clean up and modernize Guinea's economy, Mommy wasted no time setting up house and rolling up her sleeves at her new job, a senior position at the United Nations International Children's Emergency Fund (UNICEF) mission. She helped redraft the republic's constitution and designed health programs for its children. "Vaccination day was a real success," Mommy wrote me one winter. "Everybody was very happy and we vaccinated 58,000 kids or more."

MY LIFE DRIFTED AWAY from my mother's and the distance between Potomac and Guinea accommodated new secrets. One afternoon, headed to my doctor's appointment in DC, I stopped at a McDonald's for a vanilla milkshake. I planned to savor it, scooping the last delicious slosh into my mouth with a straw, on my long blood-commute home alone.

I placed my order at the counter and went to the bathroom. Suddenly I heard the bathroom bolt lock, then felt a hand on my shoulder. A bigger boy stood behind me, blocking the door. A massive Afro jutted from underneath his McDonald's visor. I was shaken by his good looks—muscles popping under a too-small polo shirt. He looked at least eighteen. Maybe early twenties? Once the lock clicked, he told me to drop my pants: he was going to suck me off. No, I said. Yes, he said. No, I said. I looked at him, confused. Why did he—so muscled, so handsome—want anything to do with me? Was this what guys in the city did? Did he think I was gay? I pushed him aside. He startled backward, eyes narrowing in surprise, then anger. I unlocked the door and ran.

I took a seat on the subway, as far from anyone as I could, alone in my head. For a second, I doubted my split escape. What if the older boy's chest and groin were as alluring as his face? And yet, I was afraid that accepting his mouth on my penis meant that I would have to go steady with him.

That blow job was impossible. The prospect of being with a guy who worked at McDonald's dazed, then rattled, me. I myself worked at Popeyes, but that guy would, I sensed, be in his dirty fast-food uniform for a long, long time. I had yet to read Marx or Mills or Gramsci or Wilson. I couldn't even define what "class" meant. But I had a keen understanding of the kind of life that Mommy and Pops had in mind for me.

Sometime later, I stopped at the nearby convenience store after my Popeyes shift to pick up toiletries. I flipped through the tabloids at the checkout counter. I was shaken by the wasted faces of Liberace, Perry Ellis, captured by a flashbulb and looking like those of criminals. The talented men issuing a double denial: "I am not a fairy, and I am not dying of the gay disease." Or a headline in the *National Enquirer*: "Rock Hudson—the REAL STORY. Shocking Reason He Hid AIDS for a YEAR." I slipped the tabloid underneath my coat. Alone in the family den that evening, I read the full spread on how Rock Hudson denied that he had the gay cancer, how the Reagans wouldn't do anything for their old friend anyway, let alone any ordinary homosexual.

I could not resist the tabloids that shamed gay men, my reading habit of self-hate. Though, in defiance, I was also devouring books that promised a taste of freedom. I lost myself in the pages of Gerald Clarke's biography of Truman Capote, into the soul of a spellbinding chipmunk of a writer from Monroeville, Alabama, who would conquer the big city, landing himself at *The New Yorker*, charming the likes of Peggy Guggenheim into long summers at her palazzo in Venice. I read how he had sleuthed and crafted a masterpiece about two disquieted drifters who murdered a family in the bowels of the American prairie in cold blood. I saw in Capote's life all the things I wanted. It was becoming clear to me that reading and writing would be my trapdoors too, my only paths to securing the life I so craved.

THE MONTHS, THE YEARS, of high school passed in this way. My siblings' and my birthdays went uncelebrated. No one had the foresight to put together dinners, the disposable cash to buy cake and candles. Letters took their place.

"Dear Rich, When we talk seriously about the world and work, I appreciate your advice, candor, and dry humour," my mother wrote me in a birthday letter. "I love it when you chuckle at the inconsistencies of the world. You are so intelligent and only you know how to get your dreams accomplished. I want you to know that I always look forward to our long talks and the silent times we spend together."

I wrote my mother prolifically in high school and she wrote me punctually and voluminously in turn. Our letters closed the emotional cavities within and between us—though only to a point.

"Dear Richie," she wrote in one. "Things are moving with the refugee settlements and I assume that corruption is a reality. As long as I keep my nose clean, I don't care about being Joan of Arc although I do get stressed out a lot seeing how much people make on children's backs! Many refugees are going back to Liberia. I do continue to love what I'm doing especially when I see it makes a difference. Pops changed the living room and dining room. It's all early Chinese and late African. It does look very nice."

It made sense to me, when I read that letter, that my mother would discuss refugee displacement and Pops's fine taste in furniture in the same breath. The Liberian refugee crisis was obviously more important to the both of us, but each item was just as newsworthy in our separation. She could pull it off in a letter, blending the heartbreaking with the comic, the global with the personal. This was the diction of our conversation and silence.

Our letters drew us closer, and yet we remained more unknown to each other than we did to our casual friends. Each one carried the weight of so many unasked questions, the pregnancy of personal experiences we left blank, all the things I would not, or could not, tell her, about my isolation in high school, getting cornered in a city toilet, my burning fear of AIDS.

I was vexed by my body: its blood, its limits, its abuse, its gifts, its monstrosity, its thirsts. My mother could not see how much I was changing.

MARCELLE, COUSCOUS, SARA, and I continued to raise one another. My senior year of high school, Couscous was enjoying his sophomore year at Yale, so I decided to apply there also. He hosted me and drove me to other college interviews. Yale, Brown, Wesleyan, Vassar, Rutgers, George Washington University: every school I applied to had to be in striking distance of a relative, or on a train or public bus route. My mother was too strict to let me get a license and drive.

Filling out my college applications, I understood that no handsome face, no dribbling skills, no head of blond hair, no trust fund, no society wife, no fat dowry wasn't going to earn me the kind of life that lived in my bones. I wanted my life to look like a perfectly turned-out ball gown, to sound like fast bebop. Smooth, easy, without sign of effort. But there was a monkey wrench. Several, in fact: black, sickle cell, secret crushes. I felt cheated. I became determined that my dark, dark skin, my uncooperative blood, and my longing for men would not snatch from me the baubles I felt were my birthright: good invitations, a nice home, success in the public eye. I would have to work extra-hard to make sure mine was mine.

It's a funny, perverse predicament to grow up an ugly black gay boy in a good suburb: I felt so deprived and so entitled at the same time. I wanted to sever myself from my upbringing. I wanted to flee as soon and as far as I could—an escape artist like Mommy.

Chapter 33

WESLEYAN UNIVERSITY WAS A LEFT-WING HOTHOUSE WITH a loose, do-what-you-want atmosphere. Setting foot on the backcountry campus, I couldn't imagine that my time there would go down as the most tumultuous in the university's century-plus existence.

In my first year, a junior was executed in a public park by his drug-dealing partners who feared his revenge after they lost him ten thousand dollars. The school was teeming with political protest. Students occupied the admissions office, demanding increased diversity on campus. Two students hurled Molotov cocktails through the window of the president's office under cover of night, igniting his antique carpet, his wooden desk, his mail. The university's boathouse, a most irresistible emblem of WASP privilege, was firebombed for unspecified political reasons. And to top it off, students burst into a university board of trustees meeting and took the agenda hostage to present their concerns: the school's investments in South Africa, its poor hiring record for faculty of color, its meager student financial aid.

Even so, the political dissent roiling the campus came with unfettered gaiety. Without warning, sleepy Foss Hill would erupt into party. I spent weeknights holding protest placards, shouting at the top of my voice, followed by weekends dancing to deep house in the basement of the Malcolm X House. Or else I was suspended upside down in the stately fraternity mansions lining High Street doing keg stands with friends, some rather tony, with nary a care in the world.

The dissonance didn't occur to me. Without thinking, I could code-switch so full, so fast, it would make your head snap.

I decided to pledge one fraternity, Delta Kappa Epsilon, since it had the reputation of throwing the best parties, and it offered first-year men free beer and excellent steak. Once we were initiated, the upperclassmen would remind us newbies that we were joining one of the oldest, proudest brotherhoods in the country: five of its national members would go on to the presidency—Rutherford B. Hayes, Theodore Roosevelt, Gerald Ford, George H. W. Bush—and, after we graduated, George W. Bush. Once I became a brother, I drank to fit in with the DKE jocks and WASPs, just as I drank to negate them. To drink was to be a man, manly men drank, and manly drinking men kept up with one another by drinking. The ability to hold one's drink was a signpost of a successful manly man who didn't need a mother.

Some of my women friends begged me to sneak them into the parties; others cringed. These were the days of Take Back the Night, date-rape awareness, especially on frat row.

From its beginnings, DKE demanded an ultra level of secrecy. Members honored an omertà never to reveal to outsiders what went on inside our nineteenth-century stone mansion standing implacably on High Street. That trust I loved as much as anything or anyone at DKE.

In the classroom, meanwhile, I was learning mostly about how systems do and don't work, which was my obsession—the constitution, the presidency, policymaking, late capitalism. The political sphere enthralled me. One summer, I interned in Washington for the Democratic Party, then another for a Senate campaign. Reading greedily, and speaking often in class, I realized how badly I wanted to be a judge, a senator, the president. But my budding and as-yet-secret attraction to men told me that I could never become a public figure, a popular leader.

It was novels also that sideswiped my political ambition. Senior year I found myself in a class called Literary Foremothers in African-American Literature. Perhaps I wanted an orderly setting in which to read *The Color Purple,* having enjoyed Whoopi Goldberg in the movie, perhaps I preferred an afternoon schedule that would respect my morning hangovers, perhaps I was curious about the professor: I don't remember why I enrolled in that class. All I know is that deep into the semester, we read a tangled, prickly tale called *Beloved,* a novel that didn't care if you got it or not.

I couldn't put the thing down. *Beloved* had a familiar strangeness, even if I didn't understand it. The story spoke to me, but I didn't know why. Reading it, I felt how language had made the ancestors' lives riskier, contingent, while the capacity to read, to know when and how to speak, had afforded this author her might. Toni Morrison's words busted open a space for freedom—in her, Sethe, me— one whose contours, whose depths, I couldn't yet figure.

NO MATTER HOW ALTRUISTIC, convivial, brainy, Wesleyan was, it came to drag on me after a couple of years. The place could placate only so much of my restlessness. The second semester of my junior year, I chased a more tactile, alien freedom across the ocean—I went to study abroad in Bath.

When I arrived, I learned that I'd been assigned to share a small flat in a row house with three roommates, also students from universities in America. My life there soon took on a predictable rhythm. By day, I reveled in Irish literature, under the supervision of a shaved-bald Irish scholar who favored black turtlenecks. I immersed myself in John Donne and the metaphysical poets, as explained by an expert trained at Oxford. At night, I went to the local pub, Chequers.

It was a cozy, run-down affair, warm lighting, walls cluttered with bric-a-brac, old wood floors dating back at least a century. This dive, smelling of crisps, ale, and piss, drew the neighborhood nightly, all ages, all types. Its air was awash with barbs and bits of slander on the locals' lives. After dinner most nights, dirty dishes piled in our sink, my roommates and I went to drink and play darts with the regulars, who may as well have lived at the pub. To most of the residents, I'm sure it seemed that I'd landed in Bath from Mars; they'd never seen a black person, they said, chuckling.

I had told my friends, my professors, my family back home fanciful tales about studying English literature in someone's motherland. That I wanted to experience a new way of learning. Instead, I shut the pub down.

Once Chequers had become too familiar, the rest of Bath opened itself up to me—its discreet courtyards, its hiding parks, its underground student bars. I roamed the streets of the Georgian city one night, the moon's sheen mixed with the streetlight, shimmering off the Avon River. The town's eighteenth-century architecture stood at attention; its neoclassical Palladian buildings blended with the Roman baths, narrow cobblestone alleys snaked into one another, and stairs dipped into basement apartments, unassuming rave houses. Lassies, their miniskirts hiked all the way up their pale thighs, stumbled out of the pubs into the misty darkness, hacking and laughing between drags on their fags. Smeared-crimson lips striving, they pecked at the boys. The girls, teetering on their heels in front of the old gray buildings, cheapened the landscape, the living Bath versus the mythic town straining to monetize its history.

The threat of adventure, my solitude, took over my tipsy thoughts. A calling, a sort of primal signal, sent me searching for my people in the dimly lit streets. I stumbled upon a pub in a side street. An elephant's head was carved into the stone facade of the building and another was painted onto the marquee. I peeked through the window and saw only men.

When I saddled up to the bar, I noticed all eyes swivel on me. Compared to Chequers, the place looked pathetic and swinish at that hour; I felt a panic to leave. But boomeranging out the front door would only attract more attention. I did my best to ignore the intense staring and ordered a snakebite.

I had barely put my lips to the pint when a man appeared from behind and pulled up a seat. He had sculpted bones for a face, a head of uncombed blond hair, and deviant, twisted teeth; he looked like one of those Shakespearean actors on *Masterpiece Theatre,* or the unruly noble in a Merchant Ivory piece. He leaned in and started a conversation. When the topic of his age came up, I almost slipped off the stool. Thirty. I was barely nineteen. But time flew in the company of this man, an antique talking. When the barman bellowed last orders, we looked at each other with beer-sotted eyes. He gathered his stuff. Again, I could see and feel the barflies staring. I could not know whether they were angry at me, an upstart stranger, for so quickly and casually departing with what was decidedly the best prize—or jealous at the man for netting the only fresh animal in the woods.

We stepped out of the bar, and I had no idea where we were headed. We roved through the late-night fog as I reveled in his pointed attention, the uncertain direction. We arrived at a building. He invited me in. To my surprise, a less handsome man sat in the parlor—waiting for him. From his pout I could tell this was no brother, cousin, or roommate. What's he doing here? I asked. That's my boyfriend. Then what am I doing here? Oh, he doesn't mind.

Before I knew it, the man was peeling off my shirt and kissing my lips, as his lover stormed out of the living room. I remember thinking, What lovely wallpaper. The man pulled me into his bedroom and threw me on the bed. When he tossed off his shirt, I felt delight looking at his lean stomach and carved pecs. Soon we were both completely nude. I remember my body startling when I saw him put on a condom. I shuddered. Was it because he had AIDS? Was it because he thought I had AIDS?

We were lost, inhaling each other, until suddenly he pinned my shoulders down and used his muscular thighs to pry my knees open, never stopping to ask my say-so for his hard thrusts, a brute violation that I did not object to. I thrashed. In my besotted fumble, I tried to ignore my fears. I concentrated on his body, shut off any awareness of my own, fixated on the attractive man on top of me. It didn't take long. That was my virginity, gone—and I do love a good wallpaper.

I had no idea what to say moments later when he kissed me good-bye. I stepped out of his flat as the sun began to rise, wearing the grin of a grimy cat caught with fish bones in his teeth.

THE ROMANS HAD BUILT Bath as a thermal spa in AD 60, then, under King George III, the town emerged in the eighteenth century as an elegant focal point of urbane English life. The city would be my base, I decided, from which to fan across the Continent during long weekends and academic breaks, burning through my meager summer-job savings. One break I boarded an old train headed to Dover. I stood on the deck of the hovercraft as it sailed from Dover to Calais, and the opal coast came closer and closer on the horizon. Inhaling Paris, weeks later, in several greedy breaths, I took a train to Le Havre, then a boat to Holland.

It was during one of my first nights in Amsterdam that I caught the attention of a nineteen-year-old Dutch boy with furious blond curls, his eyes as big as a cartoon lemur's, his skin as smooth as a newborn calf's, each of us alone in the club. He had traveled alone to the city that night from his hometown, a speck of a village that didn't even have its own post office. As I watched him dance, I saw his muscles, natural and easy.

For nights on end Rens and I kissed on the dance floor of the Exit, lost, alone together, free and unbothered by whoever might be watching us. Walking the streets holding hands, he and I cut such a dramatic figure, people stopped on the sidewalk to stare. At home, in the small hours of the night, we had body-crashing sex, lost in our shared oblivion. In the blink of an eye, we screwed on the kitchen floor of the apartment he had borrowed from his friend or in the tight twin bed of my youth hostel—anywhere, everywhere. I penetrated him bare our first time, condoms clearly visible in his friend's medicine cabinet, though neither of us said anything or gave our raw sex a second thought. From then, we never bothered to use them. We tussled like unfed animals, did not pause to dissect what was happening. My flesh tone popped against his, his against mine. Our fingers entwined near a pool of our cum, the residue of our self-erasure. It was the first time I'd experienced my body as anything other than defective or ugly.

Lying on the blankets one afternoon, on the floor of his borrowed flat, he told me how much he loathed his mother. He talked in fits and stutters—fumbling to find his English, but also because stories of affliction were fighting free from his mouth. His mother berated him. You are not fit for anything, she told him, but working this farm. University should not be wasted on you, you won't amount to much. He spoke of his town as a homogenous sinkhole, full of fearful, ugly-ass wretches, with a few exceptions; he vowed never to share a room with any of them again, even for an hour. He had grown to hate them as they hated him. There was one detail I'll never forget: he told me how his classmates tormented him because he wore dark socks, not the white tube socks that real football-playing boys wore. The only answer was a total split, and when he could escape permanently to Amsterdam, it wouldn't be a minute too soon.

He withheld none of his wounds or dreams from me. We had that bond that you share with your first true love, or that two alcoholics demand from each other, bellies saddled up to a bar—drive-by intimacy. At face value, this was a no-brainer: I had fallen for a sweet farm boy with an insatiable sex drive and a massive dick. But tangled in those blankets, we had more of a hostage-type situation, two mother-resenting terrorists taking each other prisoner, convinced we would never find a love like this again.

As Rens lay in my arms, I wondered how I could build a life—graduate school, success as an author—yoked to the trunk of a Dutch farm boy. Stroking his hair, I was mourning already a future that hadn't happened. Our love felt impossible. I could not summon the strength to tell him that I was leaving until the day before I boarded a tram for Schiphol Airport. When I abandoned him to return to my studies in Bath, I felt that my heart was still in the right place, but tiny now, cold.

• • •

TOWARD THE END OF the semester, G'mère fell sick. I rushed back
to the United States immediately after my exams. When I walked
into her hospital room, I barely recognized her emaciated figure. I
was expecting her to be delirious and incoherent, as my mother had
warned she might be. But when G'mère awakened to find me standing at the foot of her bed, she blinked her eyes and smiled widely. She
recognized me immediately. Always concerned for others, G'mère
asked, *"Comment s'est passé votre séjour à Londres?"*

Her smile, the upbeat question: I felt such relief. She was weath-
ering a minor sickness in this sterile clinic bed, I told myself, and
would be in her own by the week's end.

Just days later, G'mère died of a liver disease. Those were her last
words to me, in her proper French, "How was your sojourn to London?"

G'mère passed away on June 9, 1992. Days later, we buried her
in South Carolina, where she had joined Carmen and Pierre to live
after Sara and I had graduated from high school. It was hundreds of
miles from her homeland, to which she had never returned.

I cried at her funeral, but never again. I have not shed a single
tear, in public or private, in the decades since G'mère died.

Chapter 34

THE SUMMER THAT I GRADUATED FROM WESLEYAN, MY BEST friend, Leigh, and I hitched a ride with a mutual friend to New York City. With her shaggy hair, Leigh reminded me of Stevie Nicks. I discovered that summer that she could down whiskey late into the night, draw a small crowd to our bar booth with her magnetism. Leigh grew up in Baltimore by way of Alaska. She could thrive in city grit but also trap a pheasant and camp on a glacier. At first blush, we had nothing in common.

My move felt urgent, though long in the making. Ever since I'd secretly read about Capote in high school, I had bright fever dreams of living in New York. As our car drove into the city limits, I could see skyscrapers approaching like cocksure barcodes, teenagers bustling on sidewalks, women trilling Spanish under bodega awnings. Every part of me was famished for attainment. I swore my mouth tasted like hip-hop.

I was twenty-one. Not quite a starving artist in a garret, though full of a rebel's grit. I was so dumb and naive I didn't even know how much I didn't know.

Leigh found us, after weeks of searching, a massive loft in the East Village that was miraculously cheap. Our loft was a former Hungarian-dance studio above an independent movie theater. It had four iconic, massive windows lording over Second Avenue at Twelfth Street. We had no idea that it was where David Wojnarowicz, the legendary avant-garde artist, had lived and worked until just one year before. Wojnarowicz channeled Rimbaud in his life and shot some of his most unforgettable black-and-white self-portraits in the loft. Respected in the art world for his searing creative wit, his intense, transgressive paintings, photographs, and installations, Wojnarowicz had redefined protest art around the world, alongside his tribe of fellow East Village artists, Nan Goldin, Kiki Smith, and Peter Hujar.

In *One Day This Kid,* his signature, most iconic artwork, Wojnarowicz showed a grade-school portrait of himself. A collage caption surrounds him, a "normal"-looking nine-year-old boy: "One day this kid will talk." The piece castigates the social-political repression and antigay violence that strived to annihilate Wojnarowicz's freedoms, his self-worth, his life. And "when he begins to talk," the work vows, "men who develop a fear of this kid will attempt to silence him with strangling, fists, prison, suffocation, rape, intimidation, drugging, ropes, guns, laws, menace, roving gangs, bottles, knives, religion, decapitation, and immolation by fire."

After years of illness, Wojnarowicz had died of AIDS the year before we unpacked. A prominent member of ACT UP, Wojnarowicz had instructed friends to hang a huge banner from the loft's windows after his death and then to use that banner to lead his funeral procession: DAVID WOJNAROWICZ, 1954–1992, DIED OF AIDS DUE TO GOVERNMENT NEGLECT.

I was not aware that I was living in the iconoclastic artist's final home, but I was that kid. One day I would talk.

WE WERE CHUCKED FROM Wojnarowicz's loft two years later, thanks to a rent hike from the greedy landlord. A busted-up flat on the Lower East Side was all that I could afford next. The place was a changing, almost-hip neighborhood where I figured I'd never be bored. Leigh had found her place weeks earlier, on the very same block, Clinton Street, six buildings down. The day I moved in, the Dominican who tended bar below my apartment explained to me that the delis on my street were drug fronts.

I turned up to a neighborhood restaurant one night to have dinner with Leigh. The couple who lived next door to her decided to join us. Leaning over our food, the woman started to gag. "I feel sick," she said. "I feel sick." Leigh asked if her food was spoiled. I asked if she would be okay. Silence fell. The woman retched her dinner onto the table. "Oh," we said. The woman whispered, "I'm in withdrawal."

Their fingerprints still dusted the streets, Haring and Basquiat; they had not been dead that long. Downtown gnawed on their disquiet. Life on the Lower East Side was a discounted martini, filthy, filthy, filthy, bitter taste with a dash of dry chic. In Max Fish and the other ramshackle bars on Ludlow, where the straight boys writhed to Nine Inch Nails and could get a bag of dope quicker than they could get a cocktail, in the gay drinking holes where men got blow jobs, quick and dirty, behind black curtains, the worlds of literature and media and fashion and art and music collided, and in each introduction and each conversation and each space, people took measure of one another; fabulosity was based not on wealth but on personality, on moxie, on cleverness, on body type, on how large you could live on whatever little money you wrangled. If you had gone to Yale or worked at any job that concerned itself with counting money—accountant, banker, broker—forget it. If you were accountable to a balance sheet, even remotely, forget it. People on the Lower East Side were alive and hungry, predatory even, in a hurry to be somebody and to get places. Everyone was an understated carnival barker with a bluff. None debased themselves talking about accumulating or counting money, but all dreamed of living in their own kind of luxury. You did support the squatters who took over the crumbling buildings around Tompkins Square Park, you did understand why your friends refused to move to Brooklyn no matter how cheap the rent, but you weren't going to turn up to that art opening in Tribeca looking like who did it and why.

Heads were fogged all around—everyone was in debt or withdrawal. You spent your whole Saturday scrounging for bargains in the grimy thrift stores but didn't give a second thought to blowing hundreds on a new Vivienne Westwood shirt or the latest Prada shoe. This was when Prada was primitive and nihilistic art, graffiti for your feet—well before the Texas housewives and the Upper East Side matrons and the stockbrokers started to swaddle themselves in the stuff.

A new boy toy, Chris, and I returned from dancing at the Crowbar at an ungodly hour one night. The leaky windows in the corner of my derelict one-bedroom kept him and me shivering the next morning. We woke up cuddled under my comforter, trying to keep the fraying polyester covering our chafed heels. I peeked over the covers and did a quick catalog of the room. My jeans and tank top were strewn across the floor. My flask sat empty in a corner, its cap feet away. Chris's Tylenol lay tipped over on the nightstand. All the evidence of our late night felt so damning. I shut my eyes.

When we'd lumber out of bed, I would be the one, most days, to spy on the heroin addicts, yuppies copping in the alley beneath my bedroom window. Chris, meanwhile, would take what seemed like hours producing his news-anchor hair. He favored polo shirts and lived on the Upper East Side, where he dined out on salade Niçoise with the middle-aged gays. He had called my apartment "squalid," my sneakers "weird." Chris looked as if he'd stepped right out of somebody's country club, but when we'd met, I'd sniffed something brutish about him, something more alluring. The moment I'd met him on the dance floor, I let myself go passive, be dragged away, exhilarated by his double aura.

I came to discover how risqué in bed he was, far more experienced than I. It was almost always he who initiated sex. He grabbed me, threw me, slapped me, pinned me. That is how it went.

We'd have sweaty sex on the floor, then wage furious verbal skirmishes. We'd refuse to speak to each other for days, until something broke the ice, such as when he sent two dozen roses to my office, an apology the morning after he'd erupted in a fit of jealousy at a party in front of all our friends.

Chris and Leigh would never meet. Just as I never lumped the chicken onto the waffles, the peas onto the mashed potatoes, I kept my gay and straight friends separate.

· · ·

A BACKBENCH, NINE-TO-FIVE JOB, in the editorial department of
a company that published business journals nobody had heard of, is
all that I could finagle. Chris worked just a few blocks from me in
Midtown. He had a busy position managing operations for a company that transported automobiles around the world. I yearned to be
a writer; he counted and shipped cars.

I dreamed of writing a big literary work, my own *In Cold Blood*.
With each passing month, however, my ambitions sounded more
like delusion: what meager writing I had managed to submit in my
spare time to magazines was roundly rejected. Peddling slush essays,
playing nursemaid to Chris's ego, felt like thankless jobs. Meanwhile,
my paid job had me bored. It was all too much and too little.

My sea change came one April evening in 1994. That night, I
climbed the steps of St. John the Divine; the serenity of its Gothic
arches and stained-glass windows dazzled me. I was a shell walking,
empty, yearning for a sign. I was seeking a light to show me that my
dreams of writing had worth, and the rocket fuel to do the work. I
settled into a chair up front on the aisle near the stage. I had gotten
permission to leave work early so I could beat the crowds.

The cathedral soon spilled over with celebrants. Toni Morrison,
fresh from the Nobel ceremony, calmly walked onstage. Her appearance silenced the crowd. The cathedral, one of the five largest in the
world, was at capacity, a testament to her popularity. She stood bone
still, gave a short reading, delivered a glorious talk, and answered
questions from the audience. Afterward she collected her papers
from the podium, and I felt slipping from me my only chance to
meet the writer whose life and words I idolized. She made her way
to the stage door; I bounded in that direction to intercept her. I told
her what she meant to me and, fingers shaking, handed her my copy
of *Beloved*. I asked her to sign it.

She shook her head no, politely but firmly, and walked right
past me.

I couldn't rid the slight from my head. Trudging to the subway headed to work the next morning, my soft Walkman headphones cosseting my cold ears, fists shoved into my trench peacoat pockets, it became clear to me: if I stayed in the East Village, I'd wake up—twenty? thirty?—years later, living in a cramped walk-up, decorating a barstool like the dour middle-aged men who preyed on me at the Boiler Room. Thinking of my teenage days mopping floors at Popeyes, hearing the barflies yammer about the state of art, never having created it, I realized I needed to move on. I had a dream of California, where I could hug the sun, the ocean, the humanities, a different crop of boys. Where I could swindle the time and space to write. I decided to apply to graduate school. When I sat to take the admissions test, my internal voice, sounding just like my mother, · said, "Don't fuck this up."

I WAS LYING IN BED with Chris months later when he whispered in my ear, "I love you." That afternoon I told him that I was moving on. He pushed to know why, but I stuck to my stated reason: I had decided to go to California for graduate school. We fought bitterly that night.

Telling Chris that I was headed to Stanford was factually true, but spiritually dishonest. I could not summon the words to explain my departure. I had grown to hate him and myself. I was terrified of stagnating, desperate to prove myself. I was a sadomasochist for challenge, for discomfort. I fucked and argued acidly with this prickly creature, incapable of grasping that half the problem was me. I wasn't able to tell Chris that I did not love him or to kiss him to soothe his upset. All I could do was pour him another drink and leave the room.

Chapter 35

————

OPEN LAWNS STRETCHED ACROSS THE LANDSCAPE. NOT FAR away, closed gardens hid in the most unlikely spaces. Bubble-gum pink roses, Japanese pagodas, and sycamores decorated the intimate footpaths, palm trees swayed along the grand avenues. Above the footpaths leading to the courtyards, sandstone arches stood in formation. So many Spanish-tile roofs sprawled one after the other that I confused the plazas, the buildings around them. Everything at Stanford looked harmonized—so landscaped, so patterned, so recurrent—that I regularly got lost. I'd think I was in one garden, one department, only to discover, in delight, that I was somewhere else entirely.

I discovered extraordinary people against this backdrop. When I first saw Diane Middlebrook bound across the quad—her long legs punctuated by red knee-high leather boots, and a smartly cut leather jacket fitted to her frame—I gaped.

Diane, I would learn, was a campus legend, celebrated for her riveting, authoritative biography of Anne Sexton, a *New York Times* bestseller. She wrote nakedly about Sexton's masturbation, menstruation, drug abuse, incest, and hidden sexual affairs. The biography caused an uproar for quoting the tape-recorded therapy sessions between the suicidal poet and her psychiatrist.

Stanford offered me an irresistible chance one semester to co-teach a class with Diane, called the Literature of Transformation. We focused on instances in classic works where characters and situations transform, as well as how each classic had changed the

Western canon: Milton's *Paradise Lost*, Eliot's *Waste Land*, Woolf's *Orlando*, Hurston's *Their Eyes Were Watching God*. We helped students see how writings revamp one another, how reality refashions letters, how books alter lives.

My other main mentor at Stanford was Tim Lenoir, one of the preeminent historians of science and technology, something I knew nothing about but was fascinated to learn. Tim and I worked side by side in an emergent, exciting spin-off subfield, the digital humanities, where the technical and human sciences converge. The university was getting baptized by its surroundings, and Silicon Valley was getting regenerated by the campus, and Tim inspired me to dive into the thick of it all.

At Tim's prodding, I decided to take a graduate seminar in computer science, hoping to gain some insight into the architecture of storytelling by studying the architecture of software. Four weeks in, the class, Computer Science 378, Phenomenological Foundations of Cognition, Language and Computation, was bedeviling me, so I crept into the professor's office hours to get extra help. After explaining an assignment to me—for the third time—Professor Terry Winograd scooted his chair to his desktop computer and said, "Here. Let me show you. There's this new project I'm developing with my master's advisees, Larry and Sergey." I marveled at the cute candy letters that popped onto his screen: *Google*. Packing my book bag to leave, I couldn't understand, for the life of me, why the general public would want a "search engine," but the long-standing homework sure made more sense.

I found time too to take a class in the law school on speech, identity, and the law taught by Judith Butler. A gender-nonconforming white lesbian, Butler was the most renowned philosopher in the United States and Europe. Their book *Gender Trouble* had detonated traditional feminism, ravaged the concept of compulsory heterosexuality, and launched queer studies and queer theory. They were an extraordinary professor, who helped me revise my master's thesis into a published paper. Like Diane and Tim, Judith sat with me for hours to explain how they'd wrestled with their original discipline, in Butler's case philosophy, and how they'd forged new work, defied their fields. Observing them, I learned how little use they had for borders; they were teaching me not to imprison myself by other people's categories, nor to limit my mind to narrow, parochial academic debates.

Disciplinary boundaries, identity boxes, divisions between technology and art, moats between scholars and the public, borders between nations: I had no interest in any of them. How to do original, relevant, big: in their own dynamic ways, all three of my mentors were raising me to be a renegade. Each was teaching me how not to think or play by the rules in some of the most prestigious, rule-bound settings. Were it not for them, I would never have developed my love to *épater les bourgeois,* to challenge the Establishment even as I was entering it.

BURIED IN TEACHING and research, I faded away from Marcelle, Couscous, and Sara, and they slipped away from me. Their distant, busy lives, like mine, kept us in casual touch: Marcelle toiled as a young criminal defense attorney in Philadelphia; Sara worked at an architectural firm in DC; and Couscous worked at a small software company in Virginia.

For a while, I didn't notice the distance that had grown between me and my family; not until Palo Alto police officers came banging on my front door. A woman had reported "Richard Benjamin" missing. After one officer verified my driver's license, both of their faces relaxed with relief. They had located me, the missing person thought to be dead.

Who is this woman? I asked the police, caught up in the mystery, suddenly concerned that I was somehow not safe. One cop rifled through his notepad.

Danielle Benjamin, he said. Through his bedroom door, I could hear my roommate laughing.

The second the officers left, I phoned my mother and screamed at her. You haven't returned my phone calls for three weeks, she yelled back. She was correct, I realized. I'd been so lost in my books that I hadn't even considered my family might feel abandoned.

As far, as emphatically, as I had migrated away from my mother, her influence was kneading me undetected. She had always taught me that the best mentors come in all shapes and sizes, all genders and colors, all fields of knowledge, and never to be so provincial as to restrict my circles to people who look or think like me. She never sat me down to explain this; the lesson was in her life. I unwittingly witnessed, over time, the dazzling array of people, from Latin America to Asia, whom she learned from, and the people she took pains to mentor.

She taught me that I would learn the most when I was most uncomfortable. Education is meant to upset you, she said. And if it doesn't make you uncomfortable, you can't possibly be learning much. There is no such thing as a safe space.

My grandparents had made punishing sacrifices to learn, then put their lives at risk to teach. In my family, education has, by definition, always been dangerous. It is meant to be threatening in a braided, double sense: learning is meant to make you feel unsafe, and once you are learned, you are meant to make others unsafe. The purpose of an education is to upend received wisdom and to challenge authority.

These are the stakes of our lives: Education is power. Knowledge is freedom. No matter the prison someone aims to lock us in, we are never captive when we have a cultivated mind.

OF COURSE I MADE TIME for more than studying. Dreamers, thinkers, painters, pro skateboarders: someone was always having a house party in San Francisco. One night, I had a fling with a guy, so flirtatious, who caught my eye at a roof-deck party with his quick smile, sense of rhythm, and gift for conversation. I lay in his bed hours later, the sun rising. Getting dressed on mornings such as these, every postcoital cough, every sore throat, every muscle ache, every fever, every abrasion on my chest sent me down a spiral of shame, wondering who was going to treat the AIDS I was sure I'd just contracted.

I saw no choice other than to confront my paranoia, my shame. I searched for hematologists at Stanford Medical School, which had one of the top departments in the country. I fired off emails to the school's best blood experts with pointed questions about HIV transmission. I wanted precise data points, the exact digits to pinpoint the risk level of my recent trysts, of this and that act, of such and such bodily fluid. The few replies I received did not satisfy me. Science understands broadly the approximate risk associated to some actions, a doctor typically wrote, but I'm not going to delineate over email the infection probabilities of your night on the town.

So I begged and browbeat one of the country's premier hematologists to see me in person. The pretext I gave was my sickle cell anemia, but once I'd settled into his exam room, I spilled my secrets. Afterward, I immediately felt naked, wanted to take them back. If only the expert would talk me down from the ledge. Instead, he listened to everything I had to say in silence. Then the white man with his white hair in his white lab coat wearing his golden wedding ring looked me dead in the eyes.

"Just don't get AIDS," he said. "Not with your sickle cell anemia. It will kill you."

He walked out of the room.

For the first time ever, I was spooked into getting an HIV test. I arrived to the student health center, hoping not to run into classmates. The nurse drew my blood. She instructed me to make a follow-up appointment for three weeks later, the standard waiting period for results.

Not so long after my test, my mother caught wind from my sisters that I was gay, even after I had asked them not to tell her. Rather than talk to me or express love for me, my mother mailed me an article that she'd clipped from *The New York Times*: "HIV Rates Spiking Among Young Gay Men of Color."

Around that time, she was overseeing, to her UN peers' acclaim, scientifically advanced, culturally nuanced HIV-prevention campaigns around the world. But behind closed doors, her attitude was clear: "It's not rocket science how HIV is transmitted. Don't you dare come to me with AIDS. Educated people don't do dumb things."

IN THOSE YEARS, I was getting two kinds of education. Every break from school that I could, I parachuted back to New York, to a place called the Cock.

I remember one night when Joe and Bobby, my running buddies, leaned in and inhaled a pile of blow each from the blade of my apartment key. We licked the key's teeth and ridges to get every last bit. I could smell the drug's odor—metallic and briny. I tore a square of toilet paper, licked it, and dabbed at my nose for any lingering white dust. The last time the bouncer saw coke caked on my face, a few weeks before, he'd chucked me to the sidewalk. I started to put the bag of blow in my jeans pocket, but Bobby snatched it. He was the one who'd paid for it.

We returned to the dance floor, and then it came, that clean, lustrous something, as if I could leap off the Empire State Building, soar over the city, glide back, slowly, slowly, my feet on the dance floor. The blow let off a small bomb in my head. It demolished the detritus of my worries, cleared my brain of its confusions, its messy residue. Elated, I danced, bodies brushed against me. Boxed, tight, low ceilinged: the Cock was smaller than a rich lady's parlor.

A few hip-hop anthems later, we snorted another line in the bathroom and returned to the dance floor to groove. We admired the go-go boys as they leapt onto the bar and gyrated. They did so slowly, all the sexier; it was the rookies who danced too fast, like twitching firecrackers, duds that never explode. Bobby hadn't noticed that this time I'd managed to swipe the blow he'd purchased and put it in my pocket. I loved the jeans because they had a small discreet insert on the front right hip, just under the belt loop, perfectly sized to stash a dime bag. My uniform that year was a white Hanes undershirt and this simple pair of jeans, Dolce & Gabbana, which I had been thrilled to discover on sale for four hundred dollars in Berlin at the KaDeWe.

Most nights I checked myself in the mirror before I left the house. It was then, at the sight of my clenched face, that I could feel a jolt of longing shoot straight through me. My secrets were conspiring. I tried to focus on the night's promise and ignore my dread. I resented that Bobby didn't seem to need the coke the way I did. When he readied himself to go out, I doubt he felt his chest racing with my kind of anticipation—the desire to be swallowed by a euphoria that wouldn't come crashing down on my head. My cravings would battle my judgment all night. I pretended not to know which was going to win as I locked the apartment door.

The Cock specialized in dissolving the shame. The mood dissipated a whole history of our sexuality being negated or policed. As though Debbie Harry's lusting alto could summon from the dead the rent boys and drag queens who had consumed one another on the West Side piers. We were transported to the hot, thick summer nights when sex did not equal death, vintage seventies eroticism.

Tonight, every night, was its own special moment of utter glee. We could lick the coke flakes off each other's nostrils, dance on the bar with our pants off. No one worried about finding himself on the internet. There were no smartphones, so nobody could photograph someone's dick hanging out of his zipper, or his bare ass stuffed with a straw transporting coke. No one had their nose glued to a screen. We were fabulous when we were fabulous, and when we dressed up, we did it for ourselves, for one another. Everything was communal, exclusive, not broadcast and needy for likes.

Not everyone treasured the place. The city had raided the Cock numerous times—for noise complaints, flagrant drug use, public nudity, you name it. Mayor Giuliani was targeting the queer spaces, the racially integrated spaces, the creative spaces. The Cock tendered a grand fuck-you to "America's Mayor," to what he was doing to homogenize and "clean up" our city. Giuliani knew the owner, Mario Lopez, by name. Mario had to pay a lot of big fines to the city to keep the place going.

The Cock was the 1990s answer to Studio 54. It was the couture people, a coterie of artists, the musicians, and film directors. Almodóvar and Waters turned out on occasion. The downtown girls showed up, like Chloë Sevigny and Christina Aguilera, before she became a household name. You had the fashionistas like Alexander McQueen and David LaChapelle. Calvin Klein hung out quite a bit. Sometimes an aspiring pop princess from the piney woods of Louisiana came and danced with her male stylist. She was called Britney Spears. Laverne Cox and Honey Dijon reveled as genderbended queers. Amanda Lepore and Sophia Lamar performed. And you could hear Rufus Wainwright laugh, his voice braying like a tweaking horse. You had the hospitality kids—waiters, barbacks, dishwashers—toiling, stupendous queers who traded their soiled work clothes for glam, who took the partying to the next level. A smattering of straight boys turned up also, beautiful urchins, dirty ingenues. They came to the East Village from everywhere, from the Yakima Valley to the Mississippi Delta, to make a way out of no way. We all languished together into the wee hours like a beautiful chest of broken toys.

My poor, dear mother. Honestly. To her, assimilation to America meant excellent English and mastery of a profession. To me, apparently, it meant balancing lines off the smooth ridge of a go-go boy's stiff cock, then sniffing them away.

EMERGING FROM THE COCK as sunrise cast shadows on hard asphalt, I felt resigned to death. Aging was past my imagining. Growing up, I had no gay role models or gay father figures. The ones who could have welcomed me into adulthood had died of AIDS. My tribe was taunted by government, by Hollywood, by tabloids, by doctors, by our parents. We would not live to see forty, they said. The fear of getting AIDS became an identity itself. We did not save money, buy property, or emotionally mature, believing that one or both partners would be damned to premature decay. So why not conflagrate the candle from both ends?

I lurched in these years between Silicon Valley and the East Village. I plunged myself more deeply into work; I became a serf to King Hedonism. Alongside the sages, the company of rakes consoled me. I wanted badly to soothe my loneliness with surrogate approval, companionship, and family in the most elevated and sordid places. I had so much not to tell my mother. I seethed that she had no idea how badly I was struggling, tunneling between these worlds.

Passed out after a night
at the Cock

Chapter 36

THE JAIL CELL FILLED WITH THE STENCH OF URINE, WHICH still couldn't cover the stink of shit. A short, squat latrine sat off to the side, no toilet paper around anywhere. One man, black, lay propped against the baseboard, snoring. Another sat with his head between his knees in the corner. Another leaned against a wall, eyeing the toilet, as if deciding if he dared use it. The fourth black man was me.

Like most people arrested in Manhattan, I'd been brought to Central Booking downtown, a kind of feeder jail for the whole island. I entered the austere granite tower handcuffed, flanked by two cops. Deep in the labyrinth of underground holding cells known as the Tombs, the guards had shoved me into a cell and slammed the hulking, bulletproof metal door shut. A small transom-like window was embedded in the door. I noticed a two-way camera above the door and decided to install myself right under it. That way I could monitor the guards as they monitored me.

The core of a depleted toilet roll lay crushed on the cement floor. Flecks of tissue paper crusted the latrine bowl. A sheet of paint—or was it plaster?—peeled off the wall, dangling precariously.

Being caged with three older homeboys, gruff and manly, was not the most comfortable place to find myself. My sheer green silk shirt, still clinging to my sweaty body, and my tight jeans, the outfit I'd worn to the Roxy the night before, amounted to a bull's-eye. My tongue felt like a dead eel. I licked the insides of my cheeks and wondered when and how I could get fresh water. I needed to rinse the taste of nightlife from my mouth. From the corner of my eye, I saw my jailmate undo his pants button. I didn't think it would happen, but it did. The man pulled down his dirty jeans, squatted, and took a crap in front of us.

I hadn't slept in forty-eight hours. Even so, I found myself captive to the addict's chatter in my head. I was in withdrawal, unable to stop an onslaught of memories.

I had done so many damn-fool things. There was the summer of 1999 in San Francisco when I went home drunk with a man, another Chris, and couldn't quit him, even though I lived in that city, he in Las Vegas. We drove to Silicon Valley to drop acid at a Phish concert one weekend and, weeks later, got arrested for disorderly conduct while gambling on the Strip.

There was the turn of the millennium; I celebrated with eight friends in Paris. On New Year's Eve, we put on shiny clothes and went to the esplanade in front of the Eiffel Tower. Fireworks erupted from the landmark—vertically, horizontally, every which way. Parisians, notoriously standoffish, were kissing strangers good luck in the streets. We slithered on from a nightclub into Le Depot, a sex club, where we saw an icon of world fashion, sitting in front of a mound of cocaine as a boy toy sucked him off. At the time it seemed sublime.

Then the time my party buddy and I asked a gorgeous straight drug dealer to trade a significant purchase from us for a nice romp in the sack with him. He agreed. We took him all the way to the Upper East Side; by the time we stepped through the door, our craving for coke had vanished but our thirst for the dealer had not. We changed our mind about the coke, we told him, but we will still have you. The dealer shook his head. Give me my money, he said. I shook my head too. He walked to the kitchen and rifled through the drawers. He took out one of those big carving knives made to cut a raw tenderloin or a holiday turkey. He calmly put me in a headlock and put the point of the knife on my jugular. Don't, my buddy blurted. This is my uncle's apartment. Holding my neck still, I could see, from the corner of my left eye, the blade, a massive, shining triangle. I don't care if you do my drugs or not, said the dealer, but you have one minute to give me my money. We did. He left without another word.

There was the night only four weeks earlier when I went to the Democratic National Convention in Boston and finagled an invitation to a booze cruise of political donors sailing the Charles River. That night, I had a prime ticket to the proceedings. I missed the keynote of a new, rising superstar, one Barack Obama, because I was shit-faced somewhere near the riverbank.

My toxic antics had built up to this night. My limbs dropped in lethargy, smarted in anemic pain. I looked again at the security camera monitoring the cell, then through the small window to the outside. I was certain I would not leave the Tombs alive.

IT WILL ALWAYS PUNISH ME, the memory of how I landed in that jail cell. I've spent the balance of my life trying to forget, but sometimes a dance track, a silk party shirt, word of a police shooting, will resurrect the debacle. Two decades later, I was able to track down the dossier of the smart, capable Legal Aid lawyer who ultimately represented me. Laura meticulously investigated the episode and the crime scene and took copious notes, which I located in the Legal Aid Society's archive. A gadfly who has been told his whole life, "You sure have a terrific memory," and a scholar trained to extract documents from the obscure case files of self-protective, top-down institutions, I've now accrued several versions of what happened that night: the NYPD's, the Manhattan district attorney's, the Legal Aid Society's. This is mine:

The Roxy had three dance floors—one with house music, one with hip-hop, and a top-floor lounge with disco. That night, all three felt too crowded with other people's stale, exhaled breath. I was at that point in a night when I felt everything has been used up: the euphoria, the drugs, the best songs, and especially the air. Sweat drenching my face and body, I walked out into the dark.

Sauntering along West Eighteenth Street, I inhaled. I stopped to look at the naked sky. Like a lodestar, the dashboard of a parked vehicle caught my attention. It was the instrument panel that held my interest, inside a brand-new Mercedes sports utility vehicle. Lights, shapes, meters, glowed in a psychedelic luster. I poked my head closer to the driver's seat window and spotted another bright bauble—silver keys in the ignition. The vehicle hummed so quietly that I didn't immediately notice that it was running.

The sparkling dashboard hypnotized me. I wanted to sit on the soft leather seats. I was a fool transfixed, lusting for space, wanting to caress the keys to the spaceship. Wanting to escape myself.

Without much thought, I opened the door. I took one big step and climbed in. I shimmied my hips on the soft leather, leaned in to inspect the music selection. Then I heard the doors swing open.

Jumbles of palms and fingers gripped me by the collar of my shirt and yanked me from the driver's seat. I flew out of the car clutched by fists and was thrown onto the pavement. "I will kill you," a voice said from above. Looking up from the sidewalk, I saw three young men hovering over me. Their pupils were hard, null with rage. Soon sneakers slammed my ribs. Fists crashed my head. My cheek pulsed against the cool asphalt.

I remember those hands on me, being pulled from the car, slammed to the ground. I recall noticing how hot the Complaining Witness was, a black man perhaps two or three years younger than me. It's disturbing to appreciate how gorgeous a man is as he punches you.

I held my breath. I would not give the attackers the satisfaction of seeing me cry. I needed a plan. Either I made it back to the Roxy or I would be taken away in a body bag. I imagined myself in a *New York Post* story, one of those casualties exposed in a front-page mug shot, the tawdry scare-head announcing VICTIM KILLED OUTSIDE NIGHTCLUB. It occurred to me how thoroughly it would embarrass my mother for the rest of her life if I died in this way.

I collected all my force and found my feet underneath me. Making myself as small as I could, compact like a skier, I did a kind of crouch-run back to the Roxy. "Those guys are beating on me," I said to the bouncer, flashing him my wristband. "I'm coming back in."

For what seemed like a couple of hours after, I felt invincible, certain that those three tough guys would not annihilate me after all. All I could think to do was to order another drink. And then just another to polish off the edge.

When I emerged from the club again, it was into broad daylight. I was ready for my bed. I wished I had sunglasses. Suddenly I noticed people milling around a police cruiser and its two officers. Intrigued, I went to see what the fuss was about. Before I could ask someone what was going on, I heard a voice: "That's him! That's the one who tried to steal my Mercedes."

I recognized the face immediately—the guy who had pummeled me. "That's him!" Before I knew it, two cops had stolen a position behind me, jimmied my thin arms from my side to behind my back, and slammed me onto the hood of their cruiser. They slapped handcuffs on my wrists. "That's too tight," I shouted. "Totally unnecessary. Take it off." They ignored my words and shoved me into the back of the car. As we drove through Chelsea, the ten-minute distance from the Roxy to the precinct station, I hunched, chin to my neck, praying that none of the people out getting brunch or taking a walk that Sunday morning would see me.

On at least one point, all four versions of the event—the NYPD's, the district attorney's, the Legal Aid lawyer's, and mine—corroborate one another: I refused to be fingerprinted. I would not allow any cop to force me to submit my biometrics into the Matrix.

My wits held up under confinement; my body did not. My chest, legs, and back felt as if tiny ice picks were shanking them, the sharp, unmistakable agony from their starvation of fluid and oxygen. The zings were lightning announcing a thunderstorm. The pain pelting my legs and back was a telltale sign of a coming sickle cell crisis. The ache came so suddenly and ferociously, I could tell it was not that routine, low-grade pain that I endured about once a month.

I would not let myself die in a dirty cell. I asked the supervising cop to send me to the hospital to treat my sickle cell anemia. You're making things up, he said, not taking his eyes off his broadsheet newspaper. I started shouting to see a doctor. The cop rolled his eyes. After more noise from me, finally he folded his paper and hoisted his legs off his desk. He ordered two rookies to take me to Bellevue Hospital.

I have no recollection of sirens, traffic, a sliding-glass entrance. The only thing I recall, and distinctly, is trying to answer the emergency room staff's questions as best I could, which was difficult, since my left ankle and left wrist were shackled to the hospital gurney in NYPD's steel manacles. I was befuddled answering medical questions, degraded explaining myself as a spectacle.

Handcuff pinch, swelling bruises, congealing blood, dried-out veins. Despite the pain, my blood crisis carried an unexpected silver lining: the ER staff inadvertently provided the court confirmation that I had endured a beating. None of the police or DA records acknowledged the beating, or my hospitalization. Only my Legal Aid lawyer's notes do. My accuser had lied to the police and to the assistant district attorney, denying that he'd assaulted me, but my hospital visit documented my injuries in vivid detail.

Studying the doctor's verbatim notes, one fact now alarms me: that I asked the doctor to discharge me against his medical advice, even though I was "mentally alert" and could understand the risks he'd explained: "hypoxia, pneumonia, painful chest syndrome, brain damage, and death."

To this day, my calculation makes sense. The shame and duress of my police custody exceeded my bodily pain. Being shackled to a hospital bed at high noon during an August weekend as cops muttered things about me that I could not discern felt humiliating, distressing; the custody seemed more hazardous than the medical crisis. I decided that trying to end this police ordeal was more urgent than receiving oxygen and fluids from the attending physician, Dr. Nguyen.

I will kill you. That is what the Accuser had told me at roughly 6:11 a.m., according to the sealed record. *I'll keep you here till Christmas if I want to.* That is what the cop had told me at roughly 7:33.

In 2021, *The New York Times* reviewed more than six thousand pages of records concerning the deaths of black people in police cus-

tody in which sickle cell was raised as a cause or contributing factor
of death. They found that the genetic trait was cited in forty-seven
police custody deaths over the twenty-five years prior.

It pains me to discover how little regard everyone, including me,
had for my life, with the exception of Dr. Nguyen.

ALMOST HALF A YEAR after that night, my case was dismissed.
The plaintiff, according to the district attorney's notes, didn't honor
multiple meeting requests from her office. He didn't turn up to my
arraignment or follow up on his accusation. He was a young man
driving a brand-new gold Mercedes SUV late at night in a party district. I believe he may have been hiding something himself.

I HAVE BEEN BEATEN my whole life. The physical pain I could ignore.
That three black men, all seemingly my age, had thrashed me, aches,
as does the violence and social separation they put between us.

Those boys' eyes shone a blank black not unlike my cousin's once
had. The gulf dividing them from me was as boundless as the chasm
disjoining my cousin's life from mine. Philippe spent the same
years in prison that I spent in college. It was July 1989 that Philippe
arrived at the Franklin Correctional Facility in upstate New York; I
unpacked my belongings in my freshman dorm not long after. He
left the medium-to-maximum-security prison, completing his sentence, four and a half years later, just as I graduated and moved to
New York City. Philippe and I overlapped at opposite way stations
in the respective life maps of black boys. I adored him, and Uncle
Bernard, but never in a million years, not ever, would I have connected their battles with liquor and crack to my epic nights in gay
Manhattan. I picture Philippe, beautiful, proud, hands chained by
Reagan's America, a regime of terror that deemed whole populations
obsolete, unprofitable—disposable. When the system reduced black
and brown bodies to prison ID numbers, it never had to account
for their humanity. In that cell I worried for the first time ever that I

could become just a state numeral, my life reduced to a "black men in America" statistic, my future canceled by the juridical-industrial complex.

I spent more than ten hours in police custody, including the hospital visit. Cops arrested me outside the Roxy at 7:06 in the morning and brought me to the local precinct station. There, a cop took my mug shot. The hospital admitted me a few hours later, at 11:33, and released me at 4:40 that afternoon, when a cop drove me, shackled, back to the Chelsea precinct station. Cops transported me from the precinct station to Central Booking downtown at 5:32. Squishing in my lace-less shoes and glancing at the latrine, piled with more shit, I was certain that I had been in the Tombs for at least three days. In fact, Central Booking released me at 5:56. Despite my reflection, my nightmares stirred by withdrawal, time elapsed in this cell: twenty-four minutes, not days.

Only now, looking back, do I feel a fresh embarrassment: for protesting against a tyrannical government, my grandfather was imprisoned in solitary confinement for three months. For coke-fueled shenanigans, I was in police custody for ten hours.

How had it come to this?

Glaring at the jail guards from inside the cell, I felt keenly the pain and comedy of my position in America. Since leaving Tuckerman Lane for college, I'd been a consummate insider-outsider. I have enjoyed advantage and I have endured exclusion. We insiders know power, understand privilege more closely than those relegated to the outside. We outsiders endure turmoil because we refuse to follow the rules. The political system and our incendiary character defects keep us on the outskirts.

Mine was a reverse Horatio Alger story. I was born a creature of the Establishment, occupying the center, only to discover how viciously the margins, my family's untreated wounds, crept up on me.

Chapter 37

NOT LONG AFTER I WALKED FREE FROM THE TOMBS, SARA called with good news: she was about to deliver her first baby. An untrained ear would say she sounded ebullient, but I could hear the nerves in my twin's voice.

I hung up thrilled, fully intending to organize myself to get to DC—then forgot about the call. Days later, I received another, this time from my big sister, Marcelle: Sara had just delivered. I packed my duffel bag and awoke early the next morning with the determination of a man living out his best intentions. I arrived to Penn Station well before the train's departure hour, and it took off bright and early. Watching the mid-Atlantic suburbscape streak across the window, I felt proud. I was on track to show up for Sara, to share in this momentous occasion.

Arriving to DC, I took a cab to the apartment of an old college classmate. My friend and I had years to catch up on; we went out for a reunion dinner. I will go to bed early tonight, I told myself, inspecting the menu, to show up for Sara fresh, first thing tomorrow. But hours later, my friend and I were well into a prodigious bender that lasted all night. I awoke with a splitting headache, only to notice the midday light streaming through the curtains. I lurched up, threw on clothes, and rushed to the hospital in a taxicab.

I darted into the lobby and wondered, Where did I put Sara's room number? I realized I had not bought my twin a gift. The souvenir shop looked bare and my head throbbed; I snatched the best gift I could find and slipped the cashier ten dollars.

Sara's eyes widened with joy when she saw my face at the door of her room. Her newborn slept on her chest. I gave Sara a kiss and handed her the gift: a stuffed animal with a midriff crop top saying HAPPY BIRTHDAY!

Sara looked the thing over.

"Oh. You didn't have to. Thank you." She managed a smile.

Pops sat in the room's comfortable recliner. Sara's husband, Marcelle, and Mommy stood near her bed. My mother said nothing as I hugged Sara. Marcelle looked at me curiously. It felt to me as if both were holding their tongues to keep from commenting on my mangy entrance.

But Pops saw the gift and started to laugh. He laughed so hard his head and shoulders shook. I'm sure he found my gift ridiculous, but at least some of his outburst seemed to stem from the brain condition that was taking hold following a stroke he'd had seven years earlier.

"Shut up, Edouard!" Mommy hissed.

He only laughed harder.

I could barely look at Sara. The polyester birthday bear lay on the blanket, its crooked plastic-button eyes staring into nowhere.

TO MY SURPRISE, Sara named me the godfather to her firstborn, Jacqueline. Not long after, Leigh, coincidentally, named me godfather to her firstborn, Will, too.

Becoming a godfather is something I'd never thought to want. A godfather is not just a proxy legal guardian for a child; he is a lifelong friend and spiritual mentor. I wanted Jacqueline and Will to have childhoods free of emotional bloodshed.

The years I've spent playing with Jacqueline on Christmas mornings, or the annual birthday lunch I enjoy with Will, sledding afterward in Central Park, are gifts to the soul that no one quite intended, a surprise experience of grace. Recovery hides in places where I don't even know I want to go. These children forced me to look at myself with a ruthless honesty I never had before.

That is how I was then. I am not like that now.

Chapter 38

I WAS CLOSING OUT MY TEN-HOUR WORKDAY AT A THINK TANK that advocates for a more equitable economy in America and a better-functioning democracy. I had fought for regulators to put guardrails on Wall Street avarice, for states to increase black access to ballot boxes, for cities to combat police brutality. I had rallied to increase the federal minimum wage and against anti-black racism, in swelling movements that would soon become the Fight for Fifteen campaign and Black Lives Matter. I had just returned from touring my first book, on the growing politics of fear in America, and tasks had piled up in my office. I gathered the belongings scattered across my cluttered desk and put them in my bag. As I walked to the elevator, I caught a glimpse of the news on the large flat-screen TV pinned above the reception desk. At the word "Haiti," my body clenched. I braced myself to hear of a miracle or a catastrophe—the only ways America talks about that country.

No one could possibly have been prepared for the images that appeared: an earthquake had leveled the capital, damage far beyond anything most Americans had ever seen. Voices from those desperate for aid resounded in my ears. I looked at the noble faces, creased with resolve to help their neighbors, the faces appealing for comfort, faces that held my concern, unlike the ones I'd tuned out as a child: boat people bobbing in dinghies off Florida's coast.

The news flashed images of one damaged building after another. The presidential palace lay in ruins, its stately columns buckled, its white dome cratered. The central pavilion, main hall, and ornate

staircase collapsed into a cloud of dust. The building that my grandfather had occupied, a heap of debris. Decimated icon of a disremembered man.

An aide-mémoire without warning or logic: the news was like a
long-lost relative appearing on my doorstep. Not looking became
untenable. The next day, I watched survivors, haunted and haunting,
pleading at me from YouTube and Flickr, as though to say, *Who will
be our witness?* The worst earthquake in the Western Hemisphere
in over two hundred years, killing three hundred thousand people,
made recognition urgent. To continue my indifference toward this
country and my Haitian blood suddenly felt like a dereliction of my
humanity.

I was ready to amend my future. The moment was ripe for me
to understand what about my family's past undercut my present,
my ability to have a richer, more honest emotional life. Something
would always be off in any relationship I had until I got that first,
primal one straight.

I packed my bags for Haiti.

HAITI'S GOVERNMENT was in disarray. Some 30 percent of civil servants had died in the earthquake. Gun violence and kidnappings
spread amid the shambles. The U.S. State Department advised pro-
spective travelers to postpone their visits or to buy evacuation insurance. Two days before my scheduled flight, the eye of Hurricane
Tomas just missed the island, though torrential rains soaked the
roughly 1.3 million displaced people lucky enough to have survived
the earthquake. The flooding and turmoil exacerbated a two-week-
old cholera epidemic that was already ravaging the population.
Lacking housing, clean water, garbage removal, medical clinics, and
civil servants, the country stood in paralysis.

When I announced to my mother that I was visiting Haiti, she
begged me not to go.

I would not be deterred. Before leaving, I made appointments
at Haiti's two major national archives, so that I could inspect every

document, every object, concerning my grandfather. I hoped to catalog and study every frame of film footage capturing Daniel, every recording of his voice, in addition to ferreting out his belongings. I tracked down the addresses of two grizzled old men who had worked for him. I couldn't locate their phone numbers, so I planned to drop in on them unannounced at their homes, where I would plead for an audience. I also arranged to volunteer at a makeshift medical clinic in Cité Soleil, one of the poorest neighborhoods in the capital. I wanted to contribute whatever I could while I was there.

The night before I left, I telephoned Mommy to say goodbye.

"What time is your flight?"

"Tomorrow afternoon."

"What suit will you be wearing?"

"There'll be no suit. I'm wearing cargo shorts and a T-shirt."

"You have to wear at least a tie!" she shrieked. "You're a professor!"

I would soon land in Port-au-Prince amid an earthquake recovery, a cholera epidemic, election turbulence, and posthurricane flooding, and what my mother was concerned with was how I would come off to strangers. She said that people with my credentials had to look right.

THE JET TOUCHED DOWN in Port-au-Prince. Collecting my bags proved difficult; the baggage carousel was crowded with people kissing cheeks, dispensing hugs, bumping hips. Arriving to an airport in a European capital had always struck me as a sterile affair, marked by order and the hosts' suspicion of black and brown travelers. But when I arrived to Dakar, to Havana, and to Port-au-Prince, the arrival gates were warm and raucous—the people welcoming their returning diaspora.

Stepping out of the airport, I heard a band blare its own taste of calypso to greet the arriving travelers. I slipped five dollars into the trumpeter's upside-down hat. The passengers on the plane had spoken English and French, but as soon as I stepped out of the airport, the hard edges of Kreyòl's clacking flooded my ears. The melody, the inflection of G'mère's voice, rang all around. Thoughts of her overwhelmed me. She was everywhere.

I arrived to Port-au-Prince prepared professionally, not emotionally.

Honor?

Respect.

ON TOP OF THE earthquake recovery, epidemic, and flood damage, Haiti was also approaching a charged Election Day. It was only the third presidential election in the nation's 206-year history—not surprising, given how long colonial puppet presidents and the Duvaliers had monopolized power.

Gunshots disrupted the dark silence. In my small room in the Coconut Hotel, I could smell gunpowder and smoke. It was a few nights after I'd arrived. I sat up in bed and peeked out the window. It was a shabby place, a motel-style building surrounded by outdoor walkways, like a strip-mall Howard Johnson's. My bedroom door led directly into the night. A brown metal security gate stood between me and the street.

More gunshots.

An instant later, Ben, an American friend living in the capital, called to say he was hearing bullets. His voice shaking, he added that smoke from the streets was clouding his living room. The smoke was in my bedroom too, I told him. Police sirens wailed.

Thirty-eight candidates were running in the presidential election. Most of the protesters in the capital were in the camp of Michel Martelly, "Sweet Micky," a ribald kompa singer, bandleader, and former drug dealer, but the previous night, the sitting government, widely mistrusted, had proclaimed its own candidate, Jude Célestin, the victor in first-round balloting. Many Haitians I spoke to, across all walks of life—judges, scholars, librarians, street sweepers, cocktail waitresses—dismissed the results. International election observers also doubted the integrity of the vote. And because so many countries and global institutions had promised billions of dollars for earthquake recovery, the world was watching.

By dawn, the government had put the country on lockdown. It shuttered the airport, all public offices, and private businesses "until further notice." I read on my cell phone that the U.S. government was advising American citizens in Haiti to remain in our homes until further instruction.

Holed up among foreigners—*blans*—in the Coconut Hotel, I got cabin fever by late morning. I called a newfound friend, Rodney, a black Haitian, and asked him to come pick me up. Ben had introduced me to Rodney by the hotel pool. A taut adrenaline junkie with rippling muscles, Rodney had once been a boxer and a soldier and spoke perfect English.

When he arrived, I gave him some cash as payment for guiding me through the city. He tipped the armed hotel guard with a small bill to let us out of the security gate.

To stymie police, protesters had put barricades in the roads. They'd upended garbage dumpsters, burnt tires, and felled massive tree limbs. Rodney darted, swerved, tipped his motorcycle to dodge the dreck. Cars could not circumvent the minefields, only motorbikes and pedestrians were running the streets—and police officers riding in the cabooses of massive trucks. They stared down we motorbike riders to warn us who was boss.

I ducked my nose beneath my T-shirt, coughing at the smoke gusting from the smoldering tires. We stopped in Pétion-Ville, a residential neighborhood with upscale businesses, to investigate on foot. We spotted a crowd of men—bandannas hiding their faces—chanting and wielding tire irons. Two of them grabbed a massive cinder block and hurled it through the window of a bank. Then another.

The air exploded.

I yelped, ducking my head into my arms. "Rodney, let's go! Get on the motorcycle and let's go!"

"Hey! What's wrong with you?" Rodney barked, flicking me hard on my nose. "You scared of that gunfire?"

"I thought it was a bomb!"

"So what if it was?" he shouted. "Even if it's a bomb, I better not hear you scream again. I know my job. Really—I don't work for men who panic."

I started giggling at the absurdity of the exchange. Rodney did not. He was so offended that I'd second-guessed his judgment. I was reminded of the time I'd asked Christian, another Haitian friend, for a helmet to ride back seat on his motorcycle. A pained look had contorted his face. Imagine my gall.

Rodney and I made our way to the election bureau. As we'd suspected, UN troops were guarding the office building. The UN presence was meant to safeguard poll stations, voters, and humanitarian efforts, though it also served essentially as the corrupt government's protector. Rodney drove the motorbike fifty feet from the troops and stopped. They stood side by side in full riot gear, using their bodies and shields to buffer the election office from rock-wielding protesters. Rodney identified two middle-aged men who seemed to be in charge of the protest and asked them to have the crowd stop throwing rocks for a second—otherwise, the troops would return the favor by lobbing tear gas at us.

"*Rete tann 'jouk blan a kite,*" Rodney said, tilting his head at me. "Wait till the foreigner leaves."

They paused. I moseyed up to the troops, snapping their pictures on my iPod Touch. Decent photos. I eased closer. More pictures. Even closer. One troop lifted his machine gun and pointed it at my chest.

Satisfied with what I'd documented, I hopped back on the motorcycle.

"Can we head toward the National Palace?" I said. "I want to see the nerve center."

"Why not?"

I had not told Rodney, or anyone for that matter, who my grandfather was. I enjoyed my anonymity: nobody needed to ask me too many questions. A classic social scientist, I wanted to recede into the background. I like to work fast, hard, furious, without any attention drawn to myself.

Rodney revved the engine. Speeding through the streets, he swerved past the barricades, the blood-orange, blazing tires, the gigantic sawed-off tree trunk, the carcass of an incinerated car. By wrecking government buildings, by blocking the roads with debris, by threatening terror, the protesters had shut down the country before the government effectively could. As we jetted past the burning tires, crackling in embers, I could see the air blur and ripple around the flames. My skin stung. I stared through the smoke at the recovery-tent camps that pocked the streets. But amid the litter, the disarray, life continued. On the sidewalk nearby, some kids were using two cinder blocks as soccer goalposts. They darted about the street and sidewalk, outdribbling one another.

Soon we arrived, coughing. Shantytowns of the homeless filling the Champ de Mars. A crushed palace amid wreckage, the capital's heart appeared as broken from the previous night's pillage as from the quake's aftershocks. A crisp pain racked my chest. Natural disaster was one thing, man-made another.

Surveying the damage, Port-au-Prince, 2010

• • •

I HAD ONLY THREE close relatives remaining in Haiti: Tante Gigine, her daughter, Emeline, and Emeline's husband, Anthony, a troika of elders caring for one another in a one-story ranch house. To visit them in their remote, no-frills working-class neighborhood, I boarded a tap tap, bursting at the seams with parents and workers leaning every which way out of the caboose. I wondered whether a child might fly out of the vehicle.

When I got off, I walked from the main road to a small splinter dirt road, then down two more, until I found their home. Tante Gigine opened the door. I was surprised, touched, when she recognized me. Some holidays when I was growing up, Tante Gigine would visit us at Tuckerman Lane, bestowing everyone with gifts and her wit. I hugged her tightly; she reminded me immediately of G'mère—her beaming smile, her eyes, her voice, faint and musical like my grandmother's.

Soon after we embraced, her daughter pulled me aside and warned me about her dementia; Tante Gigine was well into her eighties.

Seated in her small courtyard, we traded pleasantries, small news from our families. My auntie could not hold a detailed or coherent conversation about the present or past, though it was not memory loss alone that hindered her. Listening to Tante Gigine, I started to comprehend why she and my other Haitian aunties never talked about our family history. Tonton Jean, her husband, had disappeared at the hands of the Duvaliers. His children would tell me months later that he'd probably died in Fort Dimanche, sometime during the 1980s. They'd grown up under a chronic cloud, an inconclusive dread, surrounding the loss of their father.

Several hours later, the sun had settled and I felt remiss, guilty at having to depart, to walk back to the tap tap depot before dark. Taking Tante Gigine's hands into mine, looking into her fatigued eyes, I saw a gorge of fortitude and resignation. Her look appeared like a levy she had paid for living decades under the Duvaliers' dictatorship after her sister had left. As I said goodbye to her for the very last time, I could not fathom that I was staring into the eyes of a woman who, in her mere twenties, had rescued my mother and her siblings from the army barracks.

MY NEXT IMPORTANT appointment was at the national archives. I could barely hold my anticipation. I expected to find original drafts of my grandfather's book manuscripts or to hold his pistol or to inspect a typewriter from his union office. I couldn't wait to see the original 35 mm film footage of his 1957 inauguration: it would be the first and only motion-picture footage I could see of my mother as a girl.

Imagine my despair at discovering that many of the items, many of his papers, had been destroyed in the earthquake. The only known film footage capturing my grandfather's presidential inauguration had also been lost. Our footprint had been erased. My mother and aunts had censored so much information about my family—and natural disaster had destroyed the rest.

THE EXCITEMENT THAT HAD overwhelmed me when I'd first arrived had ground into a sad numbness that lasted for weeks after leaving the archives. I was sitting on the poolside veranda of the Coconut Hotel, writing in my journal, when I heard an old white lady nearby ask for tea.

"I'm sorry, madame," said the Haitian waitress. "We don't have any."

Two minutes later the waitress, Nadege, set down a cup of steaming tea at my table.

"*Merci, chérie.*" I smiled.

"Hello!" bellowed the white woman, flapping her fleshy, pale arms like wings. "I thought you don't have any tea!"

The waitress startled, suddenly remembering the lady. She giggled and disappeared.

What the *blan* did not understand is that for two weeks I'd been flirting with Nadege. I'd told her how radiant her skin looks. (True.) I'd told her how smart her English sounds. (True.) I'd inquired after her family. (Sincere.) But white people just bark orders. The first time I'd requested tea from Nadege, she'd insisted there was none. The hotel is rationing tea, she'd claimed, because of the political unrest. So I flirted. By the fourth day of my months-long stay, tea had materialized and it had returned each and every morning since.

An electric-blue rag diagonally harnessing an Afro. A neck scarf tied just so. Bright plastic sunglasses perched on the nose. A sprawling meal conjured to accommodate unannounced guests. I call it Haiti-sexy. It's an ephemeral quality, a Haitian style, delivering brilliance born of constraints. Improvised, sensual, cool.

Haiti is sexy. Haitians are sexy. Haitianess is sexy. Never in my life have I been the object of such flirtation. The women batted their eyelashes at me, looked away, held my stare, looked away again. The laundress. The waitress. The cashier at the grocer. The seventy-year-old grande dame who received me at her airy home in the gracious hills of Laboule, who regaled me with tales over a two-hour lunch on her shaded patio. *Oh-oh!* Really? *Mais oui!* We laughed for hours.

Even the men, so evidently heterosexual, flirt. "Hey, baby!" some rowdy guys shouted to me one day as I walked down a street in Delmas 6. "Hey, sexy man!" They were trying to coax me onto the bar's outdoor patio. I pretended not to hear them. I noticed their reaction to my silence. They noticed me noticing them noticing me. We laughed. "Come on! Just one beer!"

Passing them by, suddenly I recognized my own Haitianess, complicit in a lifetime of silences, using reticence as a form of cunning, quietude as a kind of love language.

MY DAYS WERE DWINDLING. I could feel my curiosity burning against the clock, so I paid three long visits to a high school not far from my hotel. This school serves Delmas 6, a crowded, impoverished neighborhood. I decided to visit it not only because of its high casualties from the earthquake but to understand better the man for whom it is named.

Lycée Daniel Fignolé had been devastated. When I first arrived, I found students crammed into open-air trailers that looked like dilapidated car garages—roughly 140 students per small trailer. The school had nearly four thousand students enrolled, but only twenty-one of these makeshift outdoor classrooms.

Principal Monteçoit Louis was eager to show me around. Before becoming the school's leader in 2009, he'd spent twenty-two years teaching social studies there. The school's buildings had been pulverized to dust just months after his promotion.

That day, Principal Louis told me, he'd been preparing to leave his office when he heard a bang. "All of the sudden, everything was black. And then I felt like I was being carried away by a flow to a magnetic field, thrown and pinned against a pole. At that moment, I realized it was an earthquake. I decided to give my soul to God. I was crying, 'Jesus, Jesus, Jesus.'"

Shaking his head, casting his eyes downward, he recalled seeing his students perish. "A cinder block fell on the head of a girl. It was split open and blood was gushing out." Seven hundred students died as the roof and walls collapsed on them, and several hundred more had dropped out since. Their families became too distressed, too scared, or too poor for kids to continue their education at the once-venerable school.

The surrounding neighborhood had suffered just as gravely. "Houses fell, so many students who lived in the neighborhood lost everything, including their parents and families. Now they are still living in tents and in terrible circumstances," said Principal Louis.

He made a point of telling me that the school, founded in 1987, the year after its namesake had died, had purposely been built in this poor neighborhood.

While students across the hemisphere enjoyed computers, chemistry equipment, and the like, students at Daniel Fignolé had only notebooks and pencils. All classes—chemistry, biology, physics, social studies—were taught on chalkboards with nothing else. The school had no offices for administrators or teachers, no electricity, no telephones, no internet access, no library, no textbooks, not even a bathroom. During my second visit, when I had to relieve myself, I disappeared discreetly to a doorless outhouse with three holes in the ground, squatted, defecated, then wiped myself thoroughly with sheets of my notebook paper.

I tried to calculate the school's exact enrollment. Impossible. Attendance was transient. Kids learned in shifts; half the student body would arrive in the mornings for class, the other half would appear in the afternoon. All sported a uniform: sky-blue short-sleeved shirts and ash-gray bottoms (trousers for boys, skirts for girls).

Ezekiel, a senior whose favorite subject is philosophy, told me that the battered facilities were not the only hindrances threatening his education. The noise tormenting the outdoor classrooms, the political turmoil, the crammed space: all made it difficult for him to learn. Even the teachers added to his academic stress. "Some days there are teachers, other days there isn't even one. Sometimes the teachers don't show up—I think it's because they haven't been paid."

Talking with Ezekiel and his classmates, I thought often of L'École Fignolé. I thought too of le professeur's pupils, who had to seek out clandestine learning, off-hours and off-location, during their audacious Sunday Clubs. A monumental lesson came to me: I have the privilege to think and write about power and oppression while also earning a living.

Studying at this school requires *l'esprit calm,* Ezekiel reported—"a quiet soul." He said his favorite philosophers were Socrates and Kant. He aspired to be a sociologist, but worried that he wouldn't be able to attend college.

Ezekiel had no thorough knowledge of the man for whom his school was named. Like his classmates, he was born just about when the man had died. For the students' elders though, it was a different matter.

"Any Haitian people love Daniel Fignolé. Not like him—love him," said Jean-Yves Milliont, the school's sixtysomething security guard, who lives minutes from campus. "He worked hard for people in Haiti. He helped them."

"People say that great leaders never really die, so that's the reason a school was created in honor of Mr. Fignolé," said Principal Louis. "Every time we talk here, we tell students that he was a model, a brilliant teacher. We encourage them to learn, so they may become like him."

When Haitians got angry and confronted Papa Doc, he just cut the lights. He turned off the country's power grid, he systematically dis-educated Haitians—he literally kept them in the dark. He banned any newspapers, books, and schools that he determined to be against him. Profoundly. Stupid. Little. Man. I could hear my grandfather's voice dismissing François. Mass ignorance, extinguished transparency, the one-way flow of information, the discrediting of writers and ideas: If you suffer these, who bears witness to totalitarianism's rise? Daniel had correctly foretold exactly what a Duvalier regime would inflict.

On my final day at Lycée Daniel Fignolé, I asked Principal Louis about his dreams for the school. He paused.

"I love this institution because I helped educate many Haitian youth who are now policemen, bankers, or attend great universities here, in France, in the U.S., or in Canada," he said. "I would like for Lycée Daniel Fignolé to take back its old reputation. Everyone used to talk about this school, which had the best performance of all the public high schools. Many national valedictorians came from the Lycée Daniel Fignolé. The U.S. is known as the greatest world power because it has a solid educational system. Education raises man to the best dignity of his being. School makes the man—and the country."

TAKING A SHOWER the night before I was scheduled to leave Haiti, suddenly I could not breathe. My left arm throbbed. I sat on the tile floor of the bathroom for almost an hour to steady my body, collect my head.

When my mother had asked me to wait until "things got better" to go to Haiti, and when I read the State Department's advisory not to travel there, I'd ignored both. In the service of research, nothing had scared me. I did not fear for my ability to survive in the post-earthquake turmoil, the malaria, the cholera, the political protests, the kidnappings. I did not doubt my resourcefulness to outmaneuver those threats.

I doubted my desire to know Haiti.

Deep down, I now realize, I had been worried that Haiti would lodge its talons into my skin, that I would understand it, love it, then never again be able to distance myself from its grip. Nor my mother's. Growing up, I had always insisted to myself how different I was from her and her busted-up family. I am nothing like those deadbeats, I had told myself, cracked up in their neuroses and addictions. I had always felt my mother was defective. But what could I expect of someone who'd come from a country like that, from a father who'd disappeared?

Cracked, fading family portrait.

Children don't know their parents' ordeals.

Appreciating Haiti would mean loving all of my mother.

Chapter 39

A SILENCE ON TOP OF MY MOTHER'S HAS SHROUDED OUR history, a quietude more public, more sinister. The U.S. government has never acknowledged any role in Fignolé's ouster. Since 1957, the United States has pretended that a monster ascended to Haiti's presidency on his own. The government's reticence has done wonders: so few well-read people whom I encounter—editors, journalists, scholars, civil rights activists—understand the role the Eisenhower administration played in installing Papa Doc.

Galled by my mother's and the government's silence, I resolved to find leads elsewhere. Weeks after I returned from Haiti, I took a bus to the National Archives, just outside DC. I arrived with modest expectations as to what I might find. Maybe a campaign poster from my grandfather's historic presidential run. Or a copy of the speech he gave on democracy as president if I was lucky.

Rummaging through the archives' cavernous basement over the course of two weeks, I hit a gold mine: more than three hundred pages of memos tracking Fignolé's activities. Dating from 1946 to 1957, these "CLASSIFIED" memos were composed by top-level American diplomats in Port-au-Prince and directed to the U.S. State Department in Foggy Bottom. The memos documented in detail, and offered "threat assessment" of, Fignolé's personal actions, his speeches, his writings, his labor activities. One cable warned that Fignolé was "menacing" and thus warranted "close and constant watching." And then:

According to a usually reliable informant—

The passage that follows goes blank, blacked out with a Sharpie.

Three other documents that I uncovered were also redacted. So I filed a formal request to the State Department, in December 2010, to release the passages in their entirety. I was looking for a smoking gun.

In July 2012, the State Department denied my request to declassify the documents. I appealed immediately.

"The Panel has carefully considered the grounds on which you based your appeal," a department letter stated. "It has determined that the previously withheld portions of the four documents must continue to be withheld, in accordance with Executive Order 13526, despite the passage of time. Its release could reasonably be expected to cause serious damage to the national security of the United States."

In 2015, I sued the State Department in federal district court, under the Freedom of Information Act, to have the documents declassified. Roughly a year later, Judge Amy Berman Jackson, an Obama appointee, rejected my lawsuit and ruled in favor of the State Department. In her ruling Judge Jackson ordered half a line of one document to be released. But that was it.

The crucial passages that remained classified could, I believed, reveal the identity of the "CIA asset" who had served as an on-the-ground spy for the Eisenhower administration during the 1957 election. Determined to uncover more, I tracked down the one living English-speaking journalist who had been a firsthand witness to Haiti's 1957 civil war, the rare living Western journalist to know my grandfather personally. Bernard Diederich, by then ninety, agreed to a conversation with me. "I admired your grandfather," he told me in a recorded telephone interview. He said that he believed that the CIA informants were an "alcoholic UPI stringer" with an Italian wife—"a great cook"—as well as "a short guy married to a Frenchwoman."

I followed up: Do you remember in what "official capacity" these men served while in Haiti? What was their professional cover? But the dubious, even zany recollections offered by a declining nonagenarian led me nowhere. I wondered later if it was Diederich who'd been leading me astray. What if he was the informant shielded by the

CIA—by Judge Jackson? What if he'd been informing the CIA and deceiving me?

Since our conversation, Diederich has died.

When Daniel was expelled and Duvalier took power, it became illegal in Haiti to print Daniel's image or even speak his name. He became a codified secret. His disappearance from the historical record echoes Haiti's chronic disappearance from the United States' conscience.

According to a usually reliable informant—

Caesura. Break, pause, interruption.

SOON AFTER, I TOLD my mother that I had found once-classified State Department documents revealing how the United States had spied on her family when she was a girl. She changed the subject. I raised it again at her seventy-fifth birthday dinner at Sfoglina, an elegant trattoria, weeks later. She sat, quiet, then muttered something about how Nixon had forced her father to sign an official nondisclosure agreement that none of his family members could ever write about their arrival to America. That I should let sleeping dogs lie. I told her that she sounded evasive, that she wasn't making sense. Her eyes narrowed, her lips puckered in anger, and she threatened me not to investigate the coup. I knew better—there was no such NDA.

These conversations tested the boundaries of how far my mother and I could go to get closer to each other. I gauged how much I could share with her, especially from my findings about her father. How much could I scrape at her past, her family's failures, to get to know her more deeply? How much was I gambling the perverse comforts of our present relationship in hopes of building a bond that might or might not draw us closer? Her fear weighed on me: each detail I uncovered could harm her finespun self-image, her convoluted myths of family. By delving deeper into the research, I was risking the familiarity—something like a truce—we already have.

•   •   •

EVENTUALLY I RESIGNED myself to this maddening fact: I might never produce the smoking gun. But smoking guns materialize mostly in the movies: that's not how colonialism, imperialism, and fascism work.

Imagine my surprise, then, when I received a letter in August 2022 from the State Department, stating that it had decided to disclose all the blacked-out passages in the secret documents I had requested. My small triumph had cost four lawsuits and eleven years.

The most critical of the secret passages, from the U.S. ambassador in Haiti to the U.S. secretary of state, stated, "According to a usually reliable informant details of which CAS cabling separately army plans prior June 16 arrest Fignolé and remove him from control." CAS is shorthand for an American CIA station in a foreign country. In Haiti, as elsewhere, the CIA operated the most securely encrypted communications, more so than the embassy. An ambassador in a "hot spot" would use the CIA's better channels to relay highly sensitive information, especially involving a secret informant or concerning the embassy's relationship with that country's intelligence service. So, according to the ambassador, the CIA station in Port-au-Prince cabled Washington concerning plans for a coup, separately, under even more secure channels than the embassy's. What did those cables from the CIA station say? Who all was the CIA station cabling separately—its headquarters? the Pentagon? the White House?—and why through more secure channels? The CIA station in Haiti left no documentation that I can find.

THE TERM *blowback* first officially appeared in a then-classified 1954 CIA report. It refers to the unintended consequences suffered by everyday people from U.S. government covert activity. My family and Haiti still cope with the legacy of secret CIA intervention and U.S. gunboat diplomacy.

Dim family photos, violent silences, hand-to-mouth poverty in Crown Heights, my mother's nightmares—it's all blowback.

Chapter 40

———

MY MOTHER CALLS ME AS I WRITE THIS. I DON'T TAKE HER call. In the moment, I cannot grasp my own lifetime of putting people on mute, of going mute, my refusing to listen or speak. Unable to reach me by voice, she texts me in all caps, "HAPPY BIRTHDAY DARLING, I LOVE YOU."

There is something about our exchanges sometimes—I cannot listen to what she wants to say. I feel numb to her expressions of love as she ages, somehow baffled as to where they are coming from. It bewilders me as a grown man to hear that my mother loves me, to hear her insist on it, even during the most everyday circumstances. The messages don't feel like expressions of love, they feel like a mother reassuring herself of her own vitality. They feel like a mother, in the face of mortality, in conversation with herself, affirming her own relevance by insisting, I LOVE YOU. Sometimes, my mother says, "I love you," then pauses—indignantly waiting for the verbal reciprocation that never comes. In those moments, it sounds like a complaint, a plea. It's not that I want to hear my mother suffer. It's that I often don't want to be told that I'm loved. Many days I hate myself for not summoning the compassion and generosity for my mother that I gladly conjure for close friends and that she spent a lifetime extending to downtrodden strangers. So I don't take the call.

My mother and I are like children hiding in shadows, hoping we'll still be seen. We want our hurt to be known without having to explain it. We are too frozen to speak our pain, then resentful when its parameters, its depths, are not understood.

My whole life, my siblings accused my mother of making me her favorite. But that is not precise. The more accurate assessment is that my mother's and my sensibilities are most alike: we are best equipped to navigate each other, to circumvent each other's improvised explosive devices, to tiptoe around each other's secrets. I've often felt that my mother loves me precisely because she doesn't know me.

I am one of her known unknowns.

ONE JULY MORNING IN 2021, I woke up to news that made my chest stiffen. I'd just returned to the city from a long weekend in the country. Like so many, I was consumed with hope—the promise of more vaccines and a winding-down pandemic. Then a breaking report blindsided me: twenty-eight mercenaries had stormed the private residence of Haiti's president, Jovenel Moïse, and slaughtered him in his bed. The president was discovered by police in a pool of blood: twelve bullets in his chest, arms, right leg, and left hip, his left eye gouged out. The mercenaries ransacked his bedroom and office. His daughter, Jomarlie, heard the bullets and ran to her brother's bedroom, barely managing to survive. Martine Moïse, his wife, was shot multiple times, wounding her so badly that journalists falsely reported that she'd been killed.

Hearing the account, I thought of G'mère, alone, chain-smoking in her bedroom at Tuckerman Lane. I felt the bloodshed. I thought of how brutality is inflicted on women. So many waves of violence, political and interpersonal, had violated G'mère's body—they incited her to disremember. The violence shut down her capacity for nostalgia.

That week, I talked about the news from Haiti on NPR and MSNBC. My mother called and texted me half a dozen times a day, knowing that I was busy with work. She asked me, as casually as she could, where I was, if I had any plans to travel. After I'd told her no, puzzled by her question, she kept barraging me with messages. I demanded to know why. I could hear in her voice that open tone that she used when she was about to ask me something I might refuse her. She asked me to never again fly to Haiti or to do more investigative work there. I could hear the panic, the embarrassment in her request. She told me she was having nightmares that I'd be taken hostage in Haiti.

The sealed spaces in my heart started opening like a greased lock. When you believe that your mother doesn't love you, you feel unlovable, but also profoundly unable to love. The lack of one's love, the character of how others love and don't love, often have nothing to do with you.

When Jovenel Moïse was gunned down in his home, sixty-four years after my mother's expulsion, she was shaken all over again.

Two armed soldiers would have sufficed to kidnap her and her siblings. Forty-three soldiers took them, guns trained at their backs.

ONE EVENING YEARS AGO, Toni Morrison was scheduled to receive a social justice award at a reception in a small downtown bookstore. I thrilled at the chance to hear her speak again. I arrived early, knowing that the event would be packed. Spotting her head, a sublime coil of pewter ropes, in the back of the bookstore—who could miss it?—I tiptoed my way toward her. I clutched my dog-eared copy of *Beloved*, the same one that I've owned since my junior year in college, the one she had tartly refused to sign years earlier.

"Would you please sign this?" I sheepishly asked her.

Morrison took the book and flipped through the pages. I saw her notice my writing in the margins, the Post-its crumpled throughout the book. She quietly read them all. I was mortified. I shifted to a kind of kneel next to her wheelchair, so as not to hover above her as she read. By then, a line had formed behind me. After what seemed like an eternity, she looked up at me, held my eyes, and nodded. She shot me a sly smile, then signed my book.

That book is one of my most cherished possessions. I am certain I would not have endured as a reader or a writer were it not for its author. Through her work, Morrison gave a ragtag group of people like me the permission and inspiration to write. "There is no time for despair, no place for self-pity, no need for silence, no room for fear," Morrison once said. "If there is a book that you want to read, but it hasn't been written yet, you must be the one to write it."

Not long after that event, I reread *Beloved* for sustenance in January 2017, for that was the worst month of my life. My beloved father passed away. A white autocrat was installed as the U.S. president. Hunched over my laptop, I wrote Pops's obituary for *The Washington Post* and live-blogged Donald Trump's inauguration at the request of *The New York Times*. I toggled between drafting a loving eulogy for my father, a humanitarian champion of democracy, while reporting the investiture of Trumpism. These dual events, a personal ending, a public beginning, these two elegiac expressions, nearly severed me, each undercutting the other.

The morning after my father's funeral in Maryland, I woke my mother to say goodbye before returning to New York City. Mommy jolted out of her bed. "You're leaving? You didn't tell me you're leaving!" She grabbed me and started to wail. Sharp, wounded shrieks between labored breaths. She suddenly looked so small to me. I caressed the cuff of her nightgown. "You're leaving," she sobbed, and wouldn't let me go. This was the first time I had ever seen her so unguarded, so scared. We had just sent my father's body to be buried in Guinea and she did not want to let me go.

Lan Guinée, the hard ancestral stone / where your head will rest at last.

She was totally transparent in her love for my father and, by extension, for me.

I turned to my signed copy of *Beloved*. The first time I'd read it, as a college junior, it had flown over my head. The next time I'd read it, a young hooligan in the East Village, I could grasp its creative whispers, its social messages—if only tentatively. When I picked it up in 2017, finally I got it. I could inhabit the spirit of Sethe, mother of four, who takes a momentous decision to slaughter her last child to spare her from enslavement, the horror Sethe scarcely managed to escape.

Beloved remains the single novel with increasing resonance to our nation, to freedom, to my family, to my life. At my fifth reading of it, I was consumed by the whole conundrum of being a parent and a child, the spiritual hurt of absentee parents, the way that parents have complicated lives before having children, the way that family members go missing on each other.

It was around this time that I requested my birth certificate from the State of New York for a work assignment. Inspecting the document once it arrived, I froze. I called Sara: "You know what? You'll never guess. Remember how our triplet died? That can't be true."

I could hear Sara suck her teeth. "Of course not," she said. "I figured that out years ago."

Why had my mother fabricated a triplet for my twin and me, then killed him off? To draw pity? To guilt-trip us? To make us think that we two survivors, our lives, were providential, blessed? My survival as an infant is indeed a miracle and my life turned out charmed, saved from blood death and my habits of self-destruction in ways I may not deserve. Full of grace. Maybe it's in her, that thing that makes a mother think it's necessary to kill off one of her children, her own kind of *Beloved*. It's hard to tell whether my mother's myth, our dead triplet, is just a dingy lie—or an attempt at a gift, a lesson in harboring the spirits of the departed.

I think of Sethe, "frightened by the thought of having a baby once more. Needing to be good enough, strong enough, that caring—again. Having to stay alive just that much longer.

"'O Lord,' she thought, 'deliver me. Unless carefree, motherlove was a killer.'"

My mother rid herself of her firstborn for the first five years of her life—why? Only she really knows. I grew up with a mother who preferred parenting the world to parenting her children. It turns out her father did, too. My mother has told me that she never forgave her father, and that, as much as anything else, almost destroyed her. Porcupine quills, mountain ridges rising from the dirt of her back: this is her armor—her "policy of containment"—as corrosive as the assault on her itself. There are traumas that good people may never overcome. She might be one of those people.

Saving themselves and their children from destruction, mothers have to invent their own syntax—in language, in living.

I could never have become a functioning adult until I learned to forgive her. I am able to forgive her because I learned why she is who she is.

FOR MANY YEARS, I went on Fox News regularly as a progressive commentator. Afterward, my inbox would blow up. "Commie!" "Nigger!" "Fag!" But I would laugh off the trolls, not give them a second thought. I could read their comments in my email and across social media late at night, right before bed, then sleep like a lamb.

All these years later, I understand something darker, richer about this country I love so much.

Woodrow Wilson occupied Haiti under the pretense of building it. The sugar exec called Foggy Bottom to complain about the fiery labor leader, his "number one enemy." The State Department spied on my grandfather, then cheerfully offered him a "temporary visa." Marines seized the destroyed palace grounds to deliver earthquake relief. Commie, nigger, fag: the right-wing dog whistles that want to discredit my public voice are echoes of Eisenhower's America. They all ripple together, this country's singular uncanny ability deeply to help you and to fuck you over.

The comedy is that my family and I internalized America. We became American, we became America's story, we inhaled America's optimistic brand of historical amnesia. We can start from scratch. Just wipe it out. Fix things. There's no karma. No history. Everything's new.

It was not a story to pass on, this story of family, this story of refugees, this story of the educated meritocracy stumbling and rising, this story about who and what America is. Oftentimes, my mother liked to make a distinction between mere citizenship and deep belonging. But I have to go further than that and ask us all: What should we belong to? And who has been minding these gates of belonging? How free do we want to be?

The psychic inheritance of loss is that you know something is missing, but not what. I never knew why I became a writer until now. Writing is a restitution of remembrance to its rightful place. An act of freedom.

What happens when you have a brilliant mother is that she speaks to you in multiple pitches. Hearing my mother is a difficult, but good, thing. When talking to my mother, I learn to learn differently. Oftentimes, the curriculum is not clear. I get one prompt, and the next one comes five, ten years later. So I have to remember the structure of her sentence. But it is a necessary learning, this learning that rewires my senses. It's who my mother and I are.

Daniel's affection for his followers, theirs for him, my mother's and my double-edged bond: loving black people, deeply loving black people, is a radical act—the higher you climb a country's establishment, even more so. How can I better love my mother? If I make peace with the shame, uncover the past, if I permit a deep love for such an imperfect person, I call that loving the margins.

I picture my dying grandfather, his face tearing up inside the plane cabin, severed from his family—struggling for words, confessing that he might cry.

I picture myself at Tuckerman Lane, glaring at Mommy, trying to master my emotions, my language.

I picture my thirteen-year-old mother trapped in an army basement, boarding a Pan Am clipper.

When you've been to hell and back, she later whispered to a confused little boy, nothing can ever destroy you.

I no longer see her as defective, but as a powerful flesh-and-blood woman. She tangled with history and politics across decades, across continents. I am proud she was not destroyed. I begin to hear all the things that went unsaid and I start to write them down.

After all, this is the only love letter to my mother I am capable of writing.

Author's Note

Every person mentioned in this memoir is real. No one is fabricated. Every family member of mine and every public figure is referred to by her or his real name. However, the names of two acquaintances, with whom I partied at the Cock, have been changed.

Early in the adventure of understanding my family, my scholarly instincts kicked in. I read every serious history of Haiti I could find. I pored over every news account reporting on Daniel Fignolé in media outlets across the world. I studied the transcripts of interviews that he granted, after he'd been deposed, to a historian, which have not been published. Sprawled on my living room floor, I read every book, article, essay, government memo, and letter that Fignolé has ever written, lingering in the expressiveness of his French. I conducted roughly a dozen in-depth interviews with people who dealt with Fignolé firsthand, including one of his chief political deputies, his former private secretary, and a prominent international news correspondent in Haiti throughout the 1950s. Finally, while in Port-au-Prince, I also looked up lost relatives.

One of the poignant ironies of this story is that because the U.S. government spied on my grandfather, because of the hundreds of pages of previously classified memos on him that I found in the U.S. National Archives, I am able to thoroughly excavate his past.

What I recount about the lives of my family, and of public history, is redeemed through other sources as well. I retrieved rare information concerning Cold War U.S. history from the Allen W. Dulles Papers at Princeton University. And since Haiti was once an American territorial "possession," I also consulted rare historical sources detailing Haiti during its U.S. occupation: governors' reports, military records, property inventories, presidential proclamations and correspondence, private diaries, and public decrees. I also consulted the New York Public Library's research division, which offered many useful historical records, especially the records of the International League for Human Rights, a group that politically supported Haitian exiles, including Fignolé. I have spent years parsing this trove from the New York Public Library, Princeton University, and Harvard University, containing news articles, photographs, private papers, maps, radio broadcasts, and books. All this helped me understand and bring alive on the page what my grandfather thought, said, and did.

Researching and writing this book has been a journey of over twelve years. In that time, I went from a person who could not locate Haiti's second-largest city on a map to an authority on the country's history from 1915 to now.

While my mother is discreet, in some respects she too has lived a documented life: I culled much of her story from interviews with her friends; her high school, college, and graduate newspapers and yearbooks; interviews she granted the press as a UNICEF official; media profiles of her; and twenty years of letters that she has written to me. My extensive research informs the color of these pages, a richer landscape of Daniel Fignolé's and Danielle Benjamin's thinking and actions.

Also, I need note, I have been an amateur historian and writer since age eight; I have always been that pack rat, a hoarder of memorabilia and information. I am the person who keeps every theater program, every birthday note, every get-well card, every high school and college term paper, and, most important, every letter that a family member, lover, professor, or friend has ever written me. And since I was ten, I have been keeping a diary, off and on. This account also draws from those primary sources.

Acknowledgments

This book could not have come into being without the help and affection of family, all of whom I am so grateful for: Edouard, my late father, Maye, Ed Jr., Sara, Jacqueline, Isabelle, Tancredi, Leigh, Will, Wilder, Misha, and Aunt Jackie.

I am thankful for close friends who supported me as I wrote and never let me forget who I am: Raúl Coronado, Adam Haslett, Andrew Jacobs, Boris Khmelnitskiy, Dan Levin, and Will Schwalbe.

Thank you to dear friends who delivered ideas and critiques on this project at various junctures: Barbara Abrash, Chris Anderson, Aisha Beliso–De Jesús, Ruth Franklin, Kaiama Glover, Saidiya Hartman, Pat Mitchell, Jacqueline Novogratz, Gene Park, Gretchen Rubin, Scott Seydel, and Dani Shapiro.

In the matter of creative sanctuary, I am thankful to places that offered me congenial havens to write: Ledig House, the Bellagio Center, and Civitella. Also, I thank the institutions that offered me professional support: the Robert Silvers Foundation, the Cullman Center for Scholars and Writers at the New York Public Library, the National Endowment for the Humanities Long-Term Fellowship at the New York Public Library, the Effron Center for the Study of America at Princeton University, and the Radcliffe Institute for Advanced Study at Harvard University.

I express tremendous gratitude to Pantheon Books and the entire Pantheon team. I thank Naomi Gibbs, especially, an editor whose generous, expansive mind is matched by her precision and close attention to language, to all detail. And thank you to Markus Hoffmann and his team at Regal Hoffmann for persistently supporting this project.

Finally, I thank my mother most profusely.

Notes

Chapter 3

23 "I know the nigger": Hans Schmidt, *Maverick Marine: General Smedley D. Butler and the Contradictions of American Military History* (Lexington: University of Kentucky Press, 1987), 84.

25 "roped tightly and cruelly": Mary A. Renda, *Taking Haiti: Military Occupation and the Culture of U.S. Imperialism, 1915–1940* (Chapel Hill: University of North Carolina Press, 2001), 149.

25 An estimated 11,500 Haitians: Ibid., 10.

Chapter 4

37 "high-class muscle man": Smedley D. Butler, *War Is a Racket,* digital ed. (Rapid City, SD: Vantage Point University Press, 2010).

37 "You are likely to run": Faith Berry, *Langston Hughes: Before and Beyond Harlem* (Secaucus, NJ: Carol Publishing Group, 1992), 122.

38 "He was the joy of his students": Lyonel Paquin, *The Haitians: Class and Color Politics* (New York: Multi-Type, 1983), 133.

39 "I knew Fignolé to be very": *Collectifs Paroles, 1946–1976 [Dix-neuf cent quarante-six–dix-neuf cent soixante-seize]: Trente ans de pouvoir noir en Haïti* (Quebec: Collectifs Paroles, 1976).

39 "I ultimately loved the man": Carlo A. Desinor, *Daniel Fignolé: Un espoir vain* (Port-au-Prince: L'Imprimeur II, 1986).

Chapter 6

48 "It is time that all": Daniel Fignolé, *Chantiers,* August 1942.

48 At the United States' urging: See "Efforts to reduce the adverse effects of the termination of a cryptostegia program in Haiti sponsored by the United States," [1160] Memo: The Chargé in Haiti to the Secretary of

State," Port-au-Prince, April 14, 1944, *Foreign Relations*, 1942, 6:460. The year that Daniel founded *Chantiers*, 1942, SHADA (Société Haïtiano-Américane de Développement Agricole, a corporate agency of the Haitian government) contracted with the Rubber Reserve Company (a U.S. war agency later known as the Rubber Development Corporation) for the planting of one hundred thousand acres of Cryptostegia to cultivate rubber, displacing tens of thousands of Haitian families.

48 "the property of sixty privileged families": Fignolé, *Chantiers*, August 1942.

Chapter 8

61 "For us Marxists, the color question": Matthew J. Smith, *Red and Black in Haiti: Radicalism, Conflict, and Political Change, 1934–1957* (Chapel Hill: University of North Carolina Press, 2009), 71.

Chapter 9

63 denouncing the country's "fascist oppression": Matthew J. Smith, "VIVE 1804! The Haitian Revolution and the Revolutionary Generation of 1946," *Caribbean Quarterly* 50, no. 4 (2004): 25–41.

64 "The youth are not dangerous": Smith, *Red and Black in Haiti*, 78.

65 "1946 will be the Year": Ibid., 76.

65 "Mr. Lescot, the hour": Ibid., 65.

65 "The charismatic leader": Paquin, *Haitians*, 134.

65 "*Chantiers* had a decisive": Bernard Diederich, *The Prize: Haiti's National Palace* (New York: iUniverse, 2007), 11.

Chapter 10

67 "slight, bashful, with embers": This account is quoted directly in William Krehm, *Democracies and Tyrannies of the Caribbean in the 1940's* (Toronto: Lugus, 1999), 208.

68 "Police clashed tonight": Associated Press, "Disorder in Haiti," *New York Times*, May 14, 1946, 2.

69 "Estimé's election was received": Smith, *Red and Black in Haiti*, 98.

Chapter 11

72 "Daniel's Creole": Desinor, *Daniel Fignolé*.

74 "The greatest political weapon": Special to The New York Times, "Haitian on a Steamroller," *New York Times*, May 27, 1957, 6.

74 "Fignolé, in one half hour": Elizabeth Abbott, *Haiti: An Insider's History of the Rise and Fall of the Duvaliers* (New York: Simon & Schuster, 1988), 60.

75 "the most promising action": Baron von Holbach, "Professor Daniel Fignolé," *Haiti Sun*, January 27, 1957, 21.

76 "If anyone thinks": Smith, *Red and Black in Haiti*, 99.

76 "In 1946, le Professeur": Paquin, *Haitians*, 132.

76 "I glanced furtively": Ibid., 125.

76 "singularly non-aggressive": Robert Rotberg, *Haiti: The Politics of Squalor* (New York: Houghton Mifflin, 1971); also quoted in Paquin, *Haitians*, 127.

76 "The Moses of Port-au-Prince": *Demain*, May 22, 1946.

77 "Young teacher of the proletariat": *Rasoir*, July 1946.

78 "I thought the marines": Desinor, *Daniel Fignolé*.

Chapter 12

80 "We have formed MOP": Daniel Fignolé, *Chantiers*, June 15, 1946.

80 "Under his leadership": Smith, *Red and Black in Haiti*, 94.

80 "were to provide the early": John Marquis, *Papa Doc: Portrait of a Haitian Tyrant* (Kingston, Jamaica: LMH Publishing, 2007), 108.

82 Historians cite her: Associate Professor Grace Johnson, University of Pennsylvania, interview with the author, March 17, 2022. See also Grace Johnson, *White Gloves, Black Nation: Women, Citizenship, and Political Wayfaring in Haiti* (Chapel Hill: University of North Carolina Press, 2023).

84 "Fignolé made clear": Horatio Mooers to Ambassador, "Memorandum Regarding Call at Chancery of Daniel Fignolé," November 29, 1946, Port-au-Prince, enclosure 1, USNA, RG 59, 838.00/11-2946.

84 "remarked that he welcomed": Smith, *Red and Black in Haiti*, 94.

84 "This is a politically": Jack West, "Study of Contemporary Leftist Groups in Haiti," attachment to Harold Tittman to Secretary of State, June 11, 1948, Port-au-Prince, 4, 12, USNA, RG 59, 838.00B/6-1148.

85 "First and perhaps most": Harold Tittman to Secretary of State, "Memorandum of Conversation Between the Ambassador and Colonel Levelt," June 11, 1948, Port-au-Prince, USNA, RG 59, 838.00B/6-1148.

85 "Left-wing doctrines are": Ibid.

85 "incoherent" and "unstable": Desinor, *Daniel Fignolé*.

86 "Despite all the money": Ibid.

Chapter 14

95 Complaining of "dangerous maneuvers": Smith, *Red and Black in Haiti*, 155.

95 "anti-communist" and "pro-labor": Daniel Fignolé, *Construction*, November 21, 1951.

95 "Haiti must be anti-communist": Ibid.

99 "The most prominent student": Smith, *Red and Black in Haiti*, 157. I flesh out Smith's account through the once-classified record of U.S. operatives spying on Fignolé. See Slater C. Blackiston Jr. to Department of State, January 22, 1952, Port-au-Prince, USNA, RG 84, 350/POLITICAL AFFAIRS.

99 "I wear iron pants": Michel-Rolph Trouillot, *Haiti, State Against Nation: The Origins and Legacy of Duvalierism* (New York: Monthly Review Press, 1990), 149.

100 "For his part, Fignolé": Bernard Diederich, *Bon Papa: Haiti's Golden Years* (Port-au-Prince: Éditions Henri Deschamps, 2008), 216.

101 "What Duvalier became": Abbott, *Haiti*, 61.

Chapter 15

104 "When he was tired": Raymonde Martinez, in-person interview with the author, Coral Springs, FL, February 19, 2020.

107 "Last night, between two": Daniel Fignolé, letter to Adolphin Telson, secretary of the interior, chief of police for Port-au-Prince, October 11, 1955.

107 "Fignolé risks having": Connett to Woodward and Cabot, "Recent Political Disturbances in Haiti," January 14, 1954, Port-au-Prince, USNA, RG 59, 738.00/1-1454.

108 "Fignolé has a reputation": Robert Folsom to Department of State, January 18, 1954, Port-au-Prince, USNA, RG 59, 738.00/1-1854.

108 "Society has become": *L'Arène*, April 28, 1956.

108 "Reports of the early end": Folsom to Department of State, January 18, 1954.

Chapter 16

114 "It will be a national": See "Daniel Fignolé Dies, 71; President of Haiti Before Ouster by Duvalier," *Washington Post*, August 28, 1986, B6. See also Desinor, *Daniel Fignolé*.

115 "Mr. Fignolé emerged": Special to The New York Times, "Haiti's President Chides Aspirants," *New York Times*, March 24, 1947, 30.

117 "There was a headlong": Diederich, *Prize*, 45.

117 A rich Duvalier supporter: Abbott, *Haiti*, 66. I have corroborated this assertion also in once-classified U.S. records in the National Archives.

Chapter 17

121 "It would have been": *Le Nouvelliste*, May 27, 1957.

123 "Their dignity brought tears": Desinor, *Daniel Fignolé*.

123 "The clergy willingly": Ibid.

124 The country's gold and dollar: Paul Kennedy, "U.S., World Fund Study Aid to Haiti: But Nation under Fignole Must First Show Stability Politically," *New York Times,* June 3, 1957, 31.

125 From the debt's inception: Catherine Porter et al., "The Ransom: The Root of Haiti's Misery: Reparations to Enslavers," *New York Times,* May 20, 2022, A1.

126 "Some argue that": Daniel Fignolé, in-person interview with Robert J. Alexander, New York, May 5, 1959.

126 "We ask you, People": Translated from *Le Nouvelliste,* June 6, 1957.

126 "M. Fignolé's popularity": Kennedy, "U.S., World Fund Study," 31.

Chapter 18

127 The CIA director kicked off: This account of the meeting is culled from several primary documents that I secured, primarily "Discussion at the 325th Meeting of the National Security Council," May 27, 1957, Eisenhower Papers, 1953–61, Ann Whitman File, Dwight D. Eisenhower Library, Abilene, KS.

128 "to restore the flow": James Risen, "The C.I.A. in Iran: A Special Report: How a Plot Convulsed Iran in '53 (and in '79)," *New York Times,* April 16, 2000, 1, 13–14.

128 "I understand this fellow": "Discussion at the 325th Meeting."

129 "The number one enemy": "The New Fignolé Government in Haiti: Memorandum of Conversation, Jean Dauphin and Julian Fromer," May 27, 1957, Washington, DC, USNA, RG 59, 738.00/5-2057.

129 "the worst thing that": "Memorandum of Conversation, R. T. Davis, Julian Fromer, and Allan Stewart," May 31, 1957, Washington, DC, USNA, RG 59, 738.00/5-3157.

Chapter 19

132 "I literally don't have": Desinor, *Daniel Fignolé.*

132 "I now consider myself": "Fignolé Is Here as a Haitian Exile," *New York Times,* June 16, 1957, 21.

Chapter 20

136 "At a moment when": A copy of this letter rests in the U.S. National Archives, "Military Council of Government Succeeds Fignolé," George H. Alexander to the Department of State, June 17, 1957, Port-au-Prince, USNA, RG 59, 738.00/6-1757. It is also published in full in Paquin, *Haitians,* 304.

138 "I heard the most": Diederich, *Prize,* 56.

138 Morgue counts said: Gérard Pierre-Charles, *Radiographie d'une dictature. Haïti et Duvalier* (Montreal: Éditions Nouvelle Optique, 1973). See also "Daniel Fignolé Dies."

138 "One would have": Desinor, *Daniel Fignolé.*

139 "Every day trains": Carleton Beals, "Haiti under the Gun: On the Spot Report," *Nation,* July 6, 1957, 4.

Chapter 21

144 "pure gangsterism": Michael James, "Fignolé Accuses Army," *New York Times,* June 18, 1957, 11.

145 "One of my own pupils": Desinor, *Daniel Fignolé.*

146 Written in French: Letter from Daniel Fignolé to Dwight D. Eisenhower, June 22, 1957, New York, USNA, RG 59, 738.00/6-2257.

146 "Lunging too fast": "Fignolé Falls," *Time,* June 24, 1957, 40.

148 "It would appear that Mr. Fignolé": Roy R. Rubottom Jr., Assistant Secretary of State, letter to Joseph Swing, Commissioner of the Immigration and Naturalization Service, June 24, 1957. See also "Memorandum of Conversation—Elizabeth Schermerhorn and Julian P. Fromer, Re: Daniel Fignolé," June 24, 1957, Washington, DC, USNA, RG 59, 738.00/6-2457.

Chapter 22

150 "How can Haiti": "Presidents in Exile," *Ebony* 13, no. 4 (February 1958): 74–80.

150 "But in practice": Abbott, *Haiti,* 78.

150 "Although the defeated candidates": "Embassy's Despatches, Numbers 58 and 92," September 13, 1967, Port-au-Prince, USNA, RG 59, 738.00/9-1357.

153 "a pitiful apartment": Paquin, *Haitians,* 155.

154 "Like all of you": Ibid.

154 "The minute I set": Ibid., 156.

Chapter 23

157 "I had taught": Raymonde Martinez, in-person interview with the author, Coral Springs, FL, February 19, 2020.

158 "Seeing our mother": Ibid.

160 "Where the fuck": Ibid.

161 "It was a battle": Ibid.

Chapter 24

163 "The events in Cuba": Paquin, *Haitians,* 175.
164 "a lack of respect": Ibid.
164 "docilely made himself a": Ibid., 306.
165 "Then Fignolé came": Ibid., 177.

Chapter 27

178 "The French pulled out": Leon Dash, "Guinea's Longtime President, Ahmed Sékou Touré, Dies," *Washington Post,* March 28, 1984, C7.
179 "The social revolution": Diederich, *Bon Papa,* 196.

Chapter 28

189 "I just got a cable": U.S. Embassy, Addis Ababa, "Confidential Telegram to Secy State DC and American Embassy Conakry," November 1973.
189 "Alpha care should": Ibid.
190 "In issuing the U.S. visa": U.S. Embassy, Addis Ababa, "Confidential Telegram from US Embassy to Department of State," November 21, 1973.
191 "Following the attempted": U.S. Department of State, "Protective Services: The Benjamin Family, Operations Confidential Memorandum to the Department of State," January 4, 1974.
191 "Mrs. Benjamin indicates": U.S. Embassy, "Confidential Telegram," November 1973.

Chapter 30

211 "the person arousing": Desinor, *Daniel Fignolé.*
212 "Dignified, honorable": Fignolé's very own words, as transcribed in Robert J. Alexander's interview with Daniel Fignolé, May 5, 1959, New York.

Chapter 31

215 Daniel sat in first class: Desinor, *Daniel Fignolé.*
217 "triumphant": "Daniel Fignolé," *New York Times,* August 28, 1986, 36.
217 "Master is dying": Desinor, *Daniel Fignolé.*

Chapter 34

237 "One day this kid will talk": David Wojnarowicz, *Untitled (One Day This Kid . . .),* 1990–91, Museum of Modern Art, New York.

Chapter 35

248 Giuliani knew the owner: Mario Lopez, phone interview with the author, February 16, 2021.

Chapter 36

256 "hypoxia, pneumonia, painful": Bellevue Hospital Center Emergency Medical Services, "Patient Statement and Assessment: Richard Benjamin," New York, August 22, 2004.

256 In 2021, *The New York Times*: Michael LaForgia, "How a Genetic Trait in Black People Can Give the Police Cover," *New York Times,* May 15, 2021, A1.

Chapter 39

276 He said that he: Bernard Diederich, phone interview with the author, October 24, 2015.

277 "According to a usually": "Memorandum to Secretary of State," June 11, 1957, USNA, RG 59, 738.00/6-1157.

Select Bibliography

Archives

Archives Nationales d'Haïti, Port-au-Prince. Correspondance Département de l'interior.

Archives Nationales d'Haïti, Port-au-Prince. Correspondance Général.

Bibliothèque Haïtienne des Pères du St-Esprit (BHPSE), Port-au-Prince. Mangonés Collection.

Allen W. Dulles Papers. Seeley G. Mudd Manuscript Library, Princeton University.

Central Intelligence Agency papers, 1955–56.

Central Intelligence Agency papers, 1957–60.

Robert J. Alexander Papers. Special Collections and University Archives, Rutgers University, New Brunswick, NJ. Interview Collection, 1947–94, microfilm, IDC Publishers.

Robert J. Alexander interview with Daniel Fignolé, August 23, 1949, Port-au-Prince.

Robert J. Alexander interview with Daniel Fignolé, June 19, 1957, New York.

Robert J. Alexander interview with Daniel Fignolé, May 5, 1959, New York.

U.S. National Archives II, College Park, MD.

Records of the Department of State Relating to the Internal Affairs of Haiti, 1950–59. National Archives and Records Service, 1982. Microfilm Publication M-1246.

Organized chronologically:

Orme Wilson to Secretary of State, February 21, 1946, Port-au-Prince, USNA, RG 84, 838.00B/22146.

Horatio Mooers to Ambassador, enclosure 1, "Memorandum Regarding Call at Chancery of Daniel Fignolé," November 29, 1946, Port-au-Prince, USNA, RG 59, 838.00/11-2946.

Harold Tittman to Secretary of State, "Labor Troubles at the Plantation Dolphin," July 24, 1947, Port-au-Prince, USNA, RG 59, 838.504/7-2447.

Harold Tittman to Secretary of State, November 6, 1947, Port-au-Prince, USNA, RG 59, 838.504/11-647.

Robert H. McBride to Secretary of State, "General Comments on Developments in Haitian Labor Movement," January 14, 1948, Port-au-Prince, USNA, RG 59, 838.504/1-1448.

Jack West, "Study of Contemporary Leftist Groups in Haiti," 4, 12, attachment to Harold Tittman to Secretary of State, June 11, 1948, Port-au-Prince, USNA, RG 59, 838.00B/6-1148.

"Memorandum of Conversation between the Ambassador and Colonel Levelt," Harold Tittman to Secretary of State, June 11, 1948, Port-au-Prince, USNA, RG 59, 838.00B/6-1148.

Slater C. Blackiston Jr. to Department of State, January 22, 1952, Port-au-Prince, USNA, RG 84, 350/POLITICAL AFFAIRS.

Robert Folsom to Department of State, January 22, 1953, Port-au-Prince, USNA, RG 59, 738.00/1-2253.

Connett to Woodward and Cabot, "Recent Political Disturbances in Haiti," January 14, 1954, Port-au-Prince, USNA, RG 59, 738.00/1-1454.

Robert Folsom to Department of State, January 18, 1954, Port-au-Prince, USNA, RG 59, 738.00/1-1854.

J. Paul Barringer to Department of State, March 26, 1957, Port-au-Prince, USNA, RG 59, 738.00/3-2657.

"Memorandum of Conversations Between Chargé d'Affaires and Mr. Eric Tippenhauer," April 24, 1957, Port-au-Prince, USNA, RG 59, 738.00/4-2557.

J. Paul Barringer to Department of State, April 25, 1957, Port-au-Prince, USNA, RG 59, 738.00/4-257.

Gerald Drew to Secretary of State, May 14, 1957, Port-au-Prince, USNA, RG 59, 738.00/5-1457.

"Memorandum of Conversation, Jean Dauphin and Julian Fromer," May 20, 1957, Port-au-Prince, USNA, RG 59, 738/5-2057.

"Memorandum of Conversation, Didier Raguenet to Julian Fromer," May 29, 1957, Washington, DC, USNA, RG 59, 5-2957.

"Memorandum of Conversation, R. T. Davis, Julian Fromer, and Allan Stewart," May 31, 1957, Washington, DC, USNA, RG 59, 738.00/5-3157.

"Memorandum of Conversation, with Rubottom, Frank Cusumano,

Elmer Loughlin, and Ernest Gutierrez," June 10, 1957, Washington, DC, USNA, RG 59, 738.00/6-1057.

Hobart Spalding to Secretary of State, June 12, 1957, Port-au-Prince, USNA, RG 59, 738.00/6-1257.

George H. Alexander memorandum to Department of State, "Views of President Daniel Fignolé on Political Parties," June 13, 1957, USNA, RG 59, 738.00/6-1537.

"Gerald Drew to Secretary of State," June 16, 1957, Port-au-Prince, USNA, RG 59, 738.00/6-1657.

"Military Council of Government Succeeds Fignolé," George H. Alexander to Department of State, June 17, 1957, Port-au-Prince, USNA, RG 59, 738.00/6-1757.

Daniel Fignolé letter to Dwight D. Eisenhower, June 22, 1957, New York, USNA, RG 59, 738.00/6-2257.

"Memorandum of Conversation—Elizabeth Schermerhorn and Julian P. Fromer, Re: Daniel Fignolé," June 24, 1957, Washington, DC, USNA, RG 59, 738.00/6-2457.

John Foster Dulles, "Memorandum to the President, Re: Recognition of the New Government of Haiti," July 25, 1957, Washington, DC, Box 9, Dulles Papers, DDEL.

Anonymous to R. R. Rubottom, August 16, 1957, New York, USNA, RG 59, 738.00/8-1657.

J. Paul Barringer to Secretary of State, September 20, 1957, Port-au-Prince, USNA, RG 59, 738.00/9-2057.

"Charges of Fraud in Haitian Elections of September 22, 1957," Virgil P. Randolph to Department of State, October 24, 1957, Port-au-Prince, USNA, RG 59, 738.00/10-1457.

Interviews

In chronological order, conducted by the author:

Jean Casimir, preeminent historian, relative to Rodrigue Casimir, November 29, 2010.

Michel Hector, private secretary to Daniel Fignolé, December 14, 2010.

Bernard Diederich, journalist and eyewitness to 1957 presidential campaign, *ténèbre*, who also knew Daniel Fignolé, October 24, 2015.

Professor Matthew Smith, University College London, December 8, 2015.

Evelyne Fignolé, sister-in-law to Daniel Fignolé, widow to Necker Fignolé, February 8, 2020.

Evelyne Fignolé, niece of Daniel Fignolé, daughter to Evelyne and Necker Fignolé, February 8, 2020.

Allen "Tupper" Brown, Yale roommate and close friend to Edouard Benjamin, February 11, 2020.

Raymonde Martinez, sister to Danielle Benjamin, aunt to the author, February 19, 2020.

Jeanne Olivierri, close friend and Zeta sister to Danielle Benjamin, March 25, 2020.

Jackie Beverly, best friend and Zeta sister to Danielle Benjamin, April 3, 2020.

Naby Soumah, best friend to Edouard Benjamin Sr., April 10, 2020.

Elsie Chapman, close friend and Zeta sister to Danielle Benjamin, April 21 and June 10, 2020.

Joan Blackshear, close friend and Zeta sister to Danielle Benjamin, April 22, 2020.

Max Manigat, Haitian exile in New York City, retired Haitian scholar who traveled closely with Fignolé in northern Haiti as a young political aide during Fignolé's 1957 presidential campaign, June 10, 2020.

Edouard Benjamin Jr., brother to author, August 19, 2020.

Sara Bardin, twin sister to author, August 20, 2020.

Marcelle Tagliaferri, sister to author, August 30, 2020.

Sean Brown, cousin to author, son to (younger) Carmen Fignolé, November 8, 2020

Armando Martinez, first husband to Raymonde Martinez, December 27, 2020.

Michel Renan Martinez, eldest son to Raymonde Martinez, December 27, 2020.

Cybel Torres, eldest daughter to Raymonde Martinez, April 24, 2021.

Leigh Newman, best friend to author, April 26, 2021.

Associate Professor Grace Sanders Johnson, University of Pennsylvania, March 17, 2022.

Books

Abbott, Elizabeth. *Haiti: An Insider's History of the Rise and Fall of the Duvaliers.* New York: Simon & Schuster, 1988.

Auguste, Joseph. *La voix du M.O.P. Daniel Fignolé ou le sens d'une lutte.* Tome 1. Port-au-Prince: Éditions Delta, 1989.

Bonhomme, Colbert. *Révolution et contre-révolution en Haïti de 1946 à 1957.* Port-au-Prince: Imprimerie de l'État, 1957.

Coicou, Robert Antoine. *Les forces du bien contre les forces du mal: Les minutes d'une commission d'enquête . . . le 25 mai 1957–50 ans après.* Port-au-Prince: Éditions Nationales Acoicou, 2007.

Desinor, Carlo A. *Daniel Fignolé: Un espoir vain.* Port-au-Prince: L'Imprimeur II, 1986.

———. *De coup d'état en coup d'état*. Port-au-Prince: L'Imprimeur II, 1989.

Dubois, Laurent, Kaiama L. Glover, Nadève Ménard, Millery Polyné, and Chantalle F. Verna. *The Haiti Reader: History, Culture, Politics*. Durham, NC: Duke University Press, 2020.

Duvalier, François. *Face au peuple et á l'histoire*. Port-au-Prince: SID, 1961.

———. *Mémoires d'un leader du Tiers Monde*. Paris: Hachette, 1969.

———. *Ou, l'exemple d'une vie*. Port-au-Prince: Imprint de l'État, 1961.

Fignolé, Daniel. *Contribution á l'histoire du mouvement syndical en Haïti*. Port-au-Prince: Imprint Le Reveil, 1947.

———. *Le nord-ouest dominicain*. Port-au-Prince: Imprint A. P. Barthelemy, 1948.

———. *L'instruction publique en Haïti*. Port-au-Prince: Imprint Le Reveil, 1945.

———. *Mon mandat*. Port-au-Prince: Gazette du Palais, 1954.

———. *Notre Neybe ou leur Bahoruco?* Port-au-Prince: Bureau d'Éducation du Parti MOP, 1948.

Johnson, Grace Sanders. "La Voix des Femmes: Haitian Women's Rights, National Politics and Black Activism in Port-au-Prince and Montreal, 1934–1986." PhD diss., University of Michigan, 2013.

———. *White Gloves, Black Nation: Women, Citizenship, and Political Wayfaring in Haiti*. Chapel Hill: University of North Carolina Press, 2023.

Marquis, John. *Papa Doc: Portrait of a Haitian Tyrant*. Kingston, Jamaica: LMH Publishing, 2007.

Mathon, Alix. *Témoignage sur les évenements de 1957*. Port-au-Prince: Éditions Fardin, 1980.

Nicholls, David. *From Dessalines to Duvalier: Race, Colour and National Independence in Haiti*. New Brunswick, NJ: Rutgers University Press, 1996.

Paquin, Lyonel. *The Haitians: Class and Color Politics*. New York: Multi-Type, 1983.

Renda, Mary A. *Taking Haiti: Military Occupation and the Culture of U.S. Imperialism, 1915–1940*. Chapel Hill: University of North Carolina Press, 2001.

Schmidt, Hans. *The United States Occupation of Haiti, 1915–1934*. New Brunswick, NJ: Rutgers University Press, 1995.

Smith, Matthew J. *Red and Black in Haiti: Radicalism, Conflict, and Political Change, 1934–1957*. Chapel Hill: University of North Carolina Press, 2009.

Stotzky, Irwin P. *Silencing the Guns in Haiti: The Promise of Deliberative Democracy*. Chicago: University of Chicago Press, 1999.

Trouillot, Michel-Rolph. *Haiti, State against Nation: The Origins and Legacy of Duvalierism*. New York: Monthly Review Press, 1990.

Periodicals and Articles

Associated Press. "Haiti's President Ousted by Army; Principals in Military Coup in Haiti." *New York Times,* June 15, 1957.

Beals, Carleton. "Haiti under the Gun: On the Spot Report." *Nation*, July 6, 1957.

Bellevue Hospital Center Emergency Medical Services. "Patient Statement and Assessment: Richard Benjamin." New York, NY, August 22, 2004.

"Daniel Fignolé." *New York Times,* August 28, 1986.

"Daniel Fignolé Dies, 71; President of Haiti before Ouster by Duvalier." *Washington Post,* August 28, 1986.

Dash, Leon. "Guinea's Longtime President, Ahmed Sékou Touré, Dies." *Washington Post,* March 28, 1984, C7.

"Disorder in Haiti: Leftist Candidate Threatens Violence If Defeated." *New York Times,* May 14, 1946.

"Fignolé Is Here as Haitian Exile; Ousted President Flies to New York—Republic Quiet under the Army's Rule—Still Candidate for Election." *New York Times,* June 16, 1957.

"Haiti: Fignolé Falls." *Time,* June 24, 1957.

Kennedy, Paul. "U.S., World Fund Study Aid to Haiti: But Nation under Fignolé Must First Show Stability Politically." *New York Times,* June 3, 1957.

LaForgia, Michael. "How a Genetic Trait in Black People Can Give the Police Cover." *New York Times,* May 15, 2021.

"The Mob and Its Man Take Over in Haiti." *Life,* June 10, 1957.

Porter, Catherine, Constant Méheut, Matt Apuzzo, and Selam Gebrekidan. "The Ransom: The Root of Haiti's Misery: Reparations to Enslavers." *New York Times,* May 20, 2022.

"Presidents in Exile." *Ebony* 13, no. 4 (February 1958).

Reuters. "Obituary: Daniel Fignolé." *New York Times*, August 28, 1986.

Smith, Matthew J. "Haiti: Protest and Rebellion in the Twentieth Century." In *International Encyclopedia of Revolution and Protest: 1500—Present*, edited by Emmanuel Ness, 1514–21. Malden, MA: Wiley-Blackwell, 2009.

Wojnarowicz, David. *Untitled ("One Day This Kid . . ."),* 1990–91. Museum of Modern Art, New York.

Illustration Credits

167 "Blue and Gold," Girls' High yearbook, June 1961

169 Benjamin family collection

178 Yale University yearbook, 1964

180 Yale University yearbook, 1964

185 Benjamin family collection

197 Benjamin family collection

218 Benjamin family collection

219 Benjamin family collection

223 Benjamin family collection

250 Benjamin family collection

267 Benjamin family collection

A Note About the Author

RICH BENJAMIN is a cultural anthropologist and the author of *Searching for Whitopia*. His writing has appeared in *The New Yorker, The New York Times,* and elsewhere, and he's appeared as a commentator on MSNBC and CNN. His work has received support from the Bellagio Center, the Civitella Ranieri Foundation, Columbia Law School, the Cullman Center for Scholars and Writers, the Ford Foundation, Princeton University, the Rockefeller Foundation, the Russell Sage Foundation, and the Harvard Radcliffe Institute.

A Note on the Type

This book was set in Minion, a typeface produced by the Adobe Corporation specifically for the Macintosh personal computer and released in 1990. Designed by Robert Slimbach, Minion combines the classic characteristics of old-style faces with the full complement of weights required for modern typesetting.

Composed by North Market Street Graphics,
Lancaster, Pennsylvania

Printed and bound by Berryville Graphics,
Berryville, Virginia

Designed by Betty Lew